READERS PRAISE "AN E

"I first met the author and hiked with him for a brief time on the Appalachian Trail in southern Maine. Later, through reading his book, I hiked the entire Trail and met the real Herbert Eye. Living his dream, step by step, mountain by mountain, he tells of the beauty, adventures, trials, challenges and of the people he met durng his hike; and thus by perseverance and fortitude, discovers the hero within. Chronically detailed and described, *"An Eye on the Horizon"* could serve as an AT guide."

—Billy Thomas Leffler, AT 2000-miler—Lima, OH

"I liked your accurate trail descriptions, presented in a very factual and refreshingly non-psychoanalyticfal and non-metaphysical way. The joy you got out of hiking the trail shone through every sentence, and whatever hardship the trail dished out was born quietly and acceptingly as part of the deal. No heroics, no macho, just doing it and getting it done—and enjoying every facet of the hike down to the flowers along the way and the occasional wildlife sightings."

—Dr. Reinhard Zollitsch, Professor, University of Maine—Orono, ME

"Join the author as he experiences the joy, frustration and sadness as he pursues his dream. He describes many of the historical sites, the topography and the flora and fauna found on or near the Trail. You will become aware of the support of his family and his respect for the many volunteers and officials who maintain the Trail. Share his emotions as he completes his journey to the summof of Mt. Katahdin."

—Don Shepard, Retired School Administrator—Elyria, OH

"Your book, journal, your compassionate down-to-earth writings of your achievement of a life-long dream is, truly, a masterpiece,"

—Dorothy Mauldin ("Ankle Express") ATC Poet Laureate
Member: International Poetry Hall of Fame—Marietta, GA

"Congratulations on publishing such a fine book. You have covered things so well— the history, the beauty, the fellowship, the trials, the pain, the victories, the losses, and the achievements."

—Don Andrews, Retired State Park Administrator
Currently, Professor, University of Charleston, WV

"If you enjoy adventures, this is one of the best! I thoroughly enjoyed the book. After completing the last chapter, I felt that I had hiked the trail from beginning to end myself. I especially enjoyed the colorful historical facts the author included concerning the Appalachian Trail."

—Dallas Chadwell, Retired School Administrator, Normantown, WV

AN EYE ON THE

HORIZON

"I will lift up mine eyes unto the hills,
from whence cometh my help."
— *from Psalm 121*

AN EYE ON THE

HORIZON

An Appalachian Trail Odyssey

HERBERT F. EYE

Ridgecrest Publishers

Grafton, Ohio

An Eye on the Horizon Copyright © 1998 by Herbert F. Eye. Printed and bound in the United States of America. All rights reserved. No parts of this book may be reproduced or transmitted in any form or by any means, electrical or mechanical, including photocopying, recording or by an information storage and retrieval system—except by a reviewer who may quote brief passages in a review to be printed in a magazine or newspaper—without permission in writing from the publisher. For information, please contact Ridgecrest Publishers, P. O. Box 275, Grafton, Ohio, 44044. First printing 1997. Second printing 1998. Third printing 2000.

Although the author and publisher have made every effort to ensure the accuracy and completeness of information contained in this book, we assume no responsibility for errors, inaccuracies, omissions, or any inconsistency herein. Any slights of people, places, or organizations are unintentional.

ISBN 0-9661062-2-9
LCCN 97-92713

The poem, *"The Thru-Hikers Did It (I Walked along with Them)"* reprinted with permission from Dorothy Mauldin, member: International Poetry Hall of Fame, and ATC Poet Laureate. One-liner poem printed with permission of Bill Leffler.

Information from maps and guidebooks courtesy of Appalachian Trail Conference, Harpers Ferry, West Virginia. Information from maps and guidebooks on the White Mountains courtesy of the Appalachian Mountain Club, Boston, Massachusetts. Appalachian Trail maps courtesy National Park Service, U. S. Department of the Interior.

Author's picture on the cover was taken by the author along the Appalachian Trail on Mt. Cube, New Hampshire, with camera set on automatic exposure. Photos throughout the book were taken by the author unless otherwise indicated. Book cover layout by Herb and Joan Eye.

ACKNOWLEDGMENTS

Regarding the Trail:

Anyone who has spent time walking on the Appalachian Trail has to marvel at the foresight, development and maintenance of this great footpath. Its very existence is the result of Benton MacKaye's dream and the combined efforts of the Appalachian Trail Conference, the Confederation of local hiking and outing clubs along the Trail and the National Park Service. The hiking and outing clubs are made up of hundreds of volunteers who donate thousands of hours of service to the Trail cause each year. I am grateful to and applaud the great work of these dedicated organizations and individuals.

Regarding this Book:

I am deeply grateful for the suggestions and editing skills of the following people: Ken and Helen Black, Muriel Lytle Campbell, Dallas and Frances Chadwell, Kathy Reynolds—and last but not least my wife Joan who was not only an outstanding editor but did the layout and typesetting for this book.

This book is dedicated to Joan and our children: Melinda, David and Rodney whose love and support were with me every step— and to the memory of my brother Osbra who was an inspiration but was unable to complete the hike with me.

PREFACE

Each year millions of people break the routine of their daily lives and venture into the great outdoors. Some take periodic walks in the woods, make regular or periodic visits to public recreation areas such as local, state or national parks; take camping, hunting or fishing trips; and some hike into natural areas via a network of trails with the Appalachian Trail being the most prominent. The reasons people make these journeys vary, but a common one is to make a connection with the natural world so they can develop a better understanding of the environment and ultimately themselves.

Throughout man's history, he has learned to reap the vast natural resources of Mother Earth; and through his development of scientific technologies, he has provided for his sensual and ever-changing materialistic needs. His struggle to improve and enhance his life goes on, and the results have been remarkable. However, I believe he has been so consumed in these things that he has faltered when it comes to a better understanding of his environment and how he fits into it. John Hay, in his *In Defense of Nature*, put it very well when he said: "What we call natural resources cannot be limited to gas, oil, pulpwood or uranium—we are starving the natural resources in ourselves—the soul still needs to stretch—being needs exercise."

These thoughts certainly were uppermost in the mind of Benton MacKaye, who was the first to have a vision of an Appalachian Trail and whose name is synonymous with it. He saw the need for people to extend themselves into the natural world and believed that his vision of a trail following the Appalachian Mountain chain would provide an access to nature for millions of people from the urban areas of the eastern United States and elsewhere.

For as long as I can remember, I have had a great attraction to and respect for the natural world and was fortunate as a child growing up to have had an open front and back door to the outdoors. I grew up on a farm in southern West Virginia with thousands of acres of mountain woodland surrounding the farm. The great outdoors was always nearby beckoning me, and I took advantage of this by spending a great deal of my spare time there. I was often in the woods hunting, depending on the season. It might be game, wild honeybees, Ginseng, yellow root, mushrooms— and the list goes on. I also did a lot of camping, fishing and hiking. This early exposure bonded within me a great love for the outdoors that has lasted throughout my life and has kept bringing me back time and time again.

I learned about the Appalachian Trail as a youngster about five years after its completion in 1937 and thought that some day I would like to hike parts of it. But as I grew older, family and career commitments became foremost placing any plans for hiking it on hold. As the years passed and I approached retirement, I realized that if I were going to do any hiking, it would have to be while my health was good. In 1980, plans were made to begin the Trail in the spring of 1981. By 1987, the year of my retirement, I had made a commitment to hike the entire Trail.

During the Appalachian Trail's 60-year history, it has indeed provided what Benton MacKaye had visioned—an access to the natural world of the Appalachian Mountains from Georgia to Maine. Whether a person chooses to hike a mile, a section, a day, a week or longer, this can truly be a great experience. To those who choose to hike its entire length either on a thru-hike or a series of section-hikes over an extended period of time, it is not only remarkable but truly a journey of a lifetime.

My 2,158.8-mile hike (the official distance when I finished) of the entire Appalachian Trail was done in sections and over a period of several years. In this book I have given a detailed account of my personal experiences during the 175-day trek along this great footpath from Springer Mtn., GA, to Mt. Katahdin, ME. The following are highlighted: the physical features and facilities along the Trail, its wildlife, plant life, geologic phenomena, the ever-changing weather, history, moments of joy - sadness - concern, and last but not least the pleasure of meeting, hiking with and living with hundreds of people (from all walks of life) along the Trail. It was a great personal challenge and provided me with memories that will last forever and experiences, sights and feelings that I would like to share. This is my story…!

TABLE OF CONTENTS

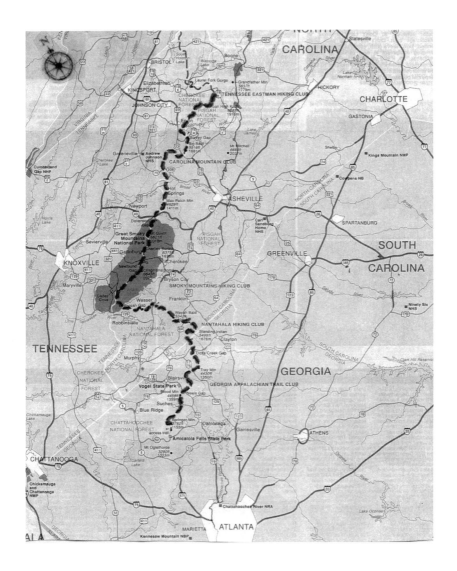

Map detail from Springer Mtn., GA, to Elk Park, NC
(Covered in Chapters one through four)
— — — — — Denotes Appalachian Trail Route
Shaded area denotes Great Smoky Mountains National Park

THE BEGINNING

*"For each bright new day is just a beginning of
what lies ahead - not what is ending."*
— *Our daughter, Melinda Fayer*

Our 1975 Ford station wagon bounced over the rough unpaved United States Forest Service (USFS) Road 28 after leaving
Georgia 52 near Dahlonega. This is one of the approaches that
hikers use to reach Springer Mtn., the southern terminus of the
Appalachian Trail (AT). The most popular approach is the 8.3-
mile blue blaze trail beginning at the Amicalola Falls State Park
Visitors Center on GA 52 between Ellijay and Dahlonega. We
chose to use the Forest Service Road, as we could go by car to
Nimblewill Gap—a point 2.2 miles from Springer Mtn.—and get
to the trailhead quicker. It was April 18, 1981—a cool, cloudy
spring morning, and the north Georgia mountain tops were
shrouded in fog. The road follows a stream for some distance
before beginning the ascent of Amicalola Mtn. to Nimblewill Gap.

There were several trout fishermen who gave us glances of curiosity as we bounced past. Our vehicle did not have much clearance compared to their high 4-by-4's which were more appropriate for the area. The road became steeper, rougher and narrower; and we began to wonder if we had made the right choice. To make it more interesting, fog engulfed us before reaching Nimblewill Gap.

Those present that morning to see us off and wish us well were my Aunt Okey who lives about 30 miles from Amicalola Falls, our 11-year-old son Rodney (who would later hike part of the Trail with me), my wife Joan, and my brother Osbra who would be my hiking companion.

After reaching Nimblewill Gap, we shouldered our heavy packs and adjusted the waist belt and shoulder straps. The pack had not seemed that heavy when I practiced putting it on and off the night before. I cautioned Joan to be very careful driving off the mountain down the steep, narrow, rough road. Neither of us knew it then, but this would be the first of scores of challenges she would have in getting me to and from trailheads from Springer to Katahdin. She would become an expert in making drives like this one, helping me plan, and keep track of my progress as I section-hiked north on the Appalachian Trail. The good-byes on that foggy April morning in the north Georgia mountains were made with both excitement and anxiety. My brother and I had been planning this trip for almost a year.

This was it—the beginning of a dream I had wanted to fulfill since age 15, an adventure that would last into the mid-nineties. When in my early teens, I wanted to join the Boy Scouts; however, because the area where I lived was very rural and there was no troop nearby, my only option was to be a Lone Scout. It was through my activities working to earn merit badges that I first learned about the Appalachian Trail. I hoped that some day I could hike some of it. I never forgot about wanting to hike on the AT as I grew older, but, because (as is the case with most everyone) we became involved in raising a family and career commitments, time could not be devoted to it.

By 1980 I had reached a point in my life when I felt I could take the time to hike some of the Trail. My brother had hiked some sections in Virginia and had shared some of his experiences with me making me even more enthused. I suggested that we go to the southern terminus of the Trail in Georgia and do some hiking there—perhaps planning to section-hike the whole Trail. He liked the idea, so we immediately began to plan a hike for the Spring of 1981.

I bought equipment and did some reading about the Trail; and the closer the time came to the date of our departure, the more excited I became. I was also excited about having my brother as a hiking companion. He was an official with the West Virginia Department of Natural Resources, a naturalist, a botanist, an expert on the outdoors and could interpret the flora and fauna along the Trail. What a great opportunity this was for me! At this point in my life, I could only devote a little time each year to the Trail which meant I would be section-hiking. I still had family and career commitments, but this would be a beginning.

So here we were on our first hiking day on the blue blaze trail approaching Springer Mountain. The fog stayed with us as we reached the summit about mid-morning. There would be no views from Springer this morning, and we learned that foggy conditions along the ridges and mountain tops were going to be a common weather phenomenon. We paused at the bronze plaque marking the southern terminus of the AT on Springer and read the inscription: "Appalachian Trail Georgia to Maine—a footpath for those who seek fellowship with the wilderness. Georgia Appalachian Trail Club, 1934." We took some pictures of the plaque and managed to get one picture of the countryside through the fog. Beside the plaque on the same rock is the first 2" by 6" vertical white painted blaze which is the official marking of the AT extending from Springer to Katahdin. This blaze is painted on any object (trees, rocks, posts, logs, etc.) large enough to accommodate its size and is usually visible from one to the other. There is also a register box on Springer, and when we signed it we noted that most of the hikers ahead of us marked "Katahdin" as their destination. I wondered how many would make it and if we ever would.

Our destination for this hike was Dick's Creek Gap where the AT crosses US 76 between Clayton and Hiawassee, GA—a distance of about 71 miles from Nimblewill Gap. We thought that 10-mile days would be manageable for us to start. Our packs were fairly heavy, and I was not sure how well I could hold up since I had not been on any type of physical-fitness program to help prepare me for the hike. However, we both had always stayed physically active, much of which had been in the outdoors.

To keep our pack weight to what we thought would be manageable, we tried to be selective in the equipment we carried. Neither of us had hiked for more than two or three days at a time, so we knew we had a lot to learn about the equipment needed for long-distance hiking. We decided we would not pack a tent because of the weight but would stay in the shelters which were spaced ten to fifteen miles apart along the Trail. However, that would change later on. This first hike would be a test run. First of all, it would tell us if we were physically able to meet the challenge of long-distance hiking and what limitations we needed to make on distance and speed. We wanted to hike at a pace that was comfortable for us giving us time to accomplish specific goals we had each set out to achieve.

The second thing we hoped to learn on this first hike was how appropriate our food, clothing and equipment we had selected would be for long-distance hiking. Through our personal outdoor experiences and reading and talking to other hikers, we had learned many common do's and don'ts. We would need to go through this experience to determine what our specific needs and preferences would be and make changes accordingly.

In selecting our food, emphasis was placed on two things: nutrition and weight, and that meant we had to think in terms of concentrated or dehydrated foods. We knew that our daily caloric intake should be high providing the increased amount of energy required. We found a good selection of dehydrated varieties containing meats, veggies, fruits and combinations. We also carried a choice of instant soups which were not only nutritious but tasty and satisfying. Bread was seldom carried due to its bulk and fragility. Most often we used bread sticks or crackers as a substitute. Occasionally, we took small canned goods which included meat, tuna, beans, etc.; but carrying these was an exception rather than the rule because of the weight and the packaging which had to be carried out.

Snacks were an important part of our food plan and included high energy items such as trail mixes made up of nuts, dried fruit, cereals and candy. We also had our favorite candy bars as well as cookies, crackers and peanut butter. Frequent snack breaks were planned to keep the calories flowing. For drinks, we used instant mixes—Tang or Gatorade for cold ones and coffee, tea, cider, or cocoa for hot ones. Not being a gourmet cook and considering conditions along the Trail, I favored food items that only required adding boiling water to rehydrate them. This cut down on preparation time and the number of utensils which had to be washed. Breakfast normally consisted of hot instant cereals such as oatmeal or Cream of Wheat fortified with honey or sugar, powdered cream and dried fruit along with coffee and Tang to drink.

The fog started to clear shortly after we left Springer, and we began to have views into the valleys. The trees and plants along the ridges were showing signs of budding, but in the valleys the tender leaves of the trees were out, showing a lot of green, which you could see diminish as elevation increased. Through this area were particles of mica glistening in the sun, looking as though someone had sprinkled tiny diamonds on the ground to add a sparkle to the Trail. This phenomenon appeared at many locations along the Trail all the way to Maine.

There is a network of side trails along the Appalachian Trail from Springer to Katahdin which are marked with a 2" by 6" painted vertical blue stripe called a blue blaze. These trails may lead to a spring, shelter, camping area, overlook or other point of interest off the AT. The first one we came to was the Benton MacKaye Trail. This was very fitting near the trailhead, because it was through MacKaye's dream and famous 1921 article entitled, "An Appalachian Trail, a Project in Regional Planning," that appeared in *Journal of the American Institute of Architects* that the AT became a reality.

We descended Springer into Stover Creek and passed through a virgin stand of large hemlock pine. As we ascended Hawk Mtn., we stopped for a break at Long Creek Falls, the first of scores of impressive waterfalls along the AT from Georgia to Maine.

We arrived at the Hawk Mtn. Shelter (our first day's destination) by late afternoon and were greeted by a gentleman from Florida who was retired and hiking a section of the Trail. He had started at Amicalola Falls and, during his second day to Hawk Mtn., had developed blisters on his feet. He had stayed over at this shelter for two days trying to doctor his blisters and rest his feet so he could move on. Most of the thru-hikers had left Springer by this date, and within the first few days many would encounter a variety of physical and/or other health problems which would necessitate delaying or aborting their hike.

After a somewhat restless night at Hawk Mtn., we were up early, ate breakfast and prepared to move on toward the Gooch Gap Shelter. The Florida hiker told us he was going to stay at the shelter another day or two giving his blisters more time to heal. We really did not like leaving him in this condition, but he assured us he would be okay, that he had plenty of food and water and would probably abort his hike at the next road crossing. We wished him well and moved on. I have often wondered when and where he left the Trail

This was Easter Sunday and we planned to hike nine miles to the Gooch Gap Shelter, taking us across three mountain peaks ranging from 3,000 to 3,300 feet. The 77 1/2-mile section of the AT in Georgia lies entirely within the Chattahoochee National Forest and crosses peaks up to 4,500 feet.

One of our goals was to study and photograph plant and animal life along the Trail. We found many spring wildflowers in bloom during this time of year along the mountain crests and valleys. Among those we took pictures of were the Silverbell or Snowdrop tree and the Sweetleaf, both of which were in full bloom and common to the southern United States. In the Blackwell Creek area, we also snapped photos of the Crested Dwarf Iris—another striking and fragrant wildflower blooming in April and May from Maryland south to Georgia.

We hiked into the Gooch Gap Shelter by mid-afternoon, and I had developed some hot spots on my feet which could become blisters if left untreated. I took care of these immediately and wondered if my shoe choice (6" hunting boots) was a good one.

We had caught up with a number of thru-hikers who were having difficulties of one kind or another: blisters, sprains, upset stomachs, and joint problems. Many were complaining about the weight of their pack, equipment not working, etc. The shelter was full of hikers, two of whom had stayed over an extra day because of foot problems. Statistics show that 80% of the thru-hikers that start at Springer Mtn. will drop out or leave the Trail within the first 100 miles. We were already seeing evidence of this within the first 20 miles.

The next morning we were up early to begin our 13-mile day which would take us to Blood Mtn. Our leg joints and feet were sore, slowing us down for a while; but we were soon moving at our usual pace. Our pack weights were heavier than they should have been. We were carrying more water than necessary as there were plenty of good sources along the Trail in Georgia and their locations were well marked. We would not have needed to carry more than one reserve quart of water at a time along this part of the Trail.

The weather had warmed up considerably by mid-morning as we crossed Ramrock Mtn. and dropped into Woody Gap. The dogwood trees were in full bloom in the Gap, and we were beginning to see a variety of other wildflowers. The Yellow Trillium and Blue Dogbane were in abundance—Spring had definitely arrived in the Blue Ridge Mountains of Georgia. As we crossed Woody Gap, we saw an interesting "commercial" sign on a tree which read: "Congratulations hikers on the first 23 miles—though you may be cold, wet, and hurting bad, don't give up. Rogers Appalachian Cottage is only 1,250 miles more." When I read that sign, I wondered how many hikers would reach that destination and if I would. It did give us a chuckle, though.

From Woody Gap we had a good climb up Big Cedar Mtn. (3,237 feet). Due to the warm weather, the climb was more difficult, and my boots continued to cause me problems. They were making my feet sore, and the downhills were murdering my toes. I knew I would have to make a change in my footwear before hiking the next section. My boots were the first items of my gear that were not passing the test on this initial trek.

Blood Mtn. (4,461 feet) is the highest peak along the AT in the state of Georgia, and Blood Mtn. Shelter is located on its summit with no water near it. Since we were planning to stay there, we had to fill our water bags and canteens from a source about a mile before we reached the summit and carry them to the shelter. This shelter is a stone structure with a dirt floor, was built by the Civilian Conservation Corps (CCC) in the 1930's and is listed on the National Register of Historic Places. The building was in rather poor condition, and I heard it has since been renovated.

The view from Blood Mtn. is, in my opinion, one of the best along the AT in Georgia. As I was viewing this vast panorama, it inspired me greatly and brought to mind the following poem which I learned in school from my third grade reader:

"The Wonderful World"

Great, wide, beautiful wonderful world,
With the wonderful water round you curled,
And the wonderful grass upon your breast,
World, you are beautifully drest.

The wonderful air is over me,
And the wonderful wind is shaking the tree—
It walks on the water, and whirls the mills,
And talks to itself on the top of the hills.

Your friendly Earth, how far do you go,
With the wheat-fields that nod and the rivers that flow,
With cities and gardens, and cliffs and isles,
And people upon you for thousands of miles?

Ah! you are so great, and I am so small,
I hardly can think of you, World, at all;
And yet within me seemed to say,
"You are more than the Earth, though you are such a dot!
You can love and think, and the Earth cannot!"
—William Brightly Rands

The weather on Blood Mtn. was outstanding—cool, crisp and clear—and I was able to capture on film one of the most beautiful sunsets I had ever seen so far. After the sun set, it became cold; and after a meal of beef stew and hot chocolate, we climbed into our snug sleeping bags and hoped for a good night's rest.

When we arose in the morning, we discovered that a mouse had carried one of Osbra's hiking socks into a crevice in the stone wall of the building. He did manage to retrieve it, however, with some difficulty. I am sure the mouse had plans to make a nest out of his sock, and what better material to make a warm, soft bed for her babies than wool. This mouse incident was the first of many that would occur as we moved north. In fact, in each of the shelters along the AT, we found that hikers devised an assortment of apparatuses and strategies to try to keep mice from invading their packs in search of food.

The temperature was in the 30's with some fog blowing across Blood Mtn. when we headed toward Low Gap Shelter, which was about 13 miles from the summit. As we began the descent of Blood Mtn. into Neels Gap, I was reminded of the Indian legend about a severe battle that was fought there between the Cherokee and Creek tribes. According to the legend, the battle was so fierce that "the hills ran red with blood." This apparently was why the Indians felt the mountain took on a red-like appearance; however, botanists say this is caused by the rust-colored lichens that grow on the rocks there.

The descent was steep, but fortunately not too long; and I was grateful for that because my boots were really giving me a fit on the downhills. We stopped at Walasi-Yi Center in Neels Gap and visited with Jeff and Dorothy Hansen, the owners. They provide rooms, meals, and have limited supplies for hikers. They also provide advice, support and encouragement to hundreds of hikers who stop at the Center each year. I made a telephone call to Joan who was visiting relatives in Atlanta. We picked up a few hiking supplies; and, as we were leaving the Center, we noted that the AT goes through the Center's archway and is the only building through which the Trail passes.

After leaving Neels Gap, we began the ascent of Levelland Mtn. and met a thru-hiker (John Crisman) who was camped in a small clearing near the base of the mountain. He had developed a knee problem and stayed over a couple of days to recover. He later caught up with us and hiked along to Dick's Creek Gap. As we hiked across Levelland Mtn. and over to the Cowrock Mtn. area, I was becoming more impressed with the topography of the north Georgia mountains. I had not expected them to be as steep or as rough as they were or that the scenery along the crest of these mountains would be so stimulating.

Interesting through the Cowrock Mtn. area was the presence of many fallen chestnut trees (American Chestnut), and we were surprised to see so many of the old ones still standing. In some areas, you could walk on the dead logs on the forest floor for hundreds of feet. This reminded me of the days when my brother and I would see how far we could walk on logs in the forest without touching the ground in the woods near our farm in West Virginia. According to what I could learn by talking to older people and through reading, this was one of the last areas in the American forest where the chestnut blight hit, explaining why the old trees and logs are still around.

As we descended the steep Cowrock Mtn. into Tesnatee Gap where the scenic Richard Russell Highway crosses, the weather remained clear. These steep descents continued to irritate my feet. I had to keep my toes well padded, as they were jamming into the toes of my boots. By now, I had learned the need to have a special type of boot for this kind of hiking, and it definitely would not be a hunting boot; because they were too heavy, and their design did not provide proper foot protection. If a study were made about why many people have to abort their long-distance hike early, a high percentage would be related to footwear—improper type, size or lack of break-in time.

We continued hiking over a series of mountains with elevations ranging between 3,300-3,600 feet and could see the green in the valleys indicating springtime was well under way there. We were tired, hungry and sore when we reached the Low Gap Shelter. John Crisman arrived later; and before dusk, we were joined by a thru-hiker from New England and two grandmothers who were section-hiking. We spent an enjoyable evening sharing food and stories and developing strategies on how we were going to keep the mice out of our packs during the night. These shelter mice had become well educated as to the contents of hikers' packs, where the goodies were located and to the many tricks devised to keep them out. By 9:00, we were all in our cozy sleeping bags side by side still exchanging stories and conversation. It was a gorgeous evening with the stars glistening through the trees, but that would change by morning.

We were up at daybreak and looked out of the shelter into a sea of fog that was so dense that visibility was reduced to just a few feet. The trees, which were only a few feet in front of the shelter, were hardly visible. It was hard to believe that the weather had made such a change overnight. We quickly prepared breakfast, packed up and began what would be a long hard day. Our plan was to hike to the Montray Shelter on Tray Mtn., which would be 15 miles—the longest so far on this trip—and the weather certainly did not look favorable. We would be crossing another series of gaps and mountains with hefty climbs over Blue Mtn., Rocky Mtn. and Tray Mtn. with elevations ranging from 4,000 to 4,400 feet.

We hiked in dense fog all day crossing through areas that would have provided great views into the valleys and across the mountains, but all we could see was a short distance ahead of us at a time. We kept pushing on not able to see where we were going or where we had been. When we began the ascent of Tray Mtn., which was three miles from our destination for the day, a misty cold rain began. The rain did not matter that much, because we were already wet; but what did matter was that it was getting colder the higher we climbed up the mountain.

Montray Shelter is located one-half mile north of the summit of Tray Mtn. (4,000 feet) where we arrived late in the day—wet, cold and extremely tired. I was cold and shivering and immediately changed into dry clothes and quickly got into my sleeping bag to warm up. No doubt, I was in the first stages of hypothermia. (I have since learned that a hiker died of hypothermia in this same shelter in November, 1984.) I never warmed up until I had a cup of hot soup and tea and then stayed in my sleeping bag all evening.

This incident made me realize that the cotton clothing we were wearing was not appropriate for the weather we would be experiencing on the AT. Not only does cotton, when wet, cause heat loss from the body, but it is difficult to get dry under Trail conditions. Part of our clothing had not passed the test on this first hike, and we knew we would be making changes in our wardrobe before the next one. We had also underestimated the weather on these high ridges and peaks during springtime. Cold, wet windy conditions are common during the spring months, and snow is not out of the realm of possibility.

We were joined by John Crisman who had been hiking with us since Neels Gap and later by a southbound hiker who was a minister from Salem, North Carolina. It was a cold rainy night on Tray Mtn., conditions I would experience many times before reaching Katahdin.

The next morning was as foggy as it was the preceding morning, and we took extra time to prepare a hearty breakfast of hot oatmeal, coffee, and Tang and to organize our gear—much of which was still wet. We had not planned a long day and were hoping the weather would clear so we could dry out. No views or photographs were possible before we left Montray Shelter at 9:00 AM, and the fog did not start to clear until we reached Wolfpen Gap about a mile from the shelter. The atmosphere cleared by the time we reached the summit of Young Lick Knob, about another mile further; however, there was still fog in the valleys. We could look back on Tray Mtn., our first view of that mountain, and regretted not being able to take pictures from its lofty peak on a clear day. Stone Mtn. near Atlanta is visible, and Standing Indian Mtn. and the Smokies are visible to the north. I was so impressed with Tray Mtn., even though we crossed it during the worst weather conditions, that I vowed to return and rehike this section (which I did with our son Rodney in the spring of 1983).

When we reached the swag of the Blue Ridge, the fog completely cleared from the valley. It turned out to be a gorgeous day with great sweeping panoramas. What a feeling of relief to be out of the depressing fog we had experienced for the last two days!

We arrived at Addis Gap Shelter by early afternoon in bright sunshine. Being early in the day, we had time to dry out, rest, and kick back to enjoy the sun and the fellowship of the hikers who were already there and those who would be arriving throughout the afternoon. The area around the shelter looked like my mother's yard on wash day. Hikers had clothes and gear hanging on lines and tree limbs and spread out on the ground and rocks everywhere to try to get them dry in the warm sunshine. Later that afternoon we built a big fire in the rock fireplace in front of the shelter and all sat around it soaking up the heat.

The two grandmothers who had spent the night with us at the Low Gap Shelter and were hiking from road crossing to road crossing joined us later. They brought hot dogs, and the rest of us pooled our leftovers and came up with a satisfying evening meal. Before bedtime, we even had popcorn that was prepared over the open fire. That night the shelter was filled with hikers, and two pitched their tents nearby.

The next day was our last on this section of the AT. We left Addis Gap Shelter at 7:30 AM, heading for Dick's Creek Gap where Joan was scheduled to pick us up. The weather remained clear, and we were able to have good views and pictures going across Kelly Knob and Powell Mtn. We arrived at Dick's Creek Gap before noon where we were greeted by Joan and Rodney. The two thru-hikers joined us before we reached the station wagon and asked if we would take them into Hiawassee, GA, to pick up mail and supplies.

On the way into town, Joan told us there was some Easter candy in a basket in the back of the car, but the only problem was it had been sitting in the warm car and the chocolate had melted and mixed in with the artificial grass in the basket. No problem for candy-craving hikers! We ate the candy and no doubt some of the artificial grass, too. On the way into Hiawassee, part of the contents of one of the hiker's packs (which had been tied to the top of the station wagon) fell out, but we did not know this until we reached town. When he discovered some items missing from his pack, we made a quick trip back and found his pants and sleeping bag by the highway, and felt fortunate to have retrieved them. After they picked up their mail and supplies, we drove them back to the trailhead and wished them well. That fall we received a postcard from John Crisman indicating he had finished the Trail.

We photographed a number of interesting plants and wildflowers through this section of Georgia. Following are some that were visible daily: the Umbrella Leaf with its large peltate leaf, the Star Chickweed with its star-like flowers, the Nodding Trillium, Dogwood, Galax and Lousewort, all common in the southern Appalachians. In some areas along the Trail, there were hundreds of some of these plants and/or flowers growing in clusters or gardens, such as the Trillium. It was as though they had purposely been planted in that fashion just for hikers to enjoy.

The section of the AT from Springer Mtn. to Dick's Creek Gap was my first introduction to hiking on the AT. It was a great experience and the beginning of an adventure of which I had long dreamed. I was inspired by the Trail in Georgia. It was a picturesque and challenging section crossing some of its highest peaks. The fine condition of the Trail reflected the diligent work and care which was being done by the Georgia Appalachian Trail Club, consisting of a team of volunteers who managed the shelters and Trail through this area. This is the first of a network of 32 Trail-maintaining clubs coordinated by the Appalachian Trail Conference (ATC) with the home office in Harpers Ferry, West Virginia. These clubs and other volunteer groups oversee the maintenance of the AT from Georgia to Maine and cannot be commended enough for their fine services.

Herb and Osbra at Nimblewill Gap near the
Springer Mountain Trailhead in Georgia

Photo by Joan Eye

TOP: Official bronze plaque and first white blaze marking Southern
    Terminus of the Appalachian Trail on Springer Mountain.
BOTTOM: American Chestnut logs on the forest floor along the
    Appalachian Trail near Blue Mtn., Georgia

FOGGY MOUNTAIN TOPS

"The ultimate purpose? There are three things:
(1) to walk; (2) to see; (3) to see what you see."
    —*Benton MacKaye*

Before beginning the hike from Dick's Creek through the Nantahala Mountains of North Carolina in June, 1982, I spent some time researching long-distance hiking equipment in backpacker shops in our area. I made several changes in my equipment—the first of which was hiking boots. I also eliminated most of the cotton clothing and added warmer and lighter weight fabrics. We decided that a two-man tent would be included on this hike, as there were several times during the first one that we could have used it. Some changes were made in food and cooking equipment, including the stove. We wanted to carry several pieces of photographic equipment, so it was necessary to reduce our pack weight in order to carry the gear we felt we would need. Our solution was to plant a food cache at Wayah Gap which was near the middle of the section we planned to hike, thus reducing our food weight by one-half.

The mountains of northern Georgia and western North Carolina are noted for their outstanding exhibits of wildflowers, particularly in late spring and early summer. We wanted to photograph the Flame Azaleas, Smooth Azaleas, rhododendrons, Mountain Laurel, and a variety of other flowering plants common here this time of year. The AT leaves the Chattahoochee National Forest at the North Carolina state line and enters the Nantahala National Forest, staying within its boundaries to the Little Tennessee River at Fontana, North Carolina.

We left Dick's Creek at noon and headed to a campsite near the North Carolina/Georgia state line at Bly Gap. The afternoon was warm and pleasant, and we enjoyed hiking through and photographing large fields of ferns, moss and other plants along the AT near Cowart Gap, Plumorchard Gap, and As Knob (yes, As is the correct name—I would like to know the history behind that name). The high annual rainfall through the southern mountains provides an environment where plants grow fast, large and with lush green foliage as well as colorful flowers. The AT through here truly becomes a path through one of nature's best gardens.

We reached Bly Gap in plenty of time to set up our tent, get water and prepare our evening meal over an open fire. It was an excellent place to camp with a large cleared area, good water that is close by and an excellent view. Bly Gap is on the Georgia/North Carolina state line and marked the completion of the first of fourteen states I would have to hike through before reaching Katahdin—one down and thirteen to go.

The weather had been great all afternoon and evening, but that would change during the night. We were awakened to the sound of rain on our tent about 2:00 AM, and that meant we would be carrying a wet tent the next day. By morning, the rain had subsided to a mist, and the mountains became submerged in fog.

We hiked from Bly Gap to Standing Indian Mtn. in extreme foggy wet conditions, reminding us of the Tray Mtn. section in Georgia. Our start into North Carolina was under conditions similar to those we had when beginning the Trail at Springer Mtn., and it lasted all day. We stopped briefly at the Muskrat Shelter for lunch and were unable to take pictures of the many clusters of azaleas which were in full bloom through the area, nor could we see any of the mountain ranges on the approach to Standing Indian Mtn.

Since the weather was not favorable for photography (or hiking for that matter), we decided to end our day early and stay at the Standing Indian Shelter at the base of the mountain by a rustling stream. We were hoping for a clear day when hiking over this mountain (5,498 feet) which is known as "The Grandstand of the Southern Appalachians." We were looking forward to views from its summit into the Tallulah River Gorge and back over the Blue Ridge in Georgia. We had the shelter to ourselves that night and were lulled to sleep by the rippling water of the stream.

By morning the rain had stopped, but the fog was still hanging around. We were sure that the higher we ascended the mountain, which was about two miles from the shelter, the more dense the fog would become. We were right—as we crested out, the visibility was at zero—what a disappointment! There was no need to take the 500-foot side trail to the summit.

The fog did not start to clear until we reached a vista near Betty's Creek Gap, and it was from this point that we experienced our first view of the valleys and mountains since leaving Bly Gap. Our plan for the day was a 15-mile hike to Big Spring Shelter just off the north crest of Albert Mtn., which was in view from the vista near Betty's Creek Gap.

Our Trail profile map and guide book alerted us to expect a steep, rocky quarter-mile scramble to the summit of Albert Mtn. How right they were! It was the toughest quarter-mile we had on the AT so far, but the view was very rewarding from the fire tower at an elevation of 5,250 feet. There was a panorama of the near and distant mountains including the watershed of the Little Tennessee River. Not only did we have many good shots of the mountains and valleys but also striking photos of the floral displays of azaleas and rhododendrons in the area.

The Big Spring Shelter was one-half mile off the summit of Albert Mtn. and not in the greatest condition. No doubt the USFS and Nantahala Hiking Club (who are volunteer maintainers for the Trail from Bly Gap to the Nantahala River at Wesser) have plans for renovation in the near future. The weather the following day was excellent for photography and hiking—clear and cool. This was a 13 1/2-mile day from Big Spring Shelter to Siler Bald Shelter and provided us with more outstanding displays of Flame Azaleas in red, orange and yellow and huge rhododendrons. We also saw Mountain Laurel with its clusters of small, white cup-shaped blossoms.

This area of North Carolina was Cherokee Indian country before the intrusion by the white man. There were many Indian settlements along the river with Indian trails crossing the mountains in the gaps. Eventually, settlers moved into the area and built homes, and plots of land were cleared where they could raise their families. One of these settlers was William Siler whose homestead was near Siler Mtn. which was named for him; and Albert Mtn. was named for his son.

The next day took us from Siler Bald Shelter across Siler Bald to Wayah Gap where we picked up our food cache. We then crossed Wine Spring Bald and Wayah Bald through Licking and Burnington Gaps to the Cold Spring Shelter, a 12-mile day crossing three mountains over 5,000 feet. Wayah Bald, a 5,336-foot heath bald with an observation tower on its summit, provides an outstanding panorama of the mountain ranges from Georgia to the Great Smoky Mountains. It was through this area that we first photographed the Smooth Azalea which is noted for its fragrant white vase-shaped flowers. I was very familiar with the Flame Azalea, as it is native to the mountains of West Virginia; but the Smooth Azalea was new to me and a pleasure to hike near where their fragrance filled the air.

By late afternoon, we reached the Cold Spring Shelter, an old log structure built by the CCC and located one-half mile off the summit of Copper Ridge Bald. Near the shelter is one of the finest springs we had seen thus far along the AT; and adding to the enjoyment of the spring someone had left a partially-filled bottle of red wine in the cold water. Needless to say, the wine was very refreshing with our evening meal; however, we did leave some for hikers that would follow. This was the first of many unusual finds we would make along the AT.

Our plan for the next day was to hike into the Nantahala River Gorge at Wesser, NC, crossing Copper Bald (5,200 feet) and Wesser Bald (4,627 feet). When we reached Wesser Bald, we climbed part way up the old fire tower for some views and photographs of the Nantahala Gorge, the Stecoah Range (which is the next section of Trail between the Nantahala River and Fontana Dam) and the Great Smoky Mountains.

Wesser Bald is the last high peak in the range before reaching the Nantahala River. After leaving the summit, the Trail begins a 6.5-mile descent into the gorge. It follows the ridge crest to an area referred to in the guide book as the "Jump up" after which it begins a steep descent along a narrow hogback ridge providing impressive views of the Nantahala Gorge and the Great Smoky Mountains. We had to exercise extreme care in making this descent, as a slight slip could result in a fall causing serious injury.

We had expected to spend the night at the Wesser Creek Shelter but learned that it had been replaced by the Rufus Morgan Shelter, which was less than a mile from Wesser where the AT crosses US 19. The shelter was new and had not had much use, so the firewood supply around it was adequate. Shortly after arriving there, we had a big fire going in a fireplace which we constructed of stones that we found nearby. We prepared chicken stew, one of the better dehydrated dinners we carried, and munched on some leftover snacks along with hot tea and reflected on the hike we had through the Nantahalas. We regretted missing some of the views because of fog and rain but thoroughly enjoyed the gorgeous wildflowers.

The next morning we hiked into Wesser, a small village on the Nantahala River, and had some snacks, including ice cream, as Osbra was a true ice cream fan. At the Nantahala Visitors Center, we talked with some people who had been whitewater rafting on the river. By mid-morning, Joan and Rodney arrived to pick us up.

Rodney joined me to hike the section of the AT from Wesser, NC, to the Little Tennessee River at Fontana, NC, in June, 1984. This was his second AT hiking experience, as he had accompanied me when I re-hiked the section from Dick's Creek Gap to Unicoi Gap over Tray Mtn. a year earlier.

This section of Trail crosses a part of the Nantahala Mtn. Range and had gained the reputation of being one of the most difficult sections along the AT and would be a challenge to both of us. I was especially interested to see how well Rodney would do, not only physically but how much he would enjoy the hike in general: the views, plant and animal life, the topography of the land, etc. If he were impressed with this hike, perhaps he would do other sections with me.

The hike from Wesser up and over Swim Bald was a steady hard climb; however, it was not as difficult as we had anticipated. There had been a major Trail relocation tempering some of the original steep climbs following a course up a jagged narrow ridge. However, the elevation gain to the summit of Swim Bald was about 3,500 feet in 5 1/2 miles. We made the climb without much difficulty in spite of the warm weather. The Sassafras Gap Shelter, which is located between Swim Bald and Cheoah Bald was our destination for the day.

The next morning, we were on the Trail early with an 11 1/2-mile destination of Cody Gap. We wanted extra time through this area because we would be going over Cheoah Bald (5,062 feet)— the highest mountain through this section and offering vistas that are ranked among the best in the southern Appalachians. We would also be crossing a number of gaps and ridges that we wanted to hike through at our leisure before reaching Cody Gap.

The summit of Cheoah Bald was only a mile from the Sassafras Gap Shelter, so we were on the summit early. What a way to begin the day! The view was truly spectacular with a breathtaking panorama of the Little Tennessee Valley, the Great Smoky Mountains and Cheoah-Stecoah Ranges. We spent as much time as we felt we could spare just taking in this magnificent scene and shooting many pictures in every direction. During our photo session on Cheoah Bald, we found a box by the AT with a note attached which read: "Secret Share Box." It contained an assortment of hiking foods and provided a way for hikers to discard food items they did not like. Hikers were invited to take or exchange food, so Rodney made an exchange finding one more appealing to him. I do not know who placed the box there, but it was a neat idea. I learned from my first day hiking on the AT to expect the unexpected at any time, and the "Secret Share Box" was no exception.

We left Cheoah Bald—moved and inspired by the beauty of these southern mountains. As we crossed Sweetwater Gap, we had clear and impressive views of the Yellow Creek area and Snowbird Mtn. to the west. A box turtle greeted us as we descended into Cody Gap where we planned to spend the night. Rodney was as fascinated with the little turtle as he had been with garter snakes, black snakes, squirrels, mice in the shelters and other wildlife we had been seeing. We pitched our tent in a small clearing in Cody Gap, got water, prepared a hearty meal of spaghetti and settled in for the evening.

The hike from Cody Gap to Fontana Dam was relatively uneventful. However, we did have views of Fontana Lake, the Yellow Creek Valley area and the Great Smoky Mountains stretching majestically out of sight to the east. The AT descends rather steeply from the Stecoah Range in the Little Tennessee Valley where it crosses Fontana Dam and traverses the 70-mile crest of the Great Smoky Mountains.

By early afternoon, we arrived at the "Fontana Hilton" Shelter (a name quite fitting because this was the finest shelter I had seen so far on the AT). It is located at the Fontana Dam complex where there are restrooms and free showers which we very quickly took advantage of.

We also toured the dam area and were impressed with the size of the facility. The dam was constructed on the Little Tennessee River and is part of the Tennessee Valley Authority (TVA) system. It was built during the early 1940's to produce hydroelectric power and is the highest dam east of the Mississippi River at 480 feet and created Fontana Lake which is 29 miles long. This area was of special interest to me, as my mother spent some of her early childhood in the area of Fontana Village while my grandfather was superintendent of the logging company when the virgin timber was being cut.

After exploring the complex, we returned to the shelter, fixed our evening meal and kicked back to reflect on the Trail in the Nantahalas. We would like to have had better weather when we hiked through the Standing Indian Mtn. area, but inclement weather is an inevitable part of the Trail experience.

One of the great rewards of hiking the AT is the people you meet along the way, and I am not referring just to hikers. They are people at crossroads; people out for a short walk; the ones giving you a lift into town and back; and the list goes on. Two such people joined us at the shelter later that afternoon, and we spent a delightful evening with them. They had canoed down the Nantahala Gorge to Fontana, had come down to the dam and would be going back up the lake to a point where they would be picked up. This was one of hundreds of meetings I would have with people from all walks of life on my journey along this magic path, and many of these would develop into lasting friendships.

After a restful night in one of the Trail's best "lodges," we were up early, had breakfast and packed up ready for Joan to pick us up by mid-morning. I really enjoyed having Rodney hike this segment of the Nantahalas with me and felt confident he would be hiking more of the Trail, as he had a good time and meaningful experience. On our way to our base camp, I pointed out to Rodney and Joan the rugged ridgeline of the Smokies. That would be the next challenge.

TOP: Osbra in a Rhododendron "Tunnel" near
Standing Indian Mountain, North Carolina
BOTTOM: The Chinquapin or Dwarf Chestnut in
bloom near Standing Indian Mountain

TOP: A lush fern garden along the Appalachian Trail
    near Bly Gap, North Carolina.
BOTTOM: The Secret Share Box on Cheoah Bald,
    NC. Rodney makes an exchange of a food item.

ON TOP OF OLD SMOKY

*"The Smokies are considered by botanists as
the vegetation cradle of North America."*
—*Eliot Porter*

The Great Smoky Mountains left a lasting impression on me after making a trip across them in the late 1940's. Since that time I had made this trip several times and to areas nearby, and each time I saw them I was deeply impressed. Seeing them was inspirational, but hiking along their crest and over their lofty peaks on the Appalachian Trail would be the ultimate in a Smoky Mountain adventure. I could not wait to get this section of my long AT hike under way.

The AT begins the southwestern section of the Smoky Mtns. at Fontana Dam on the Little Tennessee River and very quickly ascends to the main ridge. It then turns east following the ridge and the North Carolina/Tennessee state line to Davenport Gap on the Pigeon River covering a distance of 68.6 miles. The terrain is rugged, and the AT crosses over 30 prominent summits with many peaks over 6,000 feet. It crosses Clingman's Dome (6,643 feet) which is the highest peak in the ranges and the highest along the entire AT.

Botanists consider the Smokies to be the vegetation cradle of North America according to Eliot Porter's *Appalachian Wilderness the Great Smoky Mountains.* Thirteen hundred native species of flowering plants have been identified and more varieties of trees than in all of Europe. In addition, there are about 2,000 species of fungi, nearly 350 mosses and Liverworts and 230 lichens. As to the mammals, there are over 50 kinds of native mammals and 200 species of birds.

My brother did not hike with Rodney and me through the section between Wesser and Fontana Dam but would be joining me this time. We planned to hike the Smokies in two sections: the first beginning at Newfound Gap to Fontana Dam (north to south—37.8 miles), and the second from Newfound Gap to Davenport Gap (south to north—30.8 miles).

Hiking permits are not required anywhere on the AT; however, camping permits are required in the Great Smoky Mountains National Park because of the park's heavy use. Park officials say the permit system is necessary as an attempt to control the limited space which is available at each of the shelters. Before beginning our hike, we stopped at the Park Office (Visitor's Center) in Gatlinburg, registered and obtained the permit. The ranger advised us about a bear with cubs hanging around in the area of the Siler Bald Shelter—the first one we would be staying in.

We began the first section on a clear June morning and planned to hike across Clingman's Dome to the Siler Bald Shelter. Yes, there was another Siler Bald and another Siler Bald Shelter; and it was in the Nantahalas. This mountain and shelter were also named for a pioneer family who pastured cattle on it during the summer. I suspect they were relatives, as family members often settled in the same general locale.

The Trail from Newfound Gap to Clingman's Dome was originally built by the CCC during the 1930's as were scores of other Trail sections from Georgia to Maine. We would also see many other Trail related marks left by the CCC such as shelter construction (stone and log), bridges, and stone crib work around steep areas. I remember the CCC's as a child growing up and the work they did in the area around our farm such as building forest fire trails, fighting forest fires and road building. They were known as the CCC Boys.

There is a vast amount of rain and moisture in the Great Smoky Mountains, which stimulates extensive plant growth. All along the ridge line, we noticed that the downed trees and forest floors were covered with Wood Sorrel and mosses, indicative of a wet environment. The soil on these higher peaks is thin, making it necessary for trees to spread their root systems far from the trunk for support. Even then, strong winds, ice and snow take their toll along these higher ridges. Blow downs along the AT are a constant problem and keep Trail maintenance crews busy.

The Appalachian Trail crosses Clingman's Dome by the observation platform, and we walked out on it to take in the view and visit with some people who were curious about our hike. We descended Clingman's Dome; and before reaching Siler Bald Shelter, we met a group of northbound hikers heading for Newfound Gap. They were quite upset about an encounter they had with a bear and her three cubs near the shelter. The bear had intimidated one hiker to the point that he discarded his pack and fled. Fortunately, there were no injuries; however, it was a frightening experience for them. They warned us to be very careful when we hiked through there. I told them the ranger knew the bears were there and advised them to make a report to the Park Office about the incident.

We continued on to the shelter without sighting the bear but did see where the hiker's pack had been torn apart and debris scattered along the Trail. His canteen had been punctured by the bear's teeth. There were also bear droppings, claw marks on trees, and bark on stumps and logs that had been disturbed by the bear searching for grubs, roots, etc. After all, a bear with triplets needs all the help she can get, but not from hikers and campers feeding them. This is what has caused problems with bears in the Smokies and elsewhere.

We arrived at the shelter by late afternoon and still no bear sighting. We unloaded our packs onto the wire bunks and made a visual check around the shelter to locate the spring, restroom and firewood. The shelters in the Smokies are specially built by the National Park Service (NPS). They are made of stone, have wire bunks and a chain-link fence around the open end with a gate that can be latched to keep out the bears. Shortly, we were joined by a group of hikers from Cincinnati, Ohio; and along with the two of us, the shelter was full.

After we had completed our check of the area, we went to the spring for water. Upon returning to the shelter, we saw coming down the Trail for what she thought would be a tasty handout— yes, you guessed it—mama bear and her three little cubs. Everyone moved into the shelter and latched the gate. Feeding bears is an absolute NO-NO, and none of us was about to break this rule now. We were in the cage looking out, and no one wanted to be held hostage for too long. For the next hour, she wandered around the area in front of the shelter looking for bits of food and occasionally meandering up to the fence hoping someone would change their mind. Eventually, she and her cubs left the area, foraging her way into the nearby woods. The rest of the evening remained uneventful as far as the bears were concerned; and, to my knowledge, she did not return during the night.

By morning light, Osbra and I were up, had breakfast and were packing up trying not to disturb the other hikers so we could be on our way. But some of them (several of whom were women) wanted us to wait for them so they could hike with us. With the bears in the area, they felt more secure hiking in a group with men, so we agreed to wait for them. When they were ready, they wanted to lead, as it made them feel safer, so we said that was no problem. Well—guess who encountered the bears first—yes, they did; but we were there and kept moving without incident. This was our first bear encounter on the AT and we survived to tell about it.

Another animal causing concern in the Smokies is the wild boar or wild hog which is not native to the area. The major problem is not necessarily so much a threat to hikers as it is to the environment. However, hikers are advised to be aware of their presence. There were large areas all along the AT in the Thunderhead Mtn. area where they had rooted up the forest floor in search of roots, grubs and any kind of small wildlife they could find. We did not see any as we passed through but did hear them on several occasions. The only one we saw was a dead one which was lying across the Trail, and we were not sure if it had been shot or died of natural causes. The NPS was trying to reduce their numbers by trapping, but I question the amount of success they were having.

The hike from Siler Bald Shelter to the Russell Field Shelter was slightly under 14 miles and took us over a number of peaks and gaps with some of the peaks being balds. Thunderhead Mtn. (5,527 feet) is one of the higher mountains we crossed and offers an outstanding view of the distant mountains and valleys. Visible from Thunderhead is the large valley known as Cades Cove. This was the site of a large pioneer settlement during the nineteenth century. The National Park Service has restored many of the early homes, grist mills, etc.; and Cades Cove has become a major tourist attraction in the Smokies.

We continued on to the shelter enjoying colorful and outstanding views of the countryside. We were joined at the shelter by a number of northbound and southbound hikers—in fact, more than the shelter could accommodate, so many of them had to pitch their tents nearby. During the evening and night, we were visited by the shelter skunk making his rounds for tidbits that had been dropped where hikers had prepared their meals. No one fed him while we were there, but no doubt he had been fed because he was very tame. The hikers who were in the tents suspended their food on ropes in trees as a protective measure from bears, but we had no sightings at this shelter.

On the following day, we hiked across another series of knobs and gaps from the Russell Field Shelter to the Little Tennessee River at Fontana Dam which would complete the western section of the Smokies. The views from the knobs and ridges were outstanding, especially from the fire tower on Shuckstack Mtn. where a panorama of the southern Appalachians unfolds. To the east and north, the crestline of the Smokies is visible from Clingman's Dome to Thunderhead Mtn.; and to the south is Fontana Lake with its shoreline extending up the coves and valleys on both sides of the lake. Further south the Cheoah and Nantahala Ranges stood majestically and reminded me of my earlier hike through them. The descent of Shuckstack was long, but the Trail was on a fairly easy grade. We arrived at Fontana Dam by late afternoon completing the western half of the Great Smoky Mountains.

The eastern half of the AT route through the Great Smoky Mountains begins (south to north) at Newfound Gap where US 441 crosses the mountain from Gatlinburg, TN, to Cherokee, NC. It is considered to be the wildest and most rugged section of the Smokies. The AT traverses high peaks, some of which are over 6,000 feet and along narrow hogback ridges into deep gaps.

Since beginning at Springer Mtn., I had kept a journal which gave me a written record of my hike. I would normally make my entries in the journal during the evening by a campfire or in the shelter by flashlight or candlelight. Many times this was difficult to do because of weather, crowded conditions in the shelter, fatigue, lack of light, or I would simply not recall all the happenings of the day. Therefore, I decided to try a new method of recording my hike beginning with this section. Our son Dave and his wife Rhonda had given me a small hand-held tape recorder that used mini cassettes. I felt I could record observations, happenings, and other information as they occurred during the day making my record more detailed, more accurate and with much less effort. It would only add about one pound to my pack weight.

Adding to the enjoyment of this hike was another companion, Don Andrews, who joined us at Newfound Gap in May, 1989, to complete the Smokies and continue on with us to Hot Springs, NC. He was also an official with the West Virginia Department of Natural Resources. This made quite a threesome—two park officials and me (an educator). On this hike, we used a two-vehicle drop-off strategy, dropping one vehicle near Hot Springs, NC, at the trailhead and the other one at the Newfound Gap trailhead. This is a strategy we would use along the Trail to Virginia.

We had a 5:00 AM breakfast in Gatlinburg, planning to be on the Trail early, but when we arrived at the trailhead, the weather conditions (cold, rain, fog) were so bad we had to delay starting until 10:15. While we were waiting for the weather to clear, several travelers who were crossing the mountains stopped in the parking area and asked us many of the usual questions such as: "How far are you hiking? How heavy is your pack? Aren't you afraid of bears? How can you hike in weather like this?" When the rain subsided, we loaded our heavy packs, which contained 9-days' supply of food, and started across the parking lot toward the trailhead.

As we were passing a parked pickup camper, the window on the passenger side was rolled down, and a middle-aged man looked curiously at us and said, "Pretty heavy looking packs ye got there—where ye headed?" We told him we were going to Hot Springs on this trip and eventually to Katahdin. He said, "Hot Springs, that's nigh 80 miles—don't know where Katahdin is." We assured him we knew how far it was. Then he said, "Do ye mind if I ask ye about how old are ye anyway?" When we told him we were all near 60, he wished us good luck, shook his head and rolled up the window.

Our packs were indeed heavy—the heaviest we had carried so far—and the weather was giving us a start like we had in the Nantahalas. The 3-mile climb out of Newfound Gap up Mt. Kephart with our heavy packs took some time, a lot of energy and some sweat. However, there was a breeze, and it was cool which helped maintain our body temperatures. We planned to hike to the Pecks Corner Shelter which was 10.6 miles from Newfound Gap. Since we had a late start, we knew it would be late afternoon before we could arrive there.

By noon, we reached Charlie's Bunion, which is a rock outcropping where the AT leads around a very narrow ledge. The Trail could be extremely dangerous during inclement weather; however, there is a blue blaze trail leading around the area providing a safer route. The view from Charlie's Bunion was outstanding, as all the fog had cleared away and views of the mountains and valleys opened right up. To the west was Mt. Kephart, an area called the Jump Off, and Mt. LeConte which is almost 6,600 feet in elevation.

We ate our lunch while enjoying the view from Charlie's Bunion and then proceeded on to an area known as Sawtooth Ridge where the Trail follows along the sharp crest of the ridge. As you hike along for some distance, one foot is in North Carolina, and the other is in Tennessee. The ridges and peaks through this area were covered with spruce and fir, and what was astonishing to me was the extent of damage possibly caused by an insect infestation to these trees. We passed through large areas where all the trees were killed leaving very ugly scars in the forest and contributing to numerous blow downs across the AT. I was really disturbed by the amount of damage to this beautiful forest and hope more intense efforts are made for a better control or solution to this problem.

We arrived at the Pecks Corner Shelter about 6:00 PM and were later joined by six other hikers. This was a 12-man shelter, but nine hikers preparing their meals at one time created a bit of confusion. By the time we all had our sleeping bags spread out on the floor with the packs hanging from the ceiling, all available space in the shelter was occupied.

During the course of the evening, we got to know the other hikers through conversation and story telling as we lay side by side. They asked many questions about various plants and birds they had seen and heard along the Trail but could not identify. Osbra, being a naturalist, not only made identification but gave additional information which added more interest. Many of them were thru-hikers with Katahdin as their goal, and we would be seeing them off and on for the next two or three days. They eventually left us because they were hiking more miles each day than we were. However, they were going to resupply at Davenport Gap.

By morning, the mountains had become engulfed in dense fog, a weather phenomenon which was becoming all too familiar to us. We left the shelter by 8:00 AM and hiked in fog until noon, making it impossible to enjoy any views when we crossed Mt. Sequoyah and Mt. Chapman, both of which are over 6,000 feet. We ate our lunch at the Tri Corners Knob Shelter, and then the fog started to clear. By the time we reached Guyot Spur and Old Black, the fog had cleared and the mountains and valleys opened up once again. The five-mile descent from Old Black to the Cosby Knob Shelter was hard with our knees constantly reminding us of the heavy pack burden they were bearing.

We arrived at the shelter in the late afternoon and were ready to call it a day after crossing some of the highest peaks in the eastern Smokies with many of them exceeding 6,000 feet. Just before dusk, the Veery Thrushes moved into the open area by the shelter and serenaded us with their flute-noted melody. We would hear these thrushes at higher elevations all along the Appalachian chain.

Davenport Gap Shelter was our goal for the next day. This was an easy half-day hike and would complete the AT through the Great Smoky Mountains. We left the Cosby Knob Shelter, crossed Low Gap and had a very steep climb up Sunrise Mtn. where we had outstanding views from the summit. We took a rest break where the blue blaze trail leads over to Mt. Cammerer, and I regret not taking the time to hike over to it. I have heard that the view from the observation tower there is one of the best in the Smokies. On the 4 1/2-mile descent of Sunrise Mtn., we passed huge gardens of the Great Trillium and Umbrella Leaf plants. Osbra took many photographs of these plants and others in the area to add to his large collection of plant and wildflower pictures.

We arrived at the Davenport Gap Shelter by early afternoon and used the time to rest, catch up on our notes, organize our packs, bathe and review our plans for the days ahead. That afternoon the Park Service sent a work crew to the shelter to replace the old wire bunks with wood flooring; as many of the wires were broken and had been causing damage to hikers' sleeping bags, air mattresses, etc. In the shelter that night were eight hikers from Florida, Wisconsin, Maine, Connecticut, Ohio and West Virginia; and again several of them had spent the last two nights with us.

Since we had arrived at the shelter early, we had time to make a closer examination of the flora and wildlife around the shelter. Most of the hikers became interested as Osbra and Don pointed out and identified many plants, wildflowers and several birds and their songs. That evening after supper, as we lay stretched out in our sleeping bags, one of the hikers asked if we had Trail names.

We told him we did not. However, Don had lost one of his Reebok shoes that he had tied to his pack; and we jokingly said that he may have purposely lost the shoe to reduce his pack weight and maybe he should be called "The Reebok Man." The hiker said he had a better name, not just for him but for the three of us. He said that, since we all seemed to have a good general knowledge about many things, he thought we should be called, "The Three Wise Men." We were somewhat flattered and agreed that from now on we would be known as "The Three Wise Men."

Trail names are an important part of the hiker's experience. They provide better communication and hiker identification. It is easier to identify with one unique name than to keep track of hikers who may have the same first or last name. One that I recall being in the shelter with us that night was "The Marathon Man," and I would meet him again on the AT several years later in the White Mountains of New Hampshire.

The next day we left Davenport Gap Shelter and descended to the Pigeon River where I-40 crosses from Asheville, NC, to Knoxville, TN, completing about 235 miles from Springer Mtn. Before reaching Davenport Gap, we hiked through more colorful displays of Mountain Laurel, the largest we had seen since Springer. The Great Smoky Mountains were now behind us and had given us another meaningful hiking experience. I enjoyed them in a way I never had before and have a deeper feeling for their ruggedness and beauty.

TOP: Siler Bald Shelter in The Great Smoky Mountains—
   Typical in the Smokies with front enclosed in wire fence
   and gate for "bear protection."
BOTTOM: Wood Sorrel covers a fallen tree near Clingman's
   Dome in the Smokies.

TOP: Fog in the valleys as viewed from Kephart
Prong in The Great Smoky Mountains
BOTTOM: Blowdowns of spruce and fir near Mt.
Chapman in The Great Smoky Mountains

"HUGO" AND THE
SOUTHERN HIGHLANDS

"Hugo caused 18 billion dollars in damages."
—Media News Release

The 5-mile climb from the AT crossing of I-40 in Davenport Gap on the Pigeon River to the summit of Snowbird Mtn. was a real test of stamina and endurance. Thank goodness the weather was cool and breezy. After leaving Davenport Gap, the AT enters a new public land area (the Pisgah National Forest on the NC side and the Cherokee National Forest on the TN side) and continues on a course following the state line. We hit fog before we reached the summit of the mountain, and this was disappointing because we anticipated views and photos of the eastern Smokies from this lofty vantage point. Near the summit, we passed through and photographed Wood Betony, a member of the snapdragon family; the Great Trillium, a member of the lily family; and Wild Geranium— all quite common in the area.

The Groundhog Creek Shelter was the next one and was about 3 miles from the summit of Snowbird. This shelter would only accommodate six hikers, and we knew of at least seven that were headed there. That did not include any other northbound or southbounders that might come in. With this in mind, we pitched our tent in a cove near a spring one-half mile off the summit.

Don had developed foot problems before reaching Davenport Gap, so his hiking speed was reduced considerably. He had fallen behind on the ascent of Snowbird, so we told him we would move ahead and establish a campsite for the evening and for him to take his time. The fog had cleared after we set up camp, so Osbra and I decided to return to the summit to try again for more photos of the views and wildflowers. Once again, we were disappointed because, even though the fog was gone, there was so much blue haze we could hardly distinguish the outline of the Smokies to the west. Don did catch up with us before we got back to the campsite.

For the next 140 miles, the AT crosses through the "Big Bald Country" of North Carolina/Tennessee. This is a succession of high grassy and heath-covered peaks with elevations ranging between 5,000 and 6,000 feet.

We left our campsite early and began the hike across Max Patch Mtn. or "Bald" which is the first of these peaks. The weather was the clearest since leaving Newfound Gap, and we were grateful because of the views we were expecting. We were not disappointed. The 360-degree panorama was outstanding, one of the best we had so far along the AT. The elevation on the summit is 4,649 feet, and Mt. Mitchell (the highest point east of the Mississippi) in the Black Mountains is visible to the east. Back to the west is the jagged profile of the peaks of the Smokies. As I pivoted looking in every direction at the magnificent view I reflected once again to the first line of the poem, "Great, wide, beautiful, wonderful world."

I was not surprised to learn that the Max Patch mountain top was used in early times as a pasture for cattle and sheep. In fact, many of these higher areas were cleared and burned to create pasture for grazing. This, however, is not believed to be the reason these peaks are treeless. No one knows for sure, but some believe fire, soil conditions and weather are possible factors. What did surprise me, however, was that the vast flat area on this mountain was at one time used as a landing strip for small airplanes. The approach certainly had no obstruction in any direction, but the likelihood of fog is another matter.

Wildlife along the AT had been fascinating, as we had numerous daily sightings of a variety of animals and birds. One of these birds was the Ruffed Grouse. His "drumming" and sudden burst into flight lets you know of his presence, and on the ascent of Max Patch, we had an encounter with a Ruffed Grouse. She suddenly burst out of the brush beside the Trail and fluttered down through the woods making a sound of distress as though she had been injured. We were familiar with this strategy of luring predators away from her chicks that she had signaled to hide on the forest floor. We would see this performance repeated many times along the AT. Both the male and female use the element of surprise very effectively for their survival. Another one of their fascinating characteristics is their ability to adapt to a variety of environments. It was the one bird I saw and/or heard daily from Georgia to Maine at both low and high altitudes. They are truly a marvel of the wildlife world along the AT.

While crossing Max Patch Bald, we saw and heard the Quail (Bob White) which is not as common as the Ruffed Grouse on the AT. I had not seen or heard Quail in the part of the country where I grew up in many years. I remembered their Bob White calls in the meadows of our family farm as a youngster. I suspect the habitat and shortage of food has caused a reduction in their population in many parts of the country.

BOB WHITE

There's a plump little chap in a speckled coat,
And he sits on the zigzag rails remote,
Where he whistles at breezy bracing morn,
When the buckwheat is ripe, and stacked is the corn:
"Bob White! Bob White! Bob White!"

Is he hailing some comrade as blithe as he?
Now I wonder where Robert White can be!
O'er the billows of gold and amber grain
There is no one in sight—but, hark again:
"Bob White! Bob White! Bob White!"

Ah! I see why he calls; in the stubble there
Hide his plump little wife and babies fair!
So contented is he, and so proud of the same,
That he wants all the world to know his name:
"Bob White! Bob White! Bob White!"
                                        —George Cooper

After spending a considerable amount of time on Max Patch enjoying the view, taking a snack break and many pictures, we descended into Roaring Fork where we had planned to tent for the night. Don was still having problems with his feet, so he continued to hike at a slower pace resting often and caring for his feet. Osbra and I pitched our tent near the AT crossing of Roaring Fork Creek around 4:15 in the afternoon. We did not want to go any further, because we wanted to give Don enough time to reach camp before dark. It was two hours before he arrived, and we used this time to catch up on our notes, organize our packs, bathe and prepare for the evening meal.

Hot Springs, NC, is a Trail town with the AT going right through the middle of it. It was 17 miles from our campsite at Roaring Fork, so our plan for the next day was to hike to the Deer Park Mountain Shelter—about three miles short of Hot Springs. We were on the Trail very early, because we knew we had a long day ahead with two hefty mountains to climb, Walnut Mtn. and Bluff Mtn. Before reaching Lemon Gap, which is at the base of Walnut Mtn., we photographed the White Baneberry, a member of the buttercup family consisting of a cluster of white flowers on a stem. Osbra said this plant is sometimes called "Doll's Eyes" because the shiny white fruits resemble the China eyes once used in dolls.

The weather turned warm on the ascent of Walnut Mtn., and the perspiration really started to flow. Upon reaching the summit (4,280 feet), we felt like we had already done a day's work; yet, only 4 1/2 miles had been covered. After a rest and snack break, we continued on for a hard hot climb up Bluff Mtn. (4,629 feet). The 7 1/2-mile descent of Bluff Mtn. to the Deer Park Mountain Shelter gave our knees a good pounding. Near the shelter area, we started seeing more striking arrays of Mountain Laurel, and these would get better lower down near Hot Springs.

We arrived at the shelter in the late afternoon, about wiped out after a warm 14 miles over two high peaks and a long descent, and pitched our tent in a pine grove by the AT across from the shelter. Don had fallen behind several miles back, as his foot problem continued to plague him. He told us to move on and not to wait supper for him, because he would be late.

Before Don arrived, a northbound hiker came through headed for Hot Springs and stopped for a quick snack. He said he found a Reebok shoe in the Smokies between Cosby Knob Shelter and the Davenport Gap Shelter, and we noticed he had it tied to his pack. We recognized the shoe as Don's and told the hiker he would be coming into camp later due to foot problems. He told us he had passed Don about two miles back and that he was okay and on his way. He must have been hurting too bad to notice his shoe tied to the hiker's pack. When he arrived about 8:00 PM, we surprised him by presenting him with his long-lost shoe. It had traveled 35 miles with the other hiker—he was glad to reunite his Reeboks again. After a hearty meal around our open campfire, we retired to our tents for a well-earned night's rest.

We were up early, ate and packed up ready to go; but Don decided to stay in camp that day to try to recover from his sore feet and said he would hike into Hot Springs the following day and wait for us to pick him up at the Jesuit Hostel. After he assured us he would be okay, we left the campsite headed for Hot Springs. On the descent into Hot Springs, we passed through areas of more Mountain Laurel in full bloom, and I have never seen such striking clusters!

The AT passes right by the Jesuit Hostel in Hot Springs, and we stopped briefly to visit with some hikers who had spent the night there and who we had met the day before. We had eaten a breakfast of oatmeal, coffee and Tang at our campsite; but we felt a second breakfast of eggs, ham, biscuits and real orange juice was in order at the Smoky Mountain Restaurant in town. After that hearty breakfast, we proceeded down the street to call our wives. Osbra received word that his daughter-in-law had given birth to a bouncing baby girl—he had become a grandpa again.

Hot Springs is located on the French Broad River nestled in a valley between the Bald Mountains in western North Carolina. It's history begins with the Cherokee and Creek Indians' use of this area as a hunting ground. White settlers had also used the river and valley as a passageway through the mountains. The springs were discovered by white man through an Indian scout in the late 1700's. Later, a large hotel was built to accommodate guests who felt that minerals from bathing in and drinking water from the springs had health benefits.

For many years, the town boomed; as it had become a popular attraction to health seekers. But, like many other towns with mineral springs along the Appalachians, it lost its popularity. The advancement of medical technology made the health benefits derived from the springs available at any medical institution. Hot Springs experienced a revival during World War I when the old hotel was used to intern German prisoners—about 2,800 of them. We enjoyed Hot Springs and found the people to be friendly and helpful to hikers.

When we left in the early afternoon, the weather had turned quite warm and humid; and we knew the climb up Lover's Leap Ridge out of the valley would require a good bit of endurance and water. Before leaving the valley, we took on extra water in body and canteen to make the climb. The view of the French Broad River and Hot Springs from Lover's Leap Rock was fantastic even though there was a lot of haze. As I looked out into space across the valley, I thought of the half dozen or so other Lover's Leaps I know of in other areas. They were all so-named because of a love affair gone bad or a love triangle where one lover jumped to his or her death in despair. Such was the case with this one.

According to legend, a Cherokee Indian maiden (Mist-on-the-Mountain) jumped to her death after her lover (Magwa) was killed by a jealous rival.

After leaving Lover's Leap Ridge, the AT ascends into an open meadow near Tanyard Gap where we had excellent views back over Bluff and Max Patch Mountains. Our guide book made reference to a spring which was located just off the AT on a gated Forest Service Road near the open meadow. We needed to fill our canteens, due to our high consumption of water, and we faced another steep climb. It was a piped spring and produced the finest water we had found anywhere along the AT. We were tempted to camp near the spring and would have had it been later in the day.

When we crossed Tanyard Gap where the AT crosses highways 25 and 70, we found major road construction in progress; and we had to work our way around heavy earth-moving equipment that was in operation. It looked as though this would become a four-lane highway and another major link between Asheville, NC, and eastern Tennessee. The climb out of the gap up Rich Mtn. was not only steep, but the weather was extremely hot making it a hard climb. The area on the north side of the mountains had experienced a major forest fire in 1988 destroying much of the larger timber and with it the forest canopy that covered the Trail, causing us to feel the full force of the hot sun on the climb.

Our campsite for the night was in a cove by a spring off the summit of Rich Mtn. We shared it with a young couple we had camped with in the Smokies and met again in Hot Springs. The weather remained hot and humid even through the evening hours. We noticed a quantity of black flies as we were setting up our tent, and by the time we finished our evening meal, they became such a nuisance that we were forced to retreat to our tent for the remainder of the evening.

The warm humid weather was a prelude to two major thunderstorms we had that night, and I mean thunderstorms! You have not really experienced thunderstorms until you have survived one in a tent on top of a high mountain. I thought if the wind did not blow us away the rain would literally pound us into the mud. Believe it or not, our tent did not fall down, and our equipment stayed fairly dry. This storm was a test of our nerves and equipment, because this would not be our last encounter with storms in high mountains—we would look back on this as a mild one.

The section of Trail from Rich Mtn. to Allen Gap where we had a car parked was about 7 miles, and we planned to hike out by noon. When we left Rich Mtn., the weather was clear; but as we approached Allen Gap, it was overcast and began to rain. We reached the car just before a general rain set in, ending the section from Newfound Gap to Allen Gap the way we began it—in rain. We thanked the people who own and operate the little store in Allen Gap for permitting us to park there and then headed for Hot Springs to pick up Don. When we got to the Jesuit Hostel, Don had just arrived and was in the process of taking a shower. He was still having major problems with his feet, and we were grateful he had made it okay. Completing this section of our hike, we loaded up and headed for Newfound Gap to pick up Don's truck.

In September, 1989, Osbra and I returned to Allen Gap to hike the next section of the AT; but Don was unable to join us due to job commitments. We planned a hike from Allen Gap to the AT crossing of US 19E near Elk Park, NC, using the food-cache-drop method again so we would not have to carry the total supply of food. After making our food drop at the Whitewater Expedition Center on the Nolichucky River near Ervin, TN, we drove to Elk Park and made arrangements with Elbert Guinn, owner of the Times Square Restaurant there, to have a driver take us in our car to Allen Gap and return it to his restaurant for storage. Making all of these arrangements took most of the day, but we did manage to leave Allen Gap by 4:00 PM and hike to Little Laurel Shelter.

On our climb up Camp Creek Bald the next day, we noticed recent rains in the mountains had washed away top soil along the AT, leaving it rocky, barren and overgrown with a heavy cover of weeds and underbrush. As we moved over Big Butt Mtn. toward Flint Gap, we passed through rough rock bar areas that were heavily overgrown with brush and brambles, making hiking slow and difficult.

We met one Trail worker from the Carolina Hiking Club who was doing his best to clear some of the areas. We took time to visit with him and commend him on his fine efforts, and he advised us that a new shelter had been built at Flint Gap. Since that was our planned destination for the day, it was a pleasant surprise because our guidebook did not list a shelter there. In the 17 miles we had hiked from Allen Gap to Flint Gap, we had not met a hiker going in either direction. The only person we had seen was the lone Trail worker. It was autumn in the southern Appalachians, and we had the Trail completely to ourselves.

Due to an early start the next morning, we had crossed Devil's Fork Gap and ascended Frozen Knob before lunch. We were not at all impressed with the condition of the Trail through this area, since it was also overgrown with weeds and brush. The Trail blazes were either missing or so dim they could hardly be seen; and, because of this, we found ourselves missing the Trail several times. To make matters worse, all-terrain vehicles had been heavily used on both sides of Frozen Knob along the AT leaving ugly scars on the forest floor.

Before reaching Hogback Ridge Shelter, which was our destination for the day, the weather was showing signs of a major change. A dense fog had moved in, and it started to drizzle rain. When we arrived at the shelter, we quickly obtained our water and wood supply because it was evident it was going to be a wet night.

September 21, 1989, was a day we would not soon forget! The weather was unsettled when we left the Hogback Ridge Shelter on this September morn. Our destination was the Bald Mountain Shelter (or as referred to in Trail literature as the "Carolina Condo"), but little did we know how lucky we would be to be in that shelter on this night.

As we crossed Sam's Gap and began the ascent of Big Bald, the mountains became obscured in a blanket of dense fog, and it began to mist rain. We donned our pack covers and rain gear, as it appeared we were in for a general rain; but we would find there was nothing general about it. After crossing Low Gap on the ascent, we decided it was time for lunch but never finished before the rain set in. The higher we climbed, the harder the rain, and the more dense the fog became.

When we reached the summit, the wind became fierce with the fog so dense that visibility was zero; and we could barely read the elevation marker (5,516 feet) on the summit. We moved across the summit as quickly as we could, going almost in a run to try to get out of the extreme weather. We passed bird-banding nets where birds were caught and banded for migration study and also Greer Rock which was, according to history, the home of David Greer. He was a hermit who lived on the mountain off and on for almost 30 years in the early 1800's.

The "Carolina Condo" was about a mile from the summit, and we needed shelter immediately, as weather conditions were deteriorating with driving rain and fierce wind. Tree branches were falling, and the rain was literally stripping the leaves from the trees. There was not a stitch of our clothing that was dry, and it seemed that the rain and wind were coming from everywhere as though we were standing beneath a huge waterfall. We were grateful when we arrived at the shelter, even though all the surfaces in it were dripping wet. At least, now we had some protection from the severe wind and falling branches and trees.

We moved into a corner of the shelter which offered some protection from the wind and flying objects. The rain, however, was blowing into the shelter striking the floor and walls forming clouds of mist. Within 15 minutes after our arrival at the shelter, the rain and wind subsided; and we thought maybe the storm was over. We were stunned at the severity of the storm and how quickly it had subsided. Little did we know that we had not seen anything yet! We expected there would be a couple in the shelter that we met earlier in the day near Sam's Gap, as they indicated they were planning to spend the night on Bald Mtn. and that they would see us there. They were nowhere to be found, indicating they had moved on—did they know something we didn't?

Since we thought the storm was over, Osbra started a fire with some wood he found under the shelter. Dry wood was a scarce commodity, and we had to try to dry our clothes and gear and did manage to partially dry them and cook the evening meal before the second phase of the storm hit.

For the next ten hours, the storm pounded Big Bald Mtn. with a force we had never seen. Torrential driving rain and flying debris hammered the shelter all night. We slept very little fearing the shelter would be carried away in the fierce wind as Dorothy was in the *"Wizard of Oz."* The storm continued into the following morning, and it looked as though we would have to stay in the shelter for the next day.

The mountain top was engulfed in a sea of mist as we peered out of the shelter as daylight broke reluctantly. Branches, twigs and leaves covered the surrounding area as well as the lower floor of the shelter. Water was running in streams in every direction from the shelter and had plotted its own courses right down through the forest where it had not run previously. How grateful we were to have had the protection of the shelter during the storm, and we were not sure how it stood the force of the wind and flying debris throughout the night. Neither of us had ever experienced a storm of this magnitude in our lifetime.

As we were viewing the storm damage in the immediate area of the shelter, we wondered what the condition of the Trail would be ahead. We were sure blow downs of branches and trees, high streams and sections of severe Trail erosion would be waiting to challenge us. We also wondered if this storm had any connection to a hurricane named "Hugo" reported by the National Weather Service on the radio before we left Allen Gap. But we were over 300 miles from the coast—was it possible the storm could have come inland that far?

We were finally able to leave the shelter after 10:00 AM and hiked in foggy, wet, windy conditions across Little Bald Mtn., down into Whistling Gap, across an area known as High Rocks and down into Spring Gap where the AT crosses US 19W. As we were descending High Rocks, we wondered why we were not hearing traffic on US 19W which is a major highway through the area. Normally, as we descend into valleys where major highways cross, we begin hearing traffic a mile or more away. When we reached the highway, there was no traffic moving in either direction, so we suspected it had been closed due to flooding. The streams were all in a flood mode which meant we were wading through water off and on for the remainder of the day. In many areas, the streams had rerouted themselves and were running right down the AT.

We managed to reach the No Business Knob Shelter, which was about 10 miles from Big Bald Mtn., by late afternoon. Not a lot of mileage on this day; but, considering a late start, wet foggy weather, high water everywhere, many blow downs across the Trail, and not much sleep the night before, I guess that was not too bad. We were able to build a fire and did a better job of drying out some very wet clothing and equipment. Since we had left our food cache at the Expedition Center which might be on the river flood plain, we wondered what condition the Nolichucky River would be in with all the high streams that were tributaries. Would the Center be above the high water? Not being in contact with anyone in over 24 hours, all we could do was speculate and find out the next day when we reached the river.

We had a restful night, were on the Trail by 8:30 and had our first view of the Nolichucky River and Gorge from a high point on Temple Ridge. The river was muddy and high. On the descent into the Gorge, we met a southbound hiker—the first we had seen in two days. She was from Connecticut and was section-hiking. She informed us that the storm we had on Big Bald Mtn. was "Hurricane Hugo." She had spent that night in the shelter on Roan Mtn. and had to wade across high streams and struggle around blow downs and through eroded sections of the Trail as we had done. She had received news reports on the storm from the hostel at the Expedition Center where we left our food cache and said there had been major destruction reported up the East Coast.

We crossed the bridge over the Nolichucky River at Chestoa, TN, and proceeded up the river to the Whitewater Expedition Center to pick up our food. We were pleased to find that the water had not reached the Center and that our food was just as

we had left it. Tom Allen, a young man who was helping to oversee the Center, told us what happened to him coming up the river
road in his Datsun car the day before. The road makes a loop
down along the river bank under the railroad bridge, and the river
was over the road where he tried to ford it. His car stalled about
midway, and he had to wade out. While he was gone to the Center
to arrange for a tow, the river took his car.

The hostel at the Center seemed very inviting to us after the
wet stormy conditions we had been through the last couple of
days. We took a hot shower and hitched a ride into Ervin, TN, for
a steak dinner. Since we were unable to hitch a ride back to the
hostel, we had to walk the three miles, which we did not mind
after a good dinner and a walk along the river without the burden
of our packs. On the way back to the hostel, we met two young
men who said they had seen a car in the river and wanted to know
if we knew where it came from or who it belonged to. We told
them that Tom lost his car the day before and that we would pass
the word on to him and give him the location. Upon our return to
the hostel, we packed our supply of food for an early morning
departure for the Unakas.

It was still dark in the Nolichucky Gorge when we left the
hostel using flashlights and heading for the Cherry Gap Shelter
which was 15 miles up the Trail. Our packs were heavy from our
resupply of food, and we had a 5,500-foot elevation gain from the
Nolichucky over Unaka Mtn. to the Cherry Gap Shelter.

The hike through the high water of Jones Branch was a challenge, and more challenging were the several crossings we had to
make before starting the ascent to Curley Maple Gap. As we moved
higher up the Unaka Range, the sun came through brightly, really
lifting our spirits after several days of cloudy stormy weather; but
the temperature was cool in its aftermath. The streams and branches
were still high, but the sunshine provided a near perfect day as we
approached an area known as "beauty spot."

It was, indeed, a beauty spot and perfect weather made the
view from here truly spectacular. The storm had cleared the atmosphere giving us breathtaking views in every direction. We could
not help but take some time here while eating our lunch to enjoy

this fascinating landscape. This is one of the rewards in hiking this magnificent Trail. I was personally inspired by the view from this spot to the point of tears and would experience this same inspiration and spiritual renewal hundreds of times as I moved up the Appalachian Range. I vowed to return to this spot and bring Joan to share this wondrous place.

We reached the summit of Unaka Mtn. (5,180 feet—100 feet less than a mile) by mid afternoon and were impressed by the beautiful stand of red spruce. In fact, we were quite surprised to find such a stand this far south. The ground and the trunks of the spruce trees were covered with a bright green moss, taking on a storybook appearance.

Near the summit, placed neatly side by side and half filled with water, was a pair of almost-new, size 12, 8" boots (not hiking but more like hunting boots). We left them there with several unanswered questions. Why would someone leave an almost-new pair of boots here? Was the person a hiker, hunter or neither? Didn't the boots fit? Or were they too heavy? I am sure someone can solve this mystery. We reached the Cherry Gap Shelter before 6:00 PM after a full but certainly enjoyable hiking day. Unaka Mtn. had provided us with beauty and solitude, elements for a memorable day.

When we left Cherry Gap Shelter, the weather was unsettled. There was a heavy overcast and a cold misty rain along with a great deal of wind—quite a contrast from the day before. We were hoping for fair weather when we crossed the Roan Highlands which was another day and a half. After evaluating the weather situation and the hike ahead of us, we decided to make this a short day and give the atmosphere time to perhaps clear and give us a fresh start on the Roan Highlands the next day. We spent the night in the Clyde Smith Shelter where a general cold rain set in and continued throughout the night.

Water was dripping from the trees onto the shelter roof, and another sea of fog greeted us as we awoke and gazed out of the open front of the shelter at daybreak—not the scene we had hoped for at all. Today we would be traversing the Roan Highlands, an area we both were looking forward to with great interest. The

Roan Highlands contain one of the finest displays of natural rhodo-dendron gardens found anywhere in addition to spectacular balds or treeless grassy summits. We had hoped for clear weather when we made the crossing, but at this early hour it was not too prom-ising, and we had no choice but to move on. We crossed High Rocks and descended into Hughes Gap where 19W crosses. On the descent, lying by the Trail, we found a homemade stretcher which was constructed of poles and vines and had apparently been used to transport an ill or injured hiker from the back country.

Weather conditions did not improve as we ascended Beartown Mtn. and Roan High Knob. Dense fog and a fierce, chilly wind were constant companions as we crossed over the 6,285-foot Knob—the highest peak from this point on the AT before Mt. Washington in New Hampshire. These conditions continued as we crossed Carver's Gap and Jane Bald. We were disappointed that we could not enjoy the views or spend some time studying this unique highland area. This was another area I would like to return to, hoping to coincide with the spectacular floral displays of the Pink Catawba Rhododendron which occurs about mid June. Other plants I would like to study and photograph through here include the Flame Azalea and a rare one known as the Orange Bell Lily found near the bald areas.

The harsh weather forced us to move rapidly across the balds and down off the main ridge to the Roan Highland Shelter where we spent a cold, windy night. By morning, there were signs of clearing; and, needless to say, we were thankful. On this day's hike, we would be crossing Yellow Mtn. Gap (one of historical significance) and Little and Big Hump Mountains (both interest-ing bald areas). We noted, both on the approach to Roan Mtn. on the Hughes Gap side and on this descent from the Roan Highland Shelter, stands of Buckeye trees. There had been an abundant harvest, as there were buckeyes everywhere along the Trail; and we were not surprised that the gap near this area was appropri-ately named Buckeye Gap.

The sign in Yellow Mtn.Gap by the AT marked the area where the mountaineers crossed over the mountain to attack the British in October of 1780. According to history, Colonel Patrick Ferguson (a British officer of a force of Tories) sent word across the mountain in Tennessee that, if the mountaineers did not declare allegiance to King George III, he would "march (his) Army over the mountains, hang (their) leaders and lay (their) country waste with fire and sword." The mountaineers were offended by the message, so they organized a group of men, estimated at 1,000, marched over the mountain through Yellow Mtn. Gap to King's Mtn., NC, killed Ferguson and either killed or captured all of his men. This defeat was a turning point in the American Revolutionary War. It was from this historic background that the trail crossing the AT at Yellow Mtn. Gap was named, "The Overmountain Victory Trail."

Down a blue blaze trail 3/10 of a mile from the AT on the North Carolina side of the mountain is the Overmountain Shelter, an old barn which has been converted into a shelter for hikers and is visible from the AT on the approach up Little Hump Mtn. As we neared the summit of Little Hump, bright sunshine appeared and the clouds cleared away as if by magic. It was as though the Creator opened a curtain and was rewarding us for being tolerant of the miserable weather we had endured for the past two days. We were able to take in a beautiful panorama from Little Hump.

After crossing Bradley Gap and ascending Big Hump, the views became even better—looking back to the south and west were Grassy Ridge and Roan High Knob which we had hiked over in bad weather the day before. To the northwest we could see the Doe River Valley, and to the northeast were Whitetop and Mt. Rogers in Virginia, areas we would be going over on our next hike. Grandfather Mtn. was to the east—what a magnificent view—and we took advantage of the fantastic weather to take many pictures.

I have since learned through an article in *ATC News* that these remarkable highlands would not be available for hikers and others to enjoy now had it not been for the foresight of the Southern Appalachian Highlands Conservancy (SAHC) in Asheville, NC. It was through their efforts of raising funds to purchase properties from landowners in the highlands that kept developers from building skiing facilities and private homes in the higher elevations. What a loss this would have been—they are to be commended!

We ate lunch on Big Hump and took extra time to enjoy the view, as we had the mountain to ourselves and found this setting another difficult one to leave. This would be our last hiking day on this trip, and we wanted to extend our time and enjoy this mountain to the fullest. The descent from the summit of Big Hump onto US 19E was about five miles, and we were able to hike into the Apple House Shelter, which was one-half mile from US 19E, by 3:00 PM.

We wanted to bathe and change clothes before hiking out onto the highway, and the shelter provided a good place for that. When I went into the bottom of my pack for a fresh change of clothes, I made a surprising discovery—under the clothes in a nest made from bits of my toilet tissue were three newborn mice but no mom. I figured I had carried the babies in my pack since leaving the Clyde Smith Shelter two days hence. We knew mice got into our packs there, because the next day I discovered my toilet tissue had a hole chewed right through it. The mother mouse apparently had three babies in the pack that night and, when we packed up in the morning, we frightened her and she left the pack separating her from her babies. What to do with them? I placed them in their nest under the floor of the shelter, because there are mice in every shelter; but I doubt these babies would be adopted—oh, well, so goes another mouse story.

We hiked out on 19E by 4:00 PM and called Mr. Guinn in Elk Park to pick us up. Before leaving there, we made arrangements with him for a car drop for the next section we would be hiking in the Spring.

TOP: Hot Springs Historic marker, Hot Springs, NC.
BOTTOM: Hot Springs on the French Broad River
as viewed from Lovers Leap.

Photo by Osbra Eye

TOP: Spring Mountain Shelter near Allen Gap, North Carolina.
BOTTOM: Herb crossing footbridge over Oglesby Branch near Spring Gap after "Hugo"

Photo by Osbra Eye

TOP: Nolichucky River in flood mode after "Hugo" as viewed
   from overlook near Temple Ridge.
BOTTOM: Discarded homemade stretcher made of poles and
   used to transport sick or injured hiker near Hughes Gap, NC.

TOP: Herb on Little Hump Mountain with Big Hump Mountain
in the background   *Photo by Osbra Eye*
BOTTOM: A reminder of "Hugo" left on the face of a log along
the AT in the Mount Rogers National Recreation Area
(taken one year later).

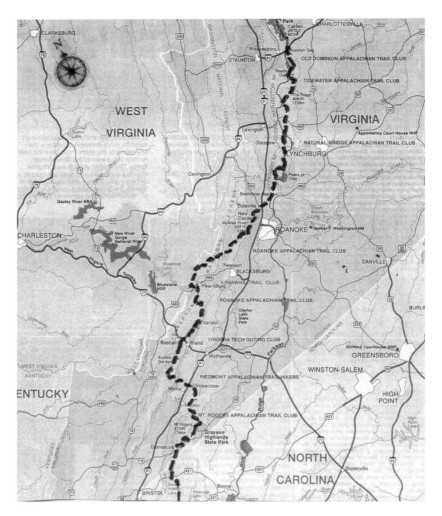

Map detail from Elk Park, NC, to Humpback Rocks, VA

(Covered in Chapters five and six)

— — — — — Denotes Appalachian Trail Route

ON PAST DAMASCUS

"The kiss of the sun for pardon, the song of the birds for mirth,
You are nearer God's heart in the garden than anywhere else
on earth."   *—John Burroughs*

On May 14, 1990, we were on the AT hiking the section from Elk Park, NC, to Troutdale, VA, about 30 miles north of Damascus, VA, a town on the Virginia/Tennessee state line. Don Andrews joined Osbra and me on this hike making "The Three Wise Men" a trio again. We used the two-vehicle strategy by placing one near the trailhead in Elk Park at the Times Square Inn Motel and the other in Troutdale. We also made a food drop near the center of this section to help make our pack weights more manageable. By the time we drove from home, made the food drop and made arrangements for the vehicles, we did not start on the Trail until 5:00 PM. The Don Nelan Shelter was four miles from the trailhead according to the Trail Guide, and that was our destination for what was left of the day. When we arrived at the shelter location around 8:00 PM, we found to our surprise that the shelter had burned; so we pitched our tents nearby giving little thought as to why it had been burned other than thinking it was probably accidental.

It was not until the next morning at the Moreland Gap Shelter that we learned what happened. A hiking couple informed us there had been a dispute between local landowners and the Park Service over property or boundary lines and that the shelter had been burned by locals in retaliation. They also said the Park Service had posted signs along the AT advising hikers not to camp through this area, to hike in groups, and to stay on the Trail. We had not seen any of the signs to this point. They could have been there and were torn down. (We did see one the following day as we were hiking across White Rock Mtn. near the fire tower.) It was also reported that fishhooks had been strung across the Trail at eye level by locals and that members of the Forest Service had been confronted on several occasions. Fortunately, we had no problem hiking through this area and were unaware of any problems until after we had passed through most of it.

After leaving Moreland Gap, we ascended White Rock Mtn. (4,105 feet), appropriately named because of the white quartzite rock which makes up the mountain. The fire tower on its summit offered rewarding views of the Iron Mtn. and Holston Mtn. ranges to the north which were areas we would hike through in the days ahead. We could also see the Roan and Unaka ranges to the south.

From White Rock Mtn., the AT descending into Laurel Fork Gorge, one of the finest in the southern Appalachians, leaves North Carolina and enters Tennessee. (The AT has followed the North Carolina/Tennessee state line since Fontana Dam.) Two states were now completed and twelve to go. The Gorge offers outstanding natural beauty, rugged geologic phenomena and a rich history. The virgin stands of hemlock, poplar, chestnut and various hardwoods once found in the gorge were timbered during the early years of the 20th century.

Huge logs were taken out by Shay steam locomotives on a narrow gauge railway. These locomotives were specially built for moving heavy loads around sharp curves and negotiating steep grades. The Shay was a locomotive which consisted of a gear train that provided power to all the wheels giving it more traction. Its turning radius was about half that of a conventional rod-driven locomotive. These features made it ideal for moving logs out of rugged areas such as Laurel Fork Gorge.

The AT follows the old railroad grade down through much of the gorge, and in three locations high trestles were constructed across the gorge when the railroad was built. These were made of wood (logs) and were engineering feats. The structures were long gone, so the AT went down the steep banks to make the crossing.

I could relate very well to this gorge and its heyday of timbering operations; because, near our family farm, the timber had been taken out in similar fashion and the narrow gauge railroad beds and many wooden trestles were still intact when I was a child. My father used to service the old Shay engines and had shared many of his experiences with me regarding the timbering operations.

Part way down the gorge, the AT leaves the old railroad bed and descends to Laurel Fork Stream at the base of Laurel Falls, a spectacular 40-foot falls of unsurpassed beauty. According to reports, 50 million gallons of water a day flow down the gorge and over this great falls creating a turbulence of wind and mist which can be felt 100 feet below the falls. This is one of the most beautiful falls along the entire AT. We stopped for an extended break below the falls taking pictures, eating a snack and just enjoying this rugged gorge. The AT continues down the Laurel Fork Stream bank for 2 tenths of a mile and returns to the old railroad bed. During high water, this part of the AT would be inaccessible. The 2.7 miles the AT follows along the banks of the Laurel Fork with its many turbulent cascades and vertical cliffs was a segment of the Trail we would not soon forget.

The ascent of Pond Mtn. out of the gorge was a test of our afternoon strength and will—a 2,000-foot elevation gain in 3 miles—and to complicate this, the temperature reached near 80 degrees. It is my understanding that the Trail has since been rerouted across Pond Mtn. to "soften" the climb and perhaps shorten the distance. Many hikers felt the old route across Pond Mtn. was "pointless" but I feel it was a part of the character of the Trail. In any event, the campsite on the summit at Pond Flats where we spent the night was in a beautiful location and had an excellent spring.

The next day's hike took us from the summit of Pond Mtn. across the Watauga Valley around Watauga Lake and up on the Iron Mountains to near the Vandeventer Shelter. Watauga Lake is part of the TVA system, and the AT follows its shoreline for 4 1/2 miles to a dam with impressive statistics: 320 feet high, 840 feet long and was completed in 1949. The lake is 16.3 miles long and .8 mile wide with a grand view from the top of the dam to the power plant which is one-half mile downstream. The geology of this valley is fascinating—when cuts were made in the mountain during the dam construction, an "edge-on" view of the great Iron Mtn. facet was exposed. Visible here are "the rock stratus of the sandstone of Iron and Holston Mountains slipped over the limestone and shales of the valleys."

After leaving the dam, the AT crosses Watauga Dam Road, begins the ascent of Iron Mtn. and follows the Iron Mtn. range for 16 miles. We hiked to the Vandeventer Shelter area which was 4 miles up the range. As we ascended the ridge, the view of the Watauga Valley and Lake stretched out beneath us for miles, and as usual the higher we climbed the better the view. To find water along the AT many times requires a steep scramble off the ridge— sometimes several hundred yards—and this was the case at this shelter, so we solved the problem by tenting in the saddle off the ridge near the spring.

The next morning we hiked up past the shelter and took in the extraordinary view of Watauga Valley from the rocks behind it. The view from here is perhaps the best than from any other shelter along the AT. The hike up the Iron Mtn. range was relatively easy with very minimal elevation changes. We met several hikers, most of whom were northbound and in a big hurry. The Annual Appalachian Trail Days' festivities were scheduled to be held on the weekend of May 19 in Damascus; and they had been trying desperately to get there so they could participate in them. At this point, we were 20 miles from Damascus and planned on arriving there on Sunday, May 21, and were sure there would still be a lot of action.

Before leaving the Iron Mtn. range, the AT crosses over Grindstaff Mtn. (4,120 feet), and near its summit is a grave and monument with the following inscription: "Uncle Nick Grindstaff—Born Dec. 26, 1851—Died July 22, 1923—lived alone, suffered alone, and died alone." Our guidebook reports that "he was an orphan at the age of three and that he was robbed and beaten when he was 26 years old while on a trip out west. Disillusioned, he became a hermit and lived the remaining 46 years of his life on Iron Mountain with only a dog as his companion." We could not help but feel sadness for Uncle Nick and many of the hardships he must have endured during those many years on Iron Mtn.

The AT leaves the Iron Mtn. range a few miles beyond Grindstaff Mtn., crosses Shady Valley, ascends Holston Mtn. and follows this range into Damascus. While crossing Shady Valley, a Ruffed Grouse burst into flight a few feet in front of me and immediately landed in the Trail and began distress calls and antics to lure me away—her usual strategy. I examined the area close by and found her chicks "frozen" but well camouflaged on the forest floor. We had been seeing and hearing grouse daily, but finding the chicks was a rarity. I photographed them and moved on without disturbing them.

The Double Spring Shelter was three miles from the Shady Valley crossing, and we planned to tent nearby because we had received accurate reports of an excellent spring there. Fortunately, our tent site was some distance from the shelter, because by nightfall it was filled with hikers who felt the need for a celebration since they were only one day from a major milepost in their hike—Damascus. From the sounds we heard, they were having a great time as they celebrated into the late evening hours, but we were not disturbed.

By leaving early the next morning, we could hike close to Damascus, thus completing additional miles while we were on the ridge and shortening the high mileage days we had planned further up the Trail. Hiking had been pleasant all the way up the Iron Mtn. range, and the Holston range was turning out the same—moderate climbs and descents, beautiful woodland consisting of large fern and mayapple gardens and abundant wildflower areas. Our packs were much lighter with our diminishing food supply, but that would change when we picked up our food cache later in the day. We had not completely run out, but our supply was getting low.

We reached the food drop location by mid morning, found it all in order under the cliff where we hid it six days before, reorganized our packs and were off to the Damascus area. At the Abington Gap Shelter, we stopped for lunch, and I made another long, steep descent off the ridge to get water—a hefty 275 yards. Holston Mtn. was a dry one with the springs well off the ridges. We found this to be true until we reached Damascus.

We had planned to tent at a campsite about 5 miles before reaching there; but, because of the scarcity of water, we continued on past the Tennessee/Virginia state line which marked another personal milepost on my northward journey on the AT—three states down and eleven to go. I had completed 450 miles of the over 2,150-mile-long Trail and was confident that my goal of hiking the entire Trail would be accomplished. The hike through Virginia would be the longest in any one of the 14 states—about 545 miles and slightly over one-quarter of the distance of the entire Trail. I was looking forward to the hike through Virginia; because, having grown up not too far from many sections of the Trail through this area, I was familiar with some of the mountains and valleys through which it passes.

Upon entering Virginia near Damascus, the AT immediately goes into the Mount Rogers National Recreation Area (MRNRA) in the Jefferson National Forest and remains there for the next 60 miles. We hiked to within two miles of Damascus to a campsite near a spring where we met a family from the area that were camping there. Later in the evening, they prepared hot dogs for us along with barbecued chicken—what a treat! This was in addition to the evening meal we had prepared on our own.

The next morning we packed up quickly, placed extra special emphasis on personal hygiene and change into fresh, clean clothes; because today we were going into Damascus for breakfast and to check out the AT festivities going on there. Wouldn't you know, it began to rain as we entered Damascus; and before we reached the Corner Cafe, we had to put on our rain gear. There were hikers everywhere, but the rain had put a damper on many of the activities. The Corner Cafe was also filled with hikers which meant we had a long wait for breakfast. During the hour we waited, they ran out of eggs, so I had a very large serving of sausage gravy and biscuits. Since the rain had squelched most of the special outdoor activities—and many were probably over anyway—we decided to move on. Before leaving Damascus, we talked to many of the hikers we had met on the Trail during the previous days.

We also had the privilege of talking with Bill Erwin, the blind hiker who accomplished the "impossible" by hiking the entire Trail and lived to tell about it in his book, *Blind Courage.* We would also meet Bill again further up the Trail in the Mt. Rogers area and were greatly inspired by his faith and courage. Hiking the entire Trail with all of our faculties is remarkable, but hiking it without eyesight is beyond comprehension bordering on divine intervention—what a feat!

It was raining steadily when we left Damascus, but as we ascended Feathercamp Ridge north of there the rain subsided; and we found ourselves hiking through a serene section of the Trail. It was well graded; the woods were open, undisturbed and peaceful. Areas like this cause me to get lost in my own thoughts.

Along the AT north of Damascus is the Virginia Creeper Railroad grade running from Abington, VA, to the North Carolina line. The old railroad grade has been made into a trail and is available to hikers, bikers and horseback riders. The AT parallels the Virginia Creeper Trail for some distance. This area in southwestern Virginia also had a history of logging and experienced a heyday from about 1910 to 1930 when millions of board feet of lumber were taken out of the mountains and valley by rail as it was in the Laurel Fork Gorge of Tennessee. The AT follows many of the old railroad beds and logging roads through this section today.

Mt. Rogers is truly a gem in southwestern Virginia with a ridge of peaks that is the highest in the state, and the AT crosses over all of them. We hiked to a camping area just across VA 601 at the foot of Whitetop Mtn., the first of these towering peaks, and de cided to tent there even though it was only mid afternoon. We wanted a fresh start the next morning up Whitetop and across Mt. Rogers. We had planned for two days to study, photograph and traverse the high ridges and make the 7-mile loop around Grayson Highlands State Park. None of us had ever been across Mt. Rogers, but we had studied about it and were anxious to make the crossing. Once again, we hoped for clear weather, but that was not to be because during the night we had a thunderstorm, ceasing before 4:00 AM and then starting again about daybreak.

We broke camp, packing up a wet tent which added weight we would have to carry across the peaks of Mt. Rogers—not a good way to start the day. The rain continued as we ascended to Buzzard Rocks. A strong wind and dense fog moved in—conditions we were all too familiar with. Once again, the higher the more extreme the weather became. Even though we had rain gear on, our clothes were soaking wet; and it was important that we keep moving to stay warm as the cold, wet windy conditions had set the stage for hypothermia.

We maintained a brisk pace across Whitetop Mtn. (5,360 feet) and dropped into Elk Garden where VA 600 crosses the MRNRA and still no break in the weather. We planned to take a lunch break at the Deep Gap Shelter two miles further on, as we needed a dry place to eat. When we arrived there, we found a concentration of hikers with tents everywhere and standing room only in the shelter. Everyone was trying to escape the harsh weather—no chance for a lunch break here or even a space for shelter, so we moved on.

There was no sign of any break in the weather, so we decided to abort the 7-mile loop through Grayson Highlands State Park. We could accomplish this by taking a blue blaze trail at Rhododendron Gap, cutting off the loop and rejoining the AT on the crest of Pine Mtn. This would shorten the day and make it possible to hike off the mountain to Troutdale where we had parked a vehicle and would end the hike for this section. The high country definitely was not the place to be in weather conditions like this. We kept moving, crossing near the summit of Mt. Rogers (5,279 feet), crossing Rhododendron Gap and Pine Mtn. as planned and made the descent past the Old Orchard Shelter (which was also packed with hikers) onto the VA 603 trailhead. It was 4 miles from there to Troutdale where my vehicle was parked, and I volunteered to make the walk (hoping to catch a ride but didn't) to pick it up. This made an exhausting 20-plus-mile day for me, my highest mileage day so far on the AT.

On October 3, 1990, Osbra and I returned to Mt. Rogers and had Joan and Osbra's wife, Naomi, drop us off at Elk Garden near the summit of Mt. Rogers (where VA 600 crosses) to rehike the section we missed through the Grayson Highlands State Park. While we were in the area, our wives joined us one day to hike down to Buzzard Rock off Whitetop Mtn. to enjoy the view.

The hike from Elk Garden up past the Deep Gap Shelter over Mt. Rogers was familiar territory to us except that the weather and views were superb, unlike our spring trip. We had lunch at Rhododendron Gap on the large boulders and enjoyed breathtaking views on this gorgeous October day. The Gap is also noted for its spectacular display of purple rhododendron which blossom during the month of June as they do on the balds of Roan Mtn. Blueberries are also prominent and ripen in August.

We saw many "wild" ponies as we traversed the high country. These are not true wild ponies but roam freely across the balds of Mt. Rogers. We were told by Park personnel that each fall some of the colts are rounded up and sold at Grayson Highlands State Park.

After leaving the Gap, we made the loop through Grayson Highland via Wilburn Ridge and passed through impressive meadows and around massive rock outcroppings. Three miles of the AT pass through this beautiful State Park. The AT then makes a sharp loop up and across Stone Mtn. with a very large, flat open summit. I was amazed at the amount of flat area there which looked large enough for an air strip. On our descent into Scales (so-named because it was the site of scales used to weigh cattle during pasturing days in the high country), we sighted the last of the wild ponies. It was not long until we were on Pine Mtn. at the junction of the blue blaze trail we had crossed from Rhododendron Gap in the spring. The rest of the hike was downhill to the familiar little parking lot on VA 603.

Mt. Rogers is truly a gem and, in my opinion, one of the finest high back country areas in the southern Appalachians. We had hiked across its lofty ridges on two occasions with the mountain in a different mood each time—a cold, rainy, foggy spring storm and a bright blue October morn—and each time I was deeply moved with its grandeur. Its panoramic views from Buzzard Rock and Whitetop Mtn., its views from the rugged peaks and cliffs of Wilburn Ridge, its open alpine meadows and the vast Rhododendron Gardens were truly inspirational. Mt. Rogers is on my list of special places along the AT that I want to return to. Since our crossing in 1990, a movement was initiated by the VA Department of Transportation to build a super highway across its high ridges. Conservationists and other environmental groups strongly objected and eventually won—NO highway—I am elated!

Our hike from VA 603 to the AT crossing of VA 16 at the MRNRA Headquarters was relatively routine and uneventful. We were, however, amazed by the amount of storm damage along the AT in this section caused by Hurricane Hugo. We had seen a great deal of damage in other areas, particularly in higher elevations to the south, but nothing compared to this. Trees of all sizes had been uprooted and/or broken off and had fallen across the AT for miles. The Trail clubs and Park Service had done a remarkable job of clearing the Trail of the hundreds of blow downs. People hiking through this section after the storm would have had to leave the Trail and hike around these areas. We continued to see major damage to the AT in the form of erosion and extensive tree damage as we moved north. The storm seemed to have "bounced" along the Appalachian chain and, when it touched down, left a trail of destruction.

TOP: Laurel Fork Falls in Laurel Fork Gorge
BOTTOM: Don Andrews and Osbra at campsite
   at Moreland Gap

TOP: Can you find the two hidden grouse chicks
   in this photograph?
BOTTOM: Rhododendron in full bloom along
   the Appalachian Trail

TOP: Osbra and Herb at Corner Cafe in Damascus
Photo by Don Andrews
BOTTOM: Deep Gap Shelter near the summit of Mt. Rogers
in the Mt. Rogers National Recreation Area

TOP: Lindamood School, 1894 one-room school
by the AT near VA 615 in The Shenandoah
BOTTOM: Chestnut Knob Shelter (The Rock
Hut) in southwestern Virginia

PAIN AND SADNESS

"No Pain—No Rain—No Maine"
—Shelter Journal along the AT

Our hikes on the AT to this point had been in the spring or early fall because of job and other commitments, but I had retired now and Osbra's job schedule had become more flexible. We could now plan hikes for other seasons of the year, and so we did for the next section. Each season is special in its own right by bringing changes in weather, plants, wildlife, views, etc., thus providing a more complete Trail experience. Another change beginning at this point was that Don would not be hiking with us since he had joined the instruction staff at Charleston University. Our Trail names would now have to be changed to "The Two Wise Men."

A late fall hike seemed appealing to both of us, so we made plans to do a part of southwestern Virginia in November, 1990. We made arrangements to leave our vehicle by a store and gift shop near the AT crossing of US 11 about 10 miles north of Marion, VA. A resident from the Adkins area, Norm Sylvester, shuttled us in our vehicle to the trailhead at the Mt. Rogers Visitors Center on VA 16, the point where we finished previously. He drove the vehicle back to the store and would be picking us up at the end of this hike where the AT crosses I-77 near Wytheville when we called him. After leaving the Visitors Center, we continued through more areas that had been heavily damaged by Hurricane Hugo. They usually did not extend for more than a few hundred feet at a time but were quite extreme and were evidence of the erratic and destructive path taken by the storm. Seeing the damage through here made us thankful that Hugo was less angry when it passed over us on Bald Mtn. in North Carolina the year before. Otherwise, we might not have been hiking through here now.

It was a crisp, clear November day with a chill in the air as we crossed over Locust and Glade Mtns. and began the descent into the Great Valley (the Shenandoah) of Virginia. We left the MRNRA and entered the Wythe District of the Jefferson National Forest. The trees were leafless exposing views which would not be visible during seasons of foliage. The forest had taken on its annual hues of grays and brown—the great outdoors had put on its winter dress. Short daylight hours, frosty nights, chilly days and the openness of the mountains and valleys would provide a new hiking experience for us—one we anxiously looked forward to. It was also a time of year when there were few hikers on the Trail. We found that most of the time we had the Trail, camping areas and shelters to ourselves.

When we reached the Chatfield Shelter (Glade Mtn. Shelter) near the crest of Glade Mtn., the temperature changed from chilly to cold, and the sky became overcast. We were in for a cold night with a good chance of precipitation, maybe even snow. The shelter was located off the ridge down in a little valley offering some protection from the wind. It was occupied by a lone hiker whose name was Mark Brokaw and, to the best of his knowledge, not related to Tom Brokaw, the newscaster. He was from Louisville, KY, had been hiking alone for some time and appeared to be glad to have company for the night.

We gathered wood and by nightfall had a huge fire going in the fireplace in front of the shelter. We had hot soup, coffee and a hearty meal of beef stew followed by a couple of hours of fellowship around the fire with Mark. In spite of the cold night with temperatures in the 20's, we were comfortable in the shelter. By dawn's early light the sky was heavily overcast, and there was a definite feel of precipitation in the air. After a good send-off breakfast at the shelter, we bid Mark adieu and were on our way. A year-and-a-half later, we would meet Mark again on the AT on the Blue Ridge south of Humpback Rocks.

The AT crosses the Big Valley of Virginia about 10 miles north of Marion and follows the ridges of Brushy Mtn. until it descends and crosses the New River at The Narrows—a distance of 88 miles. Before reaching the Big Valley, dense cloud cover began releasing a cold drizzle; and shortly, conditions changed to a very cold general rain and felt as though it might turn to snow. The closest shelter was the Davis Path Shelter which was about three miles, and we very quickly decided that would be our destination for the day.

According to our guidebook, there was no water nearby and hikers were advised to get water from a spring one mile before the shelter. By the time we arrived there, which was still early in the day, it had begun to rain hard. We did manage to gather some dry wood during the course of the afternoon and build a fire just under the overhang at the front of the shelter to dry out some extremely wet clothing and gear. The rain continued into the evening hours followed by the moving in of a cold dense fog. We were glad we chose to stay in the shelter rather than move on, as it would not have been a suitable afternoon to hike. Davis Path Shelter is located less than one-half mile from the old path that Pioneers used to cross the mountain into Davis Valley, thus the name given to the shelter.

Dawn came late the following morning as the dense fog still held its grip on the mountain, but we had stayed warm and rested through the night. We left the shelter area in fog, but as we crossed Davis Path, the fog began to clear away. As the morning progressed, all the fog cleared and the mountains and valleys opened up with views of Big Walker Mtn., Crawfish Valley and a series of distant ridges and valleys.

By mid afternoon, we had crossed Crawfish Valley and Big Walker Mtn. and stopped at the O'Lystery Community Park on VA 42 for a snack and rest break. We ascended Brushy Mtn. to the Knot Mole Branch Shelter which was our destination for the day. I thought the shelter had an interesting name and wondered about its origin. I have learned, however, that since our stay there it has been officially renamed the Knot Maul Branch Shelter. According to sources, settlers used to get knotwood from the area to make the large hand mallets called mauls that they used when splitting fence rails, posts, logs, etc. The knotwood would not splinter when driving their wooden wedges to split the logs; thus, the shelter name, "Knot Maul." I can relate to the early use of mauls, because I remember as a child my father and grandfather splitting chestnut logs with mauls driving the wedges (called Glutts) to make rails for the old "worm" fence that once encircled our farm.

During the night, a strong north wind blew across the mountains and right into the open end of the shelter along with a cold misty rain; but our insulated long johns and a stocking cap in our low-temp sleeping bags kept us cozy. The weather had cleared by morning but remained cold, and we were beginning to have some views. Hiking this time of year was indeed providing us with different experiences. With the leaves down from the trees, the woods were more open; the Trail, mountains and valleys were more exposed; the air was crisper with less haze; the Trail was carpeted with leaves; and we felt more solitude.

Two major features along the AT in this section of southwestern Virginia are Chestnut Ridge Knob and Burkes Garden. The air was crisp and clear as we ascended Chestnut Ridge—conditions we had hoped for when crossing this 4,300-foot mountain. We knew the views from the open meadows along the ridge and on the knob would be impressive, but there was another sight equally inspiring awaiting us. The misty rain we had the night before had frozen on the timber on the high ridges, and now came sunshine—what a sight to behold! Again, it seemed the Creator had rewarded us for our endurance and patience. Each tree's silvery spires jutted into the bright blue sky as if they were celebrating our arrival on the mountain. We stopped and gazed at this phenomenon in awe.

The AT follows the ridge crest through open meadows across Chestnut Knob (4,309 feet), the highest point on the mountain. We enjoyed views of Big Walker Mtn. on the right and the newly developed Beartown Wilderness area on the left. As we ascended Chestnut Knob, we watched the crystal icy spires of the trees transform like magic into droplets of water dripping from the branches and running down the tree trunks.

Nestled atop Chestnut Knob is a unique shelter built of stone that was originally used as quarters for the fire warden who used to keep vigil from the fire tower which stood there. The structure has since been renovated and used as a shelter for hikers and is referred to by them as "The Rock Hut." Another great view from the top of this mountain is Burkes Garden, a huge agricultural valley spreading for miles to the north of the Garden Mtn. escarpment.

It was 1:30 PM, and the next shelter north from Chestnut Knob was 10 1/2 miles. We could not reach the shelter by nightfall, as mid-November days are quite short. The AT descends into Walker Gap which was another mile and is the last location for water for the next 9 miles. That meant we would either have to tent in Walker Gap or pack our night's water supply to somewhere on Garden Mtn. and dry camp. It was still early, so we chose to fill our canteens and an extra water bag each and hike as far as daylight would permit and tent for the night.

We left Walker Gap ascending to the crest of Garden Mtn. The weather remained clear, but there was a great deal of wind along the ridge. We followed the Garden Mtn. escarpment having excellent views of Burkes Garden all along the Trail until late afternoon. We found a tent site well off the AT near the edge of a cliff overlooking Burkes Garden just about dusk. By the time we had the tent set up and other camp duties completed, it was dark.

We prepared our meal in the tent by candlelight and went down to a cliff afterward to sit on a rock star-gazing and watching the lights in the valley below. The wind picked up considerably, so we went back to the tent to make sure the guy lines were secure. It had been a long day, so we turned in early and lay there listening to the wind for a while before going to sleep. As the wind increased in velocity, we were awakened several times and wondered what weather conditions we would face the next day.

Our breakfast was prepared by candlelight the next morning, as we were up before daybreak, packed and on the Trail when there was barely enough light to see. We had set a goal of 17 miles and felt we needed the full day to accomplish that. A unique feature through this area is the secluded Little Wolf Creek Valley with the AT following along the creek for 2.5 miles. In this distance, the AT crosses the creek 13 times. A blue blaze trail is provided for hikers to use in times of high water. After leaving Wolf Creek, we ascended to the crest of Brushy Mtn. and followed the mountain to complete our hike at the AT crossing of I-77 near Wytheville.

Major on-going relocations have occurred along the AT during the last 20-30 years. The goals are twofold: first, to move sections of the Trail which were previously on private lands to public protected land and, second, to move sections which are on public protected lands to locations providing less damage or impact to the environment. One such area was in southwestern Virginia where the AT was moved off Big Walker Mtn. west to Brushy Mtn. The main concern here for Trail planners was the scarcity of water on Big Walker Mtn. The AT follows Brushy Mtn. on and off its ridges from near Groseclose, VA, to Pearisburg, VA, which is 88 miles.

In May, 1991, we began our hike at the AT crossing of I-77, planning to complete the section of Brushy Mtn. to Pearisburg. We would then cross the New River Valley at The Narrows and a series of mountains and valleys to near Catawba, VA. We used the two-vehicle plan dropping one at the Post Office and store in Catawba and drove the other one to the trailhead at US 52 and 21 near I-77. On our drive from Catawba, we arranged for a food drop at the 84 Lumber store in Pearisburg.

It was afternoon before we could begin the Trail. We did not plan to hike very far, as we had spent a great deal of time and energy getting there and making all the arrangements. For this hike, I tried putting cushioned insoles in my boots, as I felt my feet may be more comfortable with them. On the two previous hikes, I had developed a blister or two and believed improvements could be made on the system I was using. This was a major mistake. We hiked five miles that afternoon and pitched our tent on an old woods road well off the AT. The afternoon was warm; my pack was heavy; and my feet were not well conditioned. It usually takes a week or so of hiking to toughen them enough to stand the heavy burden of day-after-day hiking; and even then blisters can develop if caution is not exercised

By afternoon, I noticed that my feet got warmer than usual, and I had to stop more often to take off my boots and cool them. Before reaching the campsite, I developed a hot spot on the lower part of my heel. I had experienced hot spots before and knew if that problem area was not corrected, it would result in a blister. At the campsite I examined my feet carefully and they seemed okay—no blisters yet—they were not sore, but my socks were wet. That should have been my first clue.

Blisters are a common problem for long-distance hikers; in fact, most of them have experienced them at some point. It usually occurs early in the hike when the feet are not toughened to the stressful demands placed on them or when boots do not fit properly or are not well broken in. Blisters can affect hiking in the following ways: minor cases can be treated by applying tape or moleskin to the affected areas and continuing the hike; more severe cases may slow the hiker's pace or delay it; in extreme cases, the hike may have to be aborted.

The next day was warm, and our plan called for a 16-miler which would take us up Dismal Creek past Dismal Falls. The guidebook and profile map did not show any major elevation gains or losses in this section, but I had an uneasy feeling about my feet. This uneasiness became a reality about 10:00 that morning when the hot spot I had developed the day before became a blister—not a good beginning. Blisters had not been a major problem for me up to this point on the AT, and the ones I had previously were manageable. I treated the blister with moleskin and, after examination, found several more hot spots and tender areas on the bottom of both feet. I realized that the padded insoles were causing my feet to stay too hot, making the already soft skin softer and setting the stage for major blisters. I took the insoles out immediately hoping it was not too late.

The weather was hot as we started up Dismal Creek, and that was not helping my already sore feet. By the time we reached Dismal Creek Falls, I was having more discomfort in both feet. We took our packs off, rested, and I cooled my feet for a while by the falls. We decided to move on a mile or so since it was still early, and we pitched our tent in a small clearing between the AT and Dismal Creek. After another examination of my feet, it was evident that I had a major problem. The hot spots had become blisters, several of which were on the bottom of my feet. I covered the affected areas with moleskin and hoped for the best for the next day, but deep down I knew it was becoming serious and would affect my hiking comfort and speed.

A hard rain began during the night and continued right into daybreak, so we had to prepare breakfast inside the tent and then pack it up wet. The rain continued all morning. Those cushioned insoles had really done a number on my feet. I should have known better than to use them, and now the wet weather was further complicating the problem.

Our goal for the day was Docs Knob, a 14-miler, and I was not sure I could make it that far. The valleys were all fogged in as we left Dismal Creek for the ascent of Sugar Run Mtn. in a steady rain. We finally had to seek shelter under a large hemlock tree to eat lunch and then hiked in rain for the remainder of the afternoon. The persistent rain and the pain from the blisters reminded me of the quote I had seen in a shelter journal, "No rain, no pain, no Maine." When we arrived at the shelter at 5:30, there were hikers already there, and we knew more were on the way. We pitched our tent nearby knowing the shelter would be filled for the night. I doctored my feet the best I could but did not like the way they looked. Hiking all day with wet feet had caused more blisters and aggravated the existing ones. This was the first time I accepted the fact that I may have to abort the hike, as the night's rest probably would not be enough recovery time.

By the next morning, I was having so much pain that just standing was one thing, but walking was something else. I told Osbra that my condition was such that I would have to abort the hike when we reached Pearisburg and that even getting there would be a struggle. I needed to get off my feet, not just for a day or two but for an extended period of time to permit healing. To continue would be futile, as the stage was set for infection or other complications. This was a disappointment to both of us, and we would just have to come back to Pearisburg and continue at a later date.

We reached Angels Rest on the summit of Pearis Mtn. which overlooked the New River Valley and where we took a well-needed lunch break. In the meantime, two young women hiked up from Pearisburg to enjoy the view from the overlook. While talking to them, I explained my problem and asked if they knew anyone who would shuttle us to the AT crossing at I-77 or to Catawba where our vehicles were parked. They said they would be happy to, so they drove us to Catawba where we picked up Osbra's vehicle and then returned to Pearisburg for our food drop at 84 Lumber. On our drive home, I thought how unwise it was to have added padding to my boots and vowed never to let this happen to me again.

During September, 1991, Osbra and I returned to Pearisburg to continue the hike to Catawba. Again, we left one vehicle at the Post Office in Catawba and made a food drop near the AT crossing of VA 630 in the Sinking Creek Valley. On our return to Pearisburg, we left the second vehicle near the AT crossing of VA 634.

The AT crosses New River on the Senator Shumate Bridge near the city limits of Pearisburg. This is familiar territory for me, because I grew up 60 miles north of Pearisburg about ten miles from the New River Gorge. New River is one of the major river valleys the AT crosses on its 2,150-plus-mile route. It is a unique river and, even though its name is "New," geologists report it is one of the oldest rivers in the world. It begins in the mountains of North Carolina and flows north through southwestern Virginia into West Virginia and joins the Kanawha River near Charleston. It is the only major river in the United States that flows north. Its origin dates back to the Paleozoic era before much of the Appalachian Mountain ranges were formed. As the uplift of the range occurred, the river was cutting its way down in the bedrock. Evidence of this can be seen at The Narrows near where the AT crosses the river. Here the river cuts through the mountain range into West Virginia. A more impressive area of the cutting action of the river can be viewed some 60 miles north in the New River Gorge.

We left the New River Valley ascending Peters Mtn. at noon and planned to hike to the crest of the mountain where our trail guide listed a campsite and spring. With the late start, we felt that reaching that point would be a good beginning. It was a lovely sunny afternoon with a cool breeze giving us ideal conditions to climb out of the valley. I was fresh, felt good, was eager for this hike and could not help remembering the blisters I had when descending into the valley on the other side the previous spring. As we continued the ascent, we had sweeping views from The Narrows to Pearisburg and beyond and could hear a lot of activity in the valley—traffic, plants operating, trains, etc. We reached the campsite by late afternoon and were pleased with its location and spring. As night fell, a full moon rose over the valley lighting the area to almost dawnlike conditions. We sat by the campfire talking and looking down on the lights of The Narrows and Pearisburg for a while before retiring.

On the following day, our hike took us along the 12.5-mile crest of Peters Mtn. which is on the border of Virginia and West Virginia. We then dropped off the ridge along Pine Swamp to the Pine Swamp Shelter making a 14-mile day. The AT on Peters Mtn. is an outstanding section crossing through high meadows with panoramic views into West Virginia.

We found several Ginseng plants right beside the AT in the wooded areas. Its root is quite valuable and sought after by hunters during late summer and early fall when its berries turn red, making it easier to find among the other plants in the forest. We did see two men hunting Ginseng, and they reported that they had found some, so we advised them that the plants visible from the AT should be left undisturbed. When we found a plant with berries, we removed the berries making the plant harder to locate for those who might be tempted to dig the root.

When we crossed through the meadow sections of Peters Mtn. we found acres of milkweed in bloom, and they had attracted hundreds of Monarch butterflies going from one plant to the other. Monarchs are attracted to milkweed because a part of their metamorphosis takes place on the plant, and it was getting close to migrating time for them. I had never seen so many Monarchs in any one area before—a remarkable sight!

We left the crest of Peters Mtn. and began the descent to the Pine Swamp Shelter. There had been a major Trail relocation which added more distance, as is usually the case when one is made. For example, twenty years ago the entire length of the AT had been measured at a little over 2,000 miles. In September, 1996, the official distance as reported by the Appalachian Trail Conference was 2,158.8 miles. We arrived at the Pine Swamp Shelter by late afternoon, completing a 15.5-mile day. The shelter is constructed of stone and has a charming fireplace and picnic table—an enjoyable place to stay.

Big Mtn. and Potts Mtn. lay ahead of us for the following day. We crossed Sinking Creek Valley shortly after leaving the shelter and immediately began the ascent of Big Mtn. (3,700 feet). Near its crest we met two southbound hikers, the first we had seen since leaving Pearisburg. We were surprised we had not met more, as this was a picturesque section; the Trail was good, and the weather had been super. Through this section is Wind Rock (4,100 feet) which provides a panoramic view over Stony Creek and the Peters Mtn. area we had passed through earlier.

We passed a southbound hiker from Chattanooga, TN, who had spent the night in the War Spur Shelter where we were headed. He advised us that the descent from Potts Mtn. to the shelter was steep and to watch out for yellow jackets along the Trail. He was right on both counts. I had been stung by them back on Peters Mtn. The problem with yellow jackets along the Trail is that hikers aggravate them by constantly brushing against their nests in passing, keeping them in a state of irritation; and the next hiker who comes along is the one they usually zap. We each got stung as we passed their nests, so we moved along faster than planned on the steep 2-mile descent toward the shelter. It was a good thing neither of us was allergic to their stings, as this was one of many encounters we had with them on our trek north.

We had the shelter to ourselves and settled in for the night after a big meal of spaghetti and meatballs and hot cider and a campfire before bedtime. A gorgeous night it was—enhanced by the hooting of Barred Owls, "*hoohoo-hoohoo-hoohoo-hoohooaw.*" Human interpretation: "I cook for myself, who cooks for you all?" What a conversation they were having—one on each side of the shelter in the pine trees. This continued until we drifted off into a deep sleep. It seemed appropriate that, if one bird lulled us to sleep, another should wake us up; so the Whip-poor-will had the honor. He started his chants about 4:00 AM, and they seemed to have gone on for an hour or so.

Daybreak greeted us on a clear balmy morning. Our goal for the day was to complete the John Creek Valley crossing from War Spur, cross over Johns Creek Mtn. and descend into and cross Craig Valley to the AT crossing of VA 630 near where we had dropped our food cache. We then ascended Sinking Creek Mtn. and followed the ridge crest to near Sarver Cabin, the next shelter. The climb out of the valley to the summit of Johns Creek Mtn. was four miles and took us two hours. Fortunately, the weather was cool and breezy or it would have taken us longer to traverse the mountain.

After crossing Kelly Knob, the highest point on the mountain, and descending part way down the mountain toward Sinking Creek Valley, there was a stand of large Chestnut Oak trees. This was the finest stand of this variety of oak I had seen anywhere along the AT. I am always delighted when passing through forests with stands of big trees such as this and always wonder why and how these trees were spared from the loggers' axes and saws.

Little Laurel Shelter, where we stopped for lunch, is located two miles from VA 42 in the Sinking Creek Valley. Our pack weights had diminished considerably since most of our food was gone, but that would change when we crossed the valley and picked up our new supply. We reached the highway an hour after leaving Little Laurel (after missing the Trail several times going through some meadows). The weeds and high grasses had obscured much of the AT making it difficult to locate. Other hikers must have had the same problem because there were trails leading in every direction through the grass. We crossed the valley to our food cache location. We had used this method of dropping food and other supplies along the AT ahead of us a number of times, and each time we found it undisturbed by neither man nor wildlife. However, when I uncovered my supplies, I found that a mouse had gnawed a hole through one of my plastic bags of Tang and helped himself to the contents—another mouse story and more to come.

The climb out of the valley to the crest of Sinking Creek Mtn. was a challenge with our newly-replenished packs. We had taken extra water because we knew it was not available along the ridge, and that added more weight. Near the beginning of the climb up the mountain, we passed by what is considered the largest White Oak tree along the AT—it was certainly the largest I had ever seen.

The Sinking Creek Valley and Mountain area is geographically significant because, according to geologists, it is the last watershed area moving north on the AT whose waters are "Gulf bound," which means its waters will ultimately flow into the Gulf of Mexico via the Mississippi River. Sinking Creek Mtn. is also geologically interesting. It is a long, narrow rocky ridge between Sinking Creek Valley and Craig Valley and is 3,500 feet at its crest with little elevation change in the five miles that the AT follows it. Even though there are no climbs or descents, the Trail is rough following along the precipices of rock outcroppings, some of which are almost perpendicular. Many of the outcroppings jut out at 30-60-degree angles toward the west revealing stratas of rocks squeezed upward when massive forces formed the mountain. During inclement weather such as ice, snow or fog, some of these areas could be extremely hazardous.

When we reached the blue blaze trail leading off the ridge down to the spring to Sarver Cabin (.3 mile), we debated whether to go there just for resupplying water leaving our packs at the ridge crest or to hike down to the cabin and spend the night. We decided the latter was the better choice because it was already late afternoon. Also, we did not want to pack more water further up the ridge to what may turn out to be a non-existent campsite along its rocky crest. The hike down to the spring was extremely steep and we were grateful we made the right choice. We found several Ginseng plants on the descent, and some of the plants were so close to the Trail that one would brush against them when passing. It is a wonder someone had not already dug the roots; and to insure that they would not, we took the ripe berries off the plants and planted some nearby.

The spring was excellent, but Sarver Cabin was another story. According to our guidebook, the shelter was a "rehabilitated shed" which at one time had been one of the outbuildings of the Old Homestead where it was located. It did not look very appealing to us, so we pitched our tent near the spring under an old apple tree. According to legend, Sarver Cabin is haunted, having a ghost that frequents the old building. One wonders how this legend began—perhaps there was a tragedy that took place here sometime during the period when the Old Homestead was occupied by Pioneers. The moon was bright and a few days from being full, and we never saw or heard anything unusual other than an occasional apple falling from the tree and hitting our tent.

Our next day's hike would be 14 miles, taking us from the Sarver Cabin area up the remainder of Sinking Creek Mtn. crossing the Craig Creek Valley and culminating at the Pickle Branch Shelter at the base of Cove Mtn. The hike from the blue blaze leading down to Sarver along the crest of Sinking Creek Mtn. was one of the most rugged ridge lines we had hiked so far. Even though there were no climbs or descents, the rough rock scrambles made up for the lack of elevation gain. Fortunately, the weather was favorable. We took an early lunch break at the Niday Shelter (the next one north) because there had been another major Trail relocation through the upcoming Brush Mtn. section, and we knew this would increase our mileage for the afternoon.

Soon after lunch, we crossed highway 621 and began the long, hard relocation. It took us 4 1/2 hours to hike from the highway across the many ridges and valleys of Brush Mtn. Not only did the relocation add mileage, but the many steep ups and downs made an impression on our muscles and joints. We did not arrive at the Pickle Branch Shelter until 6:30 PM completing a long hard day. What we figured to be 14 miles turned out closer to 17 with terrain much more difficult than anticipated. To reach the shelter, we had to leave the AT on a blue blaze and descend one-half mile; but, once there, we found a well-kept shelter in an excellent location and shared it with two other hikers that night.

The next day, it took us 20 minutes to hike up the blue blaze to the AT from the shelter. It then ascends and follows the narrow jagged hook of Cove Mtn., and the terrain is similar to sections we had crossed the day before on Sinking Creek Mtn. As we crested out on the mountain, it began to rain; and the mountain became concealed in fog. There would be no views from this ridge crest.

We had hoped for clear weather when we crossed this mountain, as it has several rock outcroppings providing views of the Catawba Valley. One of these is a large monolith jutting into the sky known as Dragon Tooth or Buzzard Rock. Fortunately, the rain and fog cleared by the time we reached this impressive rock formation. We had our lunch on the rocks while enjoying some outstanding panoramas of the valley and then descended into VA 311 completing the Pearisburg-Catawba section of the Trail.

The AT originally followed Catawba Mtn. but was relocated across Catawba Valley to North Mtn. because of property disputes with landowners and the NPS. It then crossed the Catawba Valley again and ascended Tinker Mtn. to Scorched Earth Gap. This section of Trail was relocated back to the east side of the Catawba Valley following the crests of Catawba and Tinker Mountains. This was accomplished by the acquisition of lands by the NPS along these mountains which provided a protective corridor for the Trail. The NPS and the Trail Clubs wanted it on these ridges because they were more scenic than the North Mtn. side. I have never hiked the North Mtn. route but would have to say that the relocation does provide outstanding scenery.

Our first day of hiking through this section was from VA 311 to the Catawba Mtn. Shelter. It was October, 1991, the woods were aflame with Autumn's spectacle of bright foliage; and the sky was bright blue. What a great day to hike this section, or any section, for that matter. The AT follows a narrow backbone ridge from Lost Spectacles Gap off Cove Mtn. past the very scenic rough Devils Seat and Rawies Rest, an exposed rocky area. The hike along Catawba Mtn. took us up Saw Tooth, a sharp backbone ridge. To the right were views of Fort Lewis Mtn. and to the left Catawba Valley with North Mtn. beyond. We took extra time traversing the ridge to Catawba Shelter. The day's hike was pleasant with a cool breeze blowing across the ridge, and the scenery was outstanding. Who could ask for more, and the next day would be even better.

In my opinion, Tinker Mtn. provides scenic hiking which is difficult to surpass anywhere in the southern Appalachians, and this is the area we were anxiously looking forward to for the next day. We only planned a 9-mile day from Catawba Shelter to the next campsite at Lambert's Meadow so we would have plenty of time to photograph, study and enjoy the scenery through this area.

Our first view was from McAfee Knob (3,197 feet) on Tinker Mtn. where an overhanging rock ledge juts out into space over the Catawba Valley hundreds of feet below. The views of Catawba Valley, Roanoke Valley and the mountains beyond were truly breathtaking. After leaving the Knob, the AT follows the edge of Tinker Cliffs for one-half mile where we felt we were literally walking on the edge of the mountain. Again, we were thankful for favorable weather, because in many places the Trail was inches from the edge; and wet, icy or foggy conditions could make this area extremely hazardous.

As we moved past the Tinker Cliffs area, the AT descended through a group of large boulders known as Devil's Kitchen. Near here we could see Tinker Mtn. ahead making the loop around Carvin Cove, and we knew the AT would follow the crest of the mountain around the Cove. We had our first views of the Peaks of Otter, Apple Orchard Mtn. and other mountains across the Great Valley of the Blue Ridge where we would be hiking in the days ahead.

We descended into Scorched Earth Gap where the AT had previously crossed Catawba Valley from the North Mtn. location. Here the AT turns south where it continues around Carvin Cove. We reached Lamberts Meadow Primitive Campsite around 3:30, allowing plenty of time for our chores including pitching the tent, getting water and wood and preparing our evening meal. This had not been one of our highest mileage days but ranked high on sections of the AT we had enjoyed the most thanks to the efforts of the NPS, the ATC, and local Trail Clubs for getting the Trail back on its original course over these beautiful ridges.

On the following day, we completed the hike along Tinker Mtn. around Carvin Cove Reservoir (the water supply for the city of Roanoke), and the views from the ridge line were superb. We could look back across the Reservoir to McAfee Knob and the area of Catawba and Tinker Mtn. to the west, and the Great Valley of Virginia lay beneath us to the east and north. We could also look down on the communities of Daleville and Cloverdale where the AT crosses the Big Valley.

Before dropping off the ridge line into the valley, we had an encounter with a dog. This one was friendly, unlike some we had met. He was alone, mixed breed, charcoal color and had been well cared for but had no collar or identification. He stayed with us for the rest of the day following right behind us as though he had been with us all along. We had arranged for our wives to pick us up at the AT crossing on US 220 near Cloverdale/Troutville, and the dog followed us right to the car and wanted to go with us. It was difficult for us and our wives to leave him there, but there were many houses and people close by who could return him to his owner. He watched us out of sight as we left the parking lot.

We spent the night in our motorhome which was parked in a campground off the Blue Ridge. The following day we returned to the Cloverdale crossing and continued the hike across the Big Valley under I-81 and began the ascent of the Blue Ridge. This was our second crossing of the Big Valley on the AT. The original route had followed the Blue Ridge right on through staying on the east side of the Big Valley. The AT was displaced by the Blue Ridge Parkway, and it was moved by the USFS and the Roanoke Trail Club across the valley in 1948-49 on newly acquired Jefferson National Forest land.

By lunch time we had crossed the Big Valley and were about 8 miles into our day's hike on the Blue Ridge. It was another gorgeous October day and we had not seen many hikers. We met very few on the other side of the valley and were getting closer to the Parkway where the Trail was more accessible and where hiking traffic would increase. We reached the Wilson Creek Shelter by mid afternoon which was our goal for the day. Our guidebook indicated that the water source was from the stream below the shelter, so we took our canteens and water bags down to it (which was a quarter of a mile) and found it dry. We proceeded down the dry stream for another quarter-mile before we found any. The half-mile back up the steep ridge with our filled containers gave us a good late afternoon workout.

By 9:15 the next morning, we had reached the Blue Ridge Parkway, and the AT paralleled it for the next 7.5 miles. The Trail makes four road crossings in this 7.5-mile section; and at each crossing there were overlooks that provided excellent views of the Peaks of Otter, the Great Valley, Goose Valley and distant mountains and valleys. When we reached Bearwallow Gap, the AT led us away from the Parkway over Cove Mtn.—the second Cove Mtn. we had crossed within 50 miles. Our guidebook reported that the Gap was so-named because—you guessed it—bears wallow in a marshy area nearby to cool themselves in the summertime. We descended Cove Mtn. into Jennings Creek, had lunch at the AT crossing of VA 614 and continued on toward VA 714. After crossing Fork Mtn. we passed through another stand of big trees including Red Oak, White Oak and Pine. We hiked out at the trailhead by early afternoon finishing another section of the AT.

In May, 1992, we returned to this trailhead in the Middle Creek/ North Creek area to continue our northward hike. We used the two-vehicle method again leaving one at a campground near the trailhead, made a food drop near the AT crossing of the Parkway at Milepost 51.4, and dropped the second vehicle at the Hump-back Rocks Visitor Center on the Parkway near Rockfish Gap. The campground where we had received permission to leave one vehicle was a mile from the trailhead, so we dropped off our packs at the trailhead and flipped a coin to see who would drive the vehicle back to the campground for storage—I lost so I took the car and then walked the mile back. We always enjoyed springtime hiking because of the profusion of wildflowers along the Trail; and Osbra, being a naturalist, would be keeping his camera click-ing as usual.

Over the years, he had built up a vast collection of wildflower and plant slides, many of which he had taken along the AT. He had written many articles on plants and wildflowers which were published in the *Wonderful West Virginia* state magazine. The magazine also used scores of his photos in feature articles which appeared in it for many years, and *National Geographic* purchased and used many of his slides. When we began this hike that day in May, I had no idea this would be our last hike together.

By the time all of our arrangements were made, it was after 3:00 PM before we got under way. The AT had looped around Cove Mtn., and now it was returning to the Parkway via Bryant Ridge and Floyd Mtn. As we ascended Bryant Ridge, it began to mist rain. It had been overcast all day and had been threatening. We wanted to reach the Cornelius Creek Shelter area and would tent if it were not too wet.

We had just stopped to take a photo of Spiderwort (wildflower) when the mist changed to a general rain. By the time we crested Floyd Mtn., the weather conditions became quite cold with heavy rain, strong winds and fog. We would definitely be in the shelter. Arriving there at 6:30—wet, chilled and tired—we fixed hot drinks and changed into dry clothes. After a hot meal, we were in our sleeping bags by 8:00 PM to stay warm. The rain and wind pounded the shelter all night, and we were both awakened several times during the night when rain was blowing in on us through the open end of the shelter.

This night was reminiscent of previous ones we had experienced—Bald Mtn., Roan Mtn. Mt. Rogers, etc. The storm continued until 8:00 the next morning, so we were unable to leave until 10:00, a late start by our standards, and even then the rain still lingered. Fog and rain continued as we ascended Apple Orchard Mtn. (4,125 feet). We crossed the Parkway and reached the Thunder Hill Shelter by lunchtime. There were no views up there that day; in fact, we were lucky to find a dry place in the shelter where we could eat lunch.

The morning hike had taken us through extensive areas of rhododendron and azaleas, but we were at least a month too early to enjoy their blossoms. After lunch we descended through the Thunder Ridge Wilderness area into Petites Gap, and the inclement weather stayed with us throughout the day. Our Trail guide listed a spring 2.2 miles from Petites Gap at the site of the former Marble Spring Shelter. This would be a manageable distance for us to reach, and we were hopeful we would have better weather at a lower elevation.

We arrived at the shelter campsite at 5:30—again, wet and tired. Our distance was not that great (11.5 miles), but we had a late start and the weather had not cooperated. We pitched our tent in the Gap in the vicinity of where the Marble Spring Shelter once stood. It had been moved to Cove Mtn. The rain continued through the evening hours restricting our activities (including the preparation of our supper) to the confines of our small tent; and for the second one in a row, it rained all night.

By 9:00 AM, there were signs that there might be a break in the weather—we needed sunshine! Within half an hour, we were on the Trail again after packing up a wet tent and wet gear. We were starting late again, but we had planned a shorter mileage day anyway. This day's hike took us through the James River Face Wilderness area which, according to our guidebook, was the first wilderness area to be established in the United States. This was an outstanding natural area with the AT passing through many miles of charming woodlands.

It also took us across the James River Valley. The James is the largest waterway in the state of Virginia and, at the point where the AT crosses the river on US 501, is the lowest in central Virginia. It marks the boundary between Jefferson National Forest and the George Washington National Forest. The river is 450 miles long flowing east out of the Alleghenys and cutting its route across the Blue Ridge creating a fascinating Gorge. We hiked into the Johns Hollow Shelter 2.3 miles from Snowden Bridge where the AT crosses over the James River. In the last three days, we had seen only two hikers, and they were just out for the day.

By the next morning, the weather front had moved out, and we left Johns Hollow in sunshine. We were faced with a 2,000-foot climb (in 3 miles) out of the valley, and the views were breathtaking as we climbed past Little Rock Row up to Fuller Rocks. The vista from Fuller Rocks (2,480 feet) and Big Rocky Row (3,000 feet) of the James River Gorge was one of the finest we had seen so far on the Blue Ridge. As the day progressed, not only did we have the sunshine we had been wishing for but the temperature rose. In fact, the climb up Bluff Mtn. became quite stressful in the heat of the afternoon causing me to leave many more droplets of perspiration along the Trail.

While on this climb, we were overtaken by a young couple from Columbia, SC, who were thru-hiking the AT—Richard (Smoky) and Pam (Tweety) Hair. We would meet Pam and Richard again in the next few days, and they would become very special friends in the years to follow. Near the summit, we also met a thru-hiker from Burlington, SC, whose name was Andrew Sam ("The Medicine Man") who was a nurse; and we enjoyed his companionship while hiking with him for several miles. On the summit of Bluff Mtn. is a memorial plaque for Little Ottie Kline, a child who had become lost and perished on the mountain in the late 1800's. The mountain had taken a child's life but had given us two special friends.

We hiked off Bluff Mtn. and took a rest break at the Punch Bowl Shelter. While we were resting, Pam and Richard came along and visited with us for a while. We replenished our water supply at the shelter and moved on to pick up our food cache near the milepost on the Parkway. Our food was all intact, so we loaded up and headed for our planned campsite on Little Irish Creek four miles from our food drop location. The AT crosses Rice Mtn. before descending into Little Irish Creek, and on our descent we met a southbound hiker who looked very familiar to us. After a brief conversation, exchange and introductions (he was Mark Brokaw), we remembered sharing the Glade Mtn. Shelter with him during our fall hike in 1990. Before reaching the campsite, we passed through a small tract of impressive virgin forest which the NPS was using as an exhibit. We pitched our tent right by the creek with the trickle and rush of the water providing us a serenade throughout the night.

After a restful night by the creek, we broke camp early and proceeded around Pedlar Lake which is the water supply for the city of Lynchburg, VA, 20 miles away. The AT follows near the shoreline of the lake for three miles winding around coves and over gentle knolls and shortly reaches the Brown Creek Valley. Osbra made many stops along the creek to photograph plants and wildflowers. Along this valley were the remains of early settlements which we had seen in many of the valleys along the AT. Settlers chose these areas for their homesteads because they provided protection from the weather, were near water and had areas of flat land which they used for farming. The weather was clear, and we were seeing more and more hikers both north and southbound. Many of the northbounders were thru-hikers who were catching up with us with their 15-20-mile days.

After leaving the Brown Creek Valley, we reached US 60, a major highway crossing the Blue Ridge between Buena Vista and Lynchburg. The hike from Little Irish Creek to the highway took us longer than anticipated, not because it was difficult but because we just spent more time enjoying its natural beauty and studying the remnants of Pioneer days through the area. From the highway, we had a 2,000-foot climb in three miles to the summit of Bald Knob (another one of those bald mountains); and, since it was near noon, we ate lunch before beginning the ascent. It took us 2 1/2 hours to make the climb, as the temperature had reached near 80 degrees slowing us down considerably. We did not complain, because it was great to have warm temperatures and sunshine after the cold, wet weather we experienced a few days before. We descended into Cow Camp Gap where there was a shelter, camping area and two great springs. We had arrived early, so we used the extra time to take a bath, wash some clothes, organize our packs, build a fire and cook our evening meal.

Our next day's hike of 17 miles took us across some fine Blue Ridge country. From Cow Camp Gap we ascended Cole Mtn. (4,000 feet) with a grassy bald summit, reminiscent to areas we had crossed in the Roan Highlands. Its summit provided a panorama of Blue Ridge splendor on this crisp clear morning. We crossed Hog Camp Gap (this was farm animal territory in Pioneer days when the ridges were used for grazing) and ascended Tar Jacket Ridge—so-named, according to our guidebook, because an old mountaineer tore his jacket fleeing from angry bees.

This ridge also had an open grassy summit, and there were hundreds of feet of old stone fences which were constructed during Pioneer days. Remnants of these fences would become a familiar sight all the way along the AT into New England. A closer examination of them revealed many stones weighing hundreds of pounds that fit into their architecture. We marveled at the symmetrical placement of the stones in the walls and the amount of labor required to construct them.

Our plan for the day was to hike to the Priest Shelter near the summit of Priest Mtn. (4,063 feet), overlooking the Tye River Valley. We had a long day of crossing ridges and gaps and decided to hike down a blue blaze off the AT to tent in an area known as Crabtree meadow about a mile short of the Priest Shelter.

When we left the camping area the next morning and hiked back up to the AT, we regretted not having continued on to the shelter as was originally planned. It was a mile down to the camping area and back which would have put us at the shelter—oh well, hindsight. As we passed the shelter, we noted there was a good place to camp with a great spring nearby. This made us feel even worse—maybe next time.

The Priest is the last 4,000-footer along the AT until Vermont and is in the "Religious Range" of mountains including Little Priest, Cardinal and The Friar. After cresting the Priest we had outstanding views of the Tye River Valley. By 11:00 AM we descended the 3,000 feet from the summit of the Priest to Tye River where VA 56 crosses. The Tye River Valley was the scene of an incredible storm that hit the area during the summer of 1967. It had been reported that over 30 inches of rain fell in a six-hour period causing landslides on the mountain and a major washout in the valley. We hiked through an exposed rocky slide area which was one of the scars of the storm—and we thought Hugo was bad. The descent into Tye River was hard, but the 3,000-foot six-mile ascent out of the valley up what is known as the Three Ridges was something else.

By the time we reached the second of the Three Ridges, the temperature had soared to near 80 degrees again, and we were dripping with perspiration. We noticed dark clouds gathering, and a thunderstorm began moving across the valley. We thought we would try to hike over the highest point of the ridges to the next shelter before the storm hit, but spring storms move fast in the mountains and it caught us before we reached the summit. We did not mind the rain because we were already wet; but the lightning was a concern with continuous flashing all around us. There was nothing to get under except trees, and we wanted to stay clear of them; so we crouched down beside a large boulder and covered ourselves with our ponchos as best we could. We were at 3,000 feet, and the storm was right around us—the lightning, the thunder, the wind and the driving rain. This storm was worse than the one we were in on Walnut Mtn. in North Carolina; and, as I said then, you have not experienced a thunderstorm until you are in one on top of a mountain without cover. The forces of these storms are incredible.

We stayed put until the storm passed and then continued over the summit descending into the Maupin Field Shelter. We arrived there about 6:00 PM tired and wet after completing a difficult 15 miles across the Tye River Valley. We decided to stay in the shelter rather than the tent so we could hang our wet clothing and other gear from the ceiling to dry. The Humpback Rocks Visitor Center on the Parkway was our goal for the next day concluding this hike. It would be the last one Osbra and I would hike together.

The next morning a 45-minute hike put us into Reeds Gap where the AT swings back to the Parkway and parallels it for many miles. In crossing the Tye River Valley, the AT had swung many miles to the east. We stopped briefly at an overlook near Laurel Springs Gap; and, while we were there, Richard and Pam joined us. We had not seen them in a couple of days; in fact, we thought they had moved on ahead, but they told us they had spent the night off the Trail in a hostel (sort of) near Maupin Field Shelter. They hiked with us to near Humpback Rocks where they left us and said they were going off the Trail to spend the night in Waynesboro and resupply.

We would not see them again on the AT; but following their thru-hike and my completion of the Trail, they became special friends. This is a friendship I cherish stemming from those brief encounters with them along the AT on the Blue Ridge—another bit of Trail Magic.

We completed our day's hike and this section at the Humpback Rocks Visitor Center at 4:00 PM. We planned to hike the next section to Harpers Ferry in the fall, but that was not to be because Osbra took ill suddenly in July and passed away—what a blow!

TOP: Blisters—Oh, those aching feet! At Angels
Rest near Pearisburg, Virginia
BOTTOM: Overhanging Rock on McAfee Knob
along Tinker Cliffs in southwestern Virginia

Both photos by Osbra Eye

TOP: Osbra examining a Ginseng plant by the
   AT on Peters Mountain
BOTTOM: Hornets on Peters Mountain—
   one of the many hazards along the AT

TOP: Sarver Cabin on Sinking Creek Mtn. Legend
   has it that a ghost frequents this old structure
BOTTOM: A maple tree appears to be holding the AT
   sign in its mouth near Jennings Creek in the Blue Ridge

TOP: Pam and Richard Hair (Tweety and Smoky) with Osbra near
   Humpback Rocks—Osbra's last day hiking with me.
BOTTOM: Old rock fence near Humpback Rocks on the Blue Ridge,
   common sight along the AT from Virginia into New England.

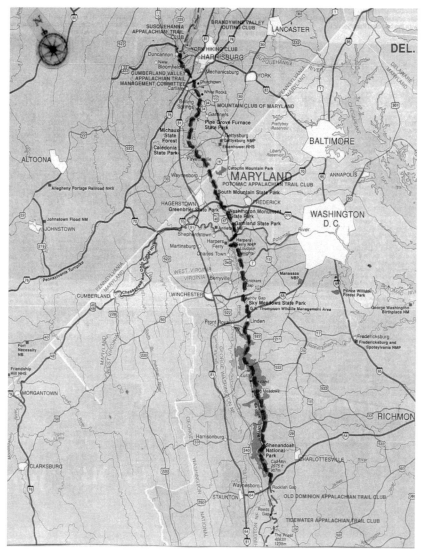

Map detail from Humpback Rocks, VA, to Duncannon, PA
(Covered in Chapter seven)

— — — — — Denotes Appalachian Trail Route

Shaded area denotes Shenandoah National Park

HALLOWED GROUND

"This is a land of many ghosts. Great armies and other
movements passed by here on the way to their destinies,
and the story of these hills is written in their blood."
—Jim Chase - Backpacker Magazine Guide to the
Appalachian Trail

Our family was devastated by Osbra's passing. His health had
been good as far as we knew, but the aneurysm had remained
hidden and struck suddenly without warning.

I was not sure I could continue the hike—at least not for a
while, and what about a hiking companion? Would I want one
and could one be found? A hiking companion should be compatible—Osbra and I were not just brothers but compatible friends
who complemented each other. After his death, I had some time
to think about the Trail and the hike and concluded that there was

no choice but to continue on—for me and for him. We had decided during the early hiking days that we wanted to hike the entire Trail. A commitment was made and I had to go on.

There still remained one major problem. Joan had not wanted me to hike alone; and, after much discussion, we resolved the problem. I really wanted to hike alone at least for a while. She agreed with conditions. She would accompany me and we would establish base camps every 75-100 miles using our motorhome for housing her. She would shuttle me to and from trailheads, and I would try to keep the number of days out to a minimum. I would slack-pack (day-hike) through areas where there were frequent road crossings. Joan would be my companion—she had only hiked a few miles of the Trail, but she was a major source of inspiration for me from the beginning. She helped in planning each hike, prepared menus and packaged foods, had shuttled us to many trailheads, had kept notes and records, typed letters, and the list goes on.

We would plan each hike together in detail. She would know where the trailhead locations were for the pick up and the approximate time to expect me. She would know the shelter and/or tenting location where I would be spending the nights and have emergency information, telephone numbers, park personnel, police, etc., for each specific hiking area. She felt comfortable with this plan even though this would mean hundreds of miles of back country travel to shuttle me and many nights alone in base camps along the way for her. On the plus side, she would see back country from Virginia to Maine that even many residents of these states never see and establish lasting friendships with people in campgrounds, in communities and with hikers at trailheads along the way. We now had a solution so I could continue on, and we began preparing for the hike Osbra and I had planned to do in the fall. (Many people have asked Joan how she could let me hike alone, and her answer to them is, "How could I not? He had a goal and a dream that needed to be fulfilled.")

In getting my pack ready for the hike, I placed a ziplock bag containing a flower, which I had taken from a floral arrangement at Osbra's funeral service, in my pack. I vowed to carry it with me daily along the AT and place it on Katahdin in his memory when I finished the Trail. I also put in my pack a metal match holder that he had carried from Springer.

The fall hike was scheduled for late September and early October, 1992, and would start at Humpback Rocks and go to Harpers Ferry, WV, completing the Virginia section of the AT. We established our first base camp at Loft Mtn. in the Shenandoah National Park. Since the AT parallels the Skyline Drive and crosses it frequently, I decided to slack-pack through the Shenandoah, a distance of over 100 miles. I began the hike with a sore knee which I had injured earlier (not while hiking), and carrying a small pack would reduce some of the stress on it. The Shenandoah was an area that I had long looked forward to hiking, and I did not want to hurry through it. I felt slack-packing would give me more time to fully enjoy the natural beauty of the Park. There would be many days of hard hiking ahead, so why not enjoy it while I could.

There was a very dense fog that September morning when Joan and I left the Loft Mtn. campsite headed south on the Skyline Drive to Humpback Rocks. Visibility was so poor that we could not drive more than 10 miles per hour safely. In spite of the extreme fog, we counted 19 deer along the Parkway—an indication of the large number of animals in the Park and the danger of car/deer collisions along the highway. Our slow travel speed caused a later arrival at the trailhead than we had planned, so I did not begin to hike until 9:00 AM.

This foggy morning was reminiscent of many others I had experienced along the AT with one exception—I was alone. When I was hiking with Osbra, I was usually out front and could often hear the tramping of his feet behind me or he might say, "Here's a plant I want to photograph and study—I'll be along later." But he was always near, and I would have to get used to not hearing this.

The dense fog seemed to crowd right in around me and the heavy moisture dripping from the trees sounded as though it was raining. There was just enough visibility to make out the Trail ahead. The dripping water was the only sound in the forest as there was no wind, not even a breeze, and no sounds of any kind of wildlife.

The AT leaves the Parkway at Humpback Rocks crossing Dobie Mtn. and descends into Mill Creek Valley. Hiking was slow with everything in the forest —the trees, large boulders and the Trail itself—appearing as grey masses without true form. Even the Mill Creek Shelter did not come into view until I was a few feet away and did not really take shape until I stepped on the porch and peered inside. It was a new shelter not even listed in my guide-book, and I was impressed with its design and construction. It would probably provide shelter for 12-16 hikers without too much crowding, one of the best I had seen so far along the AT.

After leaving the Valley, the AT ascends Elk Mtn. and swings back across the Parkway. It was through this area where I began seeing deer along the Trail. In fact, one deer came dashing out of the brush into the Trail and almost ran over me. I had made ar-rangements to meet Joan along the AT in Rockfish Gap for lunch, but when I arrived there I did not see her. It was still so foggy you could only see a few feet, so I thought she had decided against driving any more than she had to in these conditions. I ate lunch on the north side of the AT crossing of I-64 not knowing Joan was waiting on the south side of the crossing in a parking area. We were less than a hundred feet apart but could not see each other in the fog.

Rockfish Gap is near the southern terminus of the Shenandoah National Park; and for 95 miles the AT closely parallels the Sky-line Drive, the ridge line highway leading through the Park. I obtained the required back country permit at the self-registration station near the south entrance to the Park and proceeded on to the first AT crossing of the Skyline Drive at McCormick Gap, still in heavy fog and mist. I was monitoring my knee injury during this first day and hoped it would be okay with the light pack and shorter mileage; but it had been bothering me off and on during the day. After leaving McCormick Gap, I ascended Bear Den Mtn.; and upon reaching the communication towers on its summit, the fog was so dense that their outlines were barely visible. The AT was also hard to follow across the summit due to the fog and poor

Trail markings. I descended into Beagle Gap, the pick up point for the first day's hike and the first of very few times when I would be out before Joan arrived.

She was also keeping track of my knee condition, so beginning the next day we arranged for me to tie a small ribbon on the AT markers at the road crossings. This would be a signal to her that I had passed that point successfully. This system worked quite well until we were sure my knee had improved.

Heavy foggy conditions prevailed throughout the entire first day's hike approaching the Shenandoah National Park (SNP). By the second day, the weather had cleared; and after leaving Beagle Gap and ascending Calf Mtn., the ridges and valleys were sharp and clear. (It is always enlightening when the fog clears.) I crossed the National Park boundary on the north slope of Calf Mtn. and entered the Park about mid morning. The SNP is divided into three sections by two major highways crossing the Park: the Southern Section about 45 miles from Rockfish Gap to Swift Run Gap at US 33; the Central Section 34 miles from US 33 to Thornton Gap; the Northern Section about 27 miles from US 211 at Thornton Gap to US 522 near Front Royal.

I did stop briefly at the Calf Mtn. Hut for a couple of pictures and noted one of the infamous bear poles near it. Hikers are required to use these bear poles to suspend all food at least 10 feet above the ground and 4 feet horizontally. In the SNP, the three-sided structures which were referred to as shelters or lean-to's elsewhere along the AT are called "huts" here. This is the first area moving north where AT hikers are charged a fee to stay in them. The word "hut" takes on a new meaning in the White Mountains of New Hampshire and will be explained later.

As the day progressed, the temperature increased to near 80 degrees; and on the climb over an unnamed ridge after crossing Jarman Gap, I sighted a rattlesnake stretched across the Trail basking in the sun. I had seen several varieties of snakes along the AT, but this was my first rattlesnake even though I had hiked through many miles of suitable habitat. I gave him a little space, took a photo, wished him well and moved on.

Near the ridge line after crossing Sawmill Run was the first evidence I had seen of the Gypsy Moth infestation that had caused major destruction in some of the Appalachian highlands. There were acres and acres of dead oak trees along the ridges which had opened up the forest floor to a tangle of briars, underbrush, etc., along the Trail. These insects are completely changing the characteristic of the forest and apparently there is no way to stop them. Are we on the threshold of a new devastation threatening our forest similar to the blight which wiped out the American Chestnut tree during the early years of the 20th Century? I hope not—our trees are a treasured natural resource.

Many southbound hikers had commented on the excellent condition of the Trail in the Park; and from what I had seen so far, I would have to agree. The only exception was the area where the forest canopy had been destroyed by the Gypsy Moth, because there was no shade and the underbrush had taken over. In some cases, the Trail was almost completely obstructed by brush, weeds and briars.

My sore knee had flared up several times during the day, especially on the downhills. I was hoping it would not become a serious drawback to my hiking, and the next day I awoke early and found I could hardly walk. My knee was stiff and causing me a great deal of pain, and I knew if I were going to continue this hike, I would have to get off of it for a while. I did not hike that day and was not sure if one day would be enough for recovery.

The next morning I was on the Trail by 7:30 as my knee seemed much better. The day's rest had helped considerably. If all went well, I planned to hike past our base camp and perhaps even get in 14 miles. The morning was pleasant and cool, and I felt good—ideal hiking conditions. I crossed Blackrock Gap and began the ascent of Blaylock Mtn. The extent of damage the Gypsy Moths had done to the forest was hard to believe. It went on and on with every oak destroyed. The trees stood like skeletons—no leaves, no life—waiting for the elements to take them to the ground.

From the summit of Blackrock Mtn. was one of the best views so far in the Shenandoah. Also impressive was the mass of large boulders around the summit which extended down the mountain side. Geologists report that this area used to be a huge cliff that broke off and tumbled down the mountain creating this huge rock field. After leaving the Blackrock area, the AT swings back across the highway, and it was in this area that I had a second black bear sighting in the Shenandoah. He crossed the AT in front of me and very quickly disappeared into the brush. I had been seeing signs of their presence along the Trail: droppings and logs and stumps torn apart where they had foraged for insects and roots, etc. We had seen one crossing the highway the day before while returning to our base camp from the Big Meadows area.

Joan met me at the Brown Gap crossing with a hiking staff to try as an aid for my sore knee, and if it worked well I might want to continue to use it. It worked so well that I hiked past our base camp at Loft. Mtn. on to the Ivy Creek crossing allowing me to complete a 14-mile day. The staff became my companion and would stay with me all the way to Katahdin.

The following day I did not hike because of foul weather which lasted all day. It gave me another opportunity to rest my knee for the days ahead. The next day the rain and fog had cleared out, and I continued on from Ivy Creek across several ridges and gaps to the pick up point at Swift Run Gap completing 13.5 miles.

After crossing Powell Gap, I ascended Roundtop Mtn. to a rock outcropping overlooking Smith Roach Gap. I was ready for a snack break, and this place had all the amenities for a rest stop: a comfortable place to sit, a pleasant view, a nice breeze—and now another mouse story. I had taken crackers and cookies from my pack, placed the open pack behind me and sat there munching and enjoying the view. In the meantime, a mouse entered my pack (unbeknownst to me) in search of a snack for herself. Her search and escape were interrupted when I finished my snack, closed the pack, loaded up and was on my way. She was trapped inside and would have to wait for an appropriate time to escape. The time did not come until that night when I took some items from my pack in our motorhome and left it open.

The next morning, while I was having my coffee, she made her appearance on the arm of our sofa but quickly disappeared under it. After a close examination of the furniture, we found several places where she had been gathering material by gnawing tiny pieces from the fabric to build a nest. I opened the engine compartment and placed some cheese there providing a means for her to escape. She did and so goes another mouse escapade.

A notable feature along this section was the panoramic view of the Peaks of the Shenandoah from Hightop Mtn. (3,587 feet) to the south and west. There was still fog in the valleys, and from the ledges on the mountain, the peaks extended through the fog and gave an appearance of islands jutting up into the sky creating a mystic scene.

There was rainfall in the Blue Ridge again the following day, but I decided to hike in spite of it. Since beginning at Rockfish Gap, the weather had been unsettled, raining one day, clearing up for a day and then raining again. This pattern had apparently been caused, according to forecasters, by a tropical depression named Danielle moving up the East Coast.

Swift Run Gap marks the beginning of the Central Section of the Shenandoah National Park and is considered the most rugged with the highest mountains and, according to literature, the most interesting terrain in the Park—I was anxious to explore it. The rain had set in rather steadily when I left Swift Run Gap requiring my poncho and pack cover throughout the morning.

I usually take a snack break by mid morning, but I kept delaying hoping it would stop raining or that a dry place could be found. After crossing over the summit of Baldface Mtn., I finally found an overhanging oak tree which offered some protection from the persistent rain. Since it was about 11:00, an early lunch seemed more in order. After lunch, I continued on in the rain crossing Lewis Mtn. and stopped for a break at the crest of Bearfence Mtn. under an overhanging rock.

The rain just would not quit. I was wet and had been for most of the day—thank goodness the temperature was warm. The overhanging brush and weeds along the Trail kept my pant legs wet with water running into my boots keeping my feet wet. It always concerns me when I hike for extended periods of time with wet feet—the skin becomes soft and prone to blisters and that problem would not be welcome again.

We had moved our base camp from Loft Mtn. to Big Meadows near the middle of the Central Section of the Park. By the next morning the rain had subsided, and the weather had turned cool and windy. I began at Bootens Gap and hiked across Hazeltop Mtn. (3,816 feet), the highest point the AT crosses in the Park. After descending halfway down Hazeltop, I had a third Black Bear sighting. He crossed the Trail in front of me and stopped briefly to check me out and then disappeared in the underbrush. Through the section from Hazeltop to Big Meadows was an abundance of wildlife. I had seen 30 to 40 deer, most of which were near the Trail and did not pay a lot of attention to my passing; grey squirrels and birds were everywhere; I saw and heard perhaps a dozen grouse; and then there was the Black Bear. Seeing this number and varieties of wildlife through this area was a delight.

The AT crosses the Skyline Drive at Milan Gap which is the only highway crossing in the Central Section of the Park. It then swings around the perimeter of the Big Meadows Campground, our base camp for this section. I hiked into the campground by 10:00, and Joan fixed me a large breakfast—how convenient. However, this was the only time during my hike on the AT that she was able to prepare a breakfast and have it ready when I passed. She had, however, met me at trailheads many times with sandwiches for lunch.

After that big breakfast, I was off and decided to take the blue blaze up to the summit of Hawksbill Mtn. (4,050 feet). It is the highest peak in the SNP and, weatherwise, I could not have picked a better day to make the climb. The summit is .9 mile off the AT and well worth the extra time and effort. The view was absolutely outstanding—the best I had seen so far in the SNP, and it is said that the skyline of Washington, DC can be seen on a clear day. It was not, however, visible to me due to some blue haze in the distance. As I stood gazing across this marvelous landscape, my thoughts drifted back to "Great Wide Beautiful Wonderful World." Of significance on this peak is its geological makeup of green stone which is evidence of its volcanic origin and is also characteristic of many areas throughout the Park. Balsam Fir and Red Spruce are found on its summit and were the last I saw until reaching the high peaks in Vermont.

I hiked back to the AT and was descending the mountain into Hawksbill Gap when I met a southbound thru-hiker. We visited, and he indicated he was hiking into Big Meadows and would be tenting there in the campground. I told him our base camp was there and that I would look him up when I finished my hike that day. Before leaving, I asked him what his Trail name was. He introduced himself as Bill Bonaparte ("Bill and Friend"), and I said, "Bill and Friend? Is someone hiking with you?" His reply was, "Yes, Jesus." Then he asked if I had a Trail name. I paused and finally said, "Yes—just call me The Wise Man."

On the way to our camp after Joan picked me up, I told her about my meeting with Bill and that he would be camping at Big Meadows. She suggested that we locate him and invite him to join us for dinner. He graciously accepted, and we had an enjoyable evening visit with him. We were very pleased to later learn through *Trailway News* that he completed his thru-hike.

The next day's hike began at Hawksbill Gap and followed above a series of cliffs to the Skyland Lodge and Restaurant. This was a picturesque section of Trail and reflected a tremendous Trail building effort on the part of the NPS, the Potomac Appalachian Trail Club (PATC) and the CCC. Joan and I had driven up to the parking area near the Skyland Lodge to the trailhead leading over to Little Stony Man Mtn. the day before. We hiked over to the summit via the AT and a blue blaze trail and took photos of the Great Valley and many distant ridges and valleys. It was a pleasure to have Joan hike with me to one of these lofty perches.

The AT descending from Stony Man Mtn. to the Pinnacles Picnic Area was another impressive section. The Trail followed along the tops of ledges and cliffs with views of Old Rag Mtn., Stony Man and the Great Valley. When I arrived at the Pinnacles Picnic Area, Joan was waiting for me at the AT crossing with a picnic lunch. What a pleasant surprise! I left the area by noon headed for the Pinnacles summit (3,730 feet) where the view across the Pinnacles was outstanding. To the north I could see Mary's

Rock which I would be crossing before descending into Thornton Gap. The expanse of the Great Valley stretched out beneath me with the towns of New Market and Luray, the Carillon Tower near Luray Caverns and other smaller communities visible. The valleys were cloaked in green; but as I panned up the mountain side, green began to blend into fall colors. I hiked the two miles from the Pinnacles to Mary's Rock and was even more impressed with the vista from there.

Mary's Rock has an interesting history as do many of the gaps and peaks along the Blue Ridge. Sources indicate that Mary was the wife of Frances Thornton, a settler who had been given a tract of land (including Mary's Rock) extending up through Thornton Gap on the Blue Ridge. On a trip to the area, Frances gave the Rock to Mary as a wedding gift. From the outcropping on Mary's Rock, all of Thornton Gap was visible including Luray, the Park Headquarters, the Thornton Gap panorama and several miles of US 211 through the gap. The view from Mary's Rock is said to be the best in the SNP, and to be there on a bright blue October day made it even more special. I hiked the fairly steep descent into Thornton Gap by 3:00 PM, finishing the impressive and inspiring Central Section of the SNP.

On the following day we moved our base camp from Big Meadows to Mathews Arm Campground in the SNP. I decided to do a section of the Trail that afternoon in order to shorten the hikes for the next two days. Being the shortest of the three in the Shenandoah, I planned two days to traverse the Northern Section. The hike from Thornton Gap to the Pass Mtn. summit was easy and uneventful. I did stop briefly at the Pass Mtn. Hut and left a message in the log book for two hikers I had met in the Southern Section. From Pass Mtn. to the Rattlesnake overlook where Joan met me for lunch was also an easy stretch.

After leaving the overlook, I ascended Hogback Mtn., reaching an elevation of 3,500 feet and passed several points with picturesque overlooks. The AT crosses the Skyline Drive four times over the Hogback Mtn. area, and many of the ledges and outcroppings provide great panoramas across the mountains and valleys of the Blue Ridge. My knee had given me a great deal of trouble almost every day while in the Shenandoah; however, it seemed to be doing better when I hiked out at the AT crossing of the Skyline Drive between South Marshal and North Marshal Mountains completing 13 miles.

On my last hiking day in the Shenandoah, I planned a rendezvous with Joan at the AT crossing of US 522 near Front Royal in the early afternoon. After a number of ups and downs with limited views, I passed the northern boundary of the SNP.

The Shenandoah had provided me with a new hiking experience. It was the only area during the entire length of the Trail where there was a highway in such close proximity for such a distance. Yet, its countless ups and downs, its lofty peaks (some over 4,000 feet), its abundant flora and wildlife, its intriguing geology, its history and overall natural beauty will always remain a major part of my Appalachian Trail hiking memories. By early afternoon, I had reached the high fenced enclosure of the National Zoo Compound which is a 4,000-acre preserve owned by the National Zoological Park, a branch of the Smithsonian Institute. I hiked out on US 522 in Chester Gap where Joan was waiting to pick me up.

Finishing the section that early gave us time to do our shopping in nearby Front Royal. The next morning we moved our base camp to the Front Royal area so I could begin the Northern Virginia section. The AT from this point to Harpers Ferry crosses five Blue Ridge Gaps: Chester, Mannassas, Ashby, Snickers and Keys. These gaps were contact routes in Northern Virginia between the Piedmont and the Great Valley and were the scene of much military activity during the Civil War. By the time we made the move, set up camp and drove to the trailhead, it was mid day; so I only hiked 8 miles, crossing High Knob and descending into Manassas Gap.

Close to where the AT leaves US 522 in Chester Gap, I was greeted by a unique sign by the AT which read, "ENTERING RESTRICTED GROUNDS BREEDING CENTER NATIONAL ZOOLOGICAL PARK, PETS ON LEASH, NO CAMPING, NO FIRES, STAY ON TRAIL, NO TRESPASSING, VIOLATORS WILL BE EATEN." The AT continues around the perimeter of the Park which is enclosed by a high wire fence. Through the fence, I could see exotic animals grazing in the meadow areas. The AT then ascends near the summit of High Knob, which is a few hundred feet from the springs that are the headwaters of the Rappahannock River. Through this area were more piles of rocks and stone fences settlers had made clearing the land.

By early afternoon, I arrived at the Jim and Molly Denton Shelter, and what a shelter! This was, without question, the finest shelter I had seen so far on the AT. The PATC's Trail building and maintenance efforts are outstanding, but this reflects the ultimate in shelter design and facilities. This one certainly had it all: a wood deck with built-in benches, a cooking pavilion, tables, fireplace and a shower (cold) that was a marvel.

The AT crosses through some open meadows after ascending a second ridge with outstanding views of the Great Valley and the mountain ranges in West Virginia and then descends into Manassas Gap to the crossing of VA 55. It had taken longer than I planned through this section, and Joan hiked up the Trail to meet me to make sure I was okay.

The next day's hike took me through an interesting area between Manassas Gap and Ashby Gap—The G. Richard Thompson Wildlife Management Area which, according to Trail literature, is administered by the Virginia Commission of Game and Inland Fisheries. Wildlife through here consisted of deer, turkeys, grouse and squirrels; and there was also a stand of timber including oak, poplar, cherry, locust and clusters of sassafras trees—many of which were larger than normally found.

The Dick's Dome Shelter (named after its builder Dick George who is a PATC member) in this area is unique with its geodesic design—the only one like it along the entire AT. I did have a chance to visit with the caretaker while passing. Through this section is Signal Knob which is on a blue blaze trail off the AT and was used as a vantage point by soldiers during the Civil War. Before reaching Ashby Gap, the AT passes through the extreme western tip of Sky Meadows State Park and then descends into the Gap passing an old stone wall near a sign that read: "George Washington passed here." When I hiked out on US 50, Joan was walking down the road to meet me.

If you look at a profile map of the AT between Ashby Gap and Snickers Gap, a roller coaster would come to mind—I counted 13 peaks and valleys. According to the guidebook, this is the most difficult 14-mile section in northern Virginia and Maryland; and after hiking it, I would also include the northern Shenandoah.

I began the hike at Ashby Gap early and knew I would be in for a full day. After about three miles, I passed through a fine stand of young growth of Yellow Poplar (Tulip) trees. Poplar is a fast-growing tree; and in another 20 years, if left undisturbed, those trees will be achieving big status. The Rod Hollow Shelter in this area is .2 mile off the AT, so I stopped for water and a snack break. Once again, the PATC is to be commended for their outstanding efforts in shelter construction and maintenance. Located at this site was another well-designed clean shelter, a covered picnic table and fireplace, a large patio chair out front and three pads for tents—all in a well-planned setting. Great going, PATC! It would indeed be a pleasure to stay in this shelter.

The marvelous October weather—bright, clear, crisp—continued through this section. However, due to heavy forest and undergrowth cover over these ridges, there were few views except from Buzzard Hill and Bear Den Rocks. I hiked out on VA 7 in Snickers Gap in the late afternoon completing the most strenuous 14-mile section since down on the Blue Ridge. What made it so difficult were the continuous ups and downs with the AT going straight over the peaks with no assist from switchbacks. In spite of its difficulty, I enjoyed the many ridges and valleys and the challenges they presented.

On the following day, we moved our base camp from Front Royal to Harpers Ferry. That afternoon I hiked from the AT crossing of WV 9 to the junction of US 340 and Shenandoah Street in Harpers Ferry. Since this was only a 5.3-mile section, I finished it by 2:00 PM giving us the rest of the afternoon to tour historic Harpers Ferry and the surrounding countryside.

There was still the 13.5-mile section from Snickers Gap to Keys Gap to complete, so I returned there the following morning. The weather had changed from the bright blue October day I had enjoyed the day before to a rainy, foggy morning when I left Snickers Gap. This day's hike would mark another milestone on my AT journey—I would be finishing the state of Virginia and enter West Virginia for the second time (the first time was on Peters Mtn. near Pearisburg).

About four miles from Snickers Gap, I met a large hiking group that had camped at Devil's Raceway. These people were members of an outreach program with participants from all over the country. I had met other groups along the AT participating in similar programs and applaud their efforts. They were providing experiences for many who may not ever have had the opportunity, particularly young people from urban areas.

I reached the Blackburn AT Center at 11:45 in a heavy downpour of rain which had continued throughout the morning. The Center is on a blue blaze trail .3 mile off the ridge and is owned by the PATC. There was no one there, but it was open for hikers. It is really a fine facility that has a large screened porch with picnic tables, a sofa, books and various printed material for hikers to enjoy. There is also a cabin nearby which has been converted into a hostel for hikers. I ate my lunch at one of the tables while the rain came down in torrents. Thanks, PATC, for providing a comfortable, dry place for my lunch!

From the Blackburn Trail Center, I hiked to the David Lesser Shelter, another one of those newly-constructed PATC structures. This one has a large deck, deck chairs, unique log design, covered picnic tables with a fireplace and a large area for tents. Also—get this—suspended under the picnic shelter was a handcrafted porch swing adding the final touch to hiking enjoyment. Another remarkable facility—you have done it again, PATC! The Keys Gap Shelter which was very near WV 9 had been removed and replaced by this shelter which is two miles from Keys Gap.

Shelters near highways are often targets of vandalism and are frequently used by local groups. There is a movement by Trail clubs and the NPS to relocate the shelters that are in close proximity to highways in order to reduce vandalism and provide a better wilderness experience for hikers.

The hike to Keys Gap was completed by mid afternoon, officially completing my hike through the state of Virginia. There had been variety along the AT in Virginia—its high peaks and lush valleys, its abundance of wildlife, its fascinating geology, its rich history, the grandeur of the Blue Ridge and the Shenandoah. I was grateful the AT passed through this distinctive state. Four down and ten to go!

Harpers Ferry is located in the eastern Panhandle of West Virginia at the confluence of the Shenandoah and Potomac Rivers and is an area of historic significance. It became a National Historic Park in 1963 and has a Visitor Center nearby where people can take tours and obtain detailed information about its history.

After crossing the Shenandoah River, the AT continues on through Harpers Ferry passing Jefferson Rock, ruins of St. John's—the Episcopal Church, Robert Harper's house and continues on past a replica of the Engine House which was the area of the infamous John Brown's Stand. While Joan was enjoying the shops in the historic district, I hiked the .95-mile section through Harpers Ferry to the Engine House. I stopped at Jefferson Rock to enjoy the view Jefferson spoke of looking down the Shenandoah toward its confluence with the Potomac.

On the day we were there, there was a reenactment of the days preceding the election of 1860. Groups of people in costumes of the day were standing on street corners discussing issues of the times. They pretended we were not there and that time had been moved back to 1860. During the reenactment, we were approached by a young man dressed in period costume, who shook my hand, placed a copy of a Confederate $5.00 bill in it and said he appreciated my support of his candidate.

We left the historic district and stopped at the Appalachian Trail Conference Center which is in town and visited with the staff but missed seeing Jean Cashin. She was the information specialist (now retired) and referred to as "Trail Mother" to hikers. (I also missed seeing her on a second visit later.) I signed the Trail Register and browsed through their display of Trail items—books, maps, T-shirts, etc.

In May, 1993, Joan and I returned to Harpers Ferry to resume my hike. We used the same plan as the previous fall and established our first base camp at Cunningham Falls State Park, MD.

The AT leaves Harpers Ferry by crossing the Potomac River on the 600-foot Goodloe Byron Memorial Bridge Pedestrian Walkway which was built by the NPS. Even though Harpers Ferry is considered the psychological midpoint of the AT, I still had 77 miles before reaching the geographical midpoint near Pine Grove Furnace State Park in Pennsylvania. The skies were grey, and it looked and felt like rain when I left Harpers Ferry approaching the Bridge. After crossing the Potomac, I entered Maryland—five down and nine states to go.!

The Trail then follows the old C & O (Chesapeake and Ohio) Towpath running beside the abandoned canal along the Potomac River for three miles. The C & O Canal was completed in 1850 and was used as a major mode of transportation between Cumberland, MD, and Washington, D. C., until near the turn of the 20th Century. It is now a National Historic Park. As I hiked over the old towpath, I recalled studying about and seeing pictures of the old canals in my history books in school. I could picture in my mind the mules or oxen trudging along the towpath with the canal boat following behind.

The AT leaves the river valley at Weverton and, as I ascended South Mtn., it started to rain and showed signs of lasting a while. I was looking forward to the view from Weverton Cliffs across the Potomac; but when I arrived, the rain and fog obscured the view. Wet conditions continued as I reached the summit of South Mtn. and moved on up the ridge. During prolonged rains, it is sometimes difficult to find a dry place to stop for a rest or to eat—such was the case here. Before noon I finally found one under an overhanging rock extending from a large pile of boulders.

South Mtn. is another area reflecting 19th Century and Civil War history. Crompton Gap is the first gap along the AT after leaving the Potomac River Valley. The first bit of unusual history along the AT near the gap was Gath's empty tomb, and an empty tomb it is. The inscription on the plaque there reads: "During the Nineteenth Century few people bought burial lots in public cemeteries as we do today. Instead a small parcel of their own land was usually set aside as a private cemetery. If enough money was available a mausoleum tomb was built for certain family members. Gath concerned with his own burial built this lonely tomb about 20 years before his death which came on April 15, 1914, in New York City. By this time his great wealth had dwindled and the near-penniless Gath was buried in a Philadelphia, Pennsylvania, cemetery instead of his own tomb as he had desired. Gath's empty tomb mutely symbolizes the uncertainties of life, fame and fortune and the certainty of death." "Gath" was the pen name for George Alfred Townsend, a Civil War journalist who erected the 50-foot memorial in Crompton Gap honoring Civil War newspaper correspondents.

The unusual memorial is in Gathland State Park and looks somewhat like a miniature lopsided Arch de Triumph with one large arch at ground level and three small ones above with a tower extending above the top level on one side. Near the memorial and Gath's tomb are remnants of earthworks from the fierce battle that was fought in the Gap during the Civil War.

The following morning I left Crompton Gap heading along South Mtn. to the crossing of I-70. The AT follows South Mtn. across the 40-mile neck of western Maryland. Before reaching the ridge line, I hiked down a .3-mile blue blaze to the Crompton Gap Shelter to take a photo and check out the location. I had been doing this all along the Trail for my own photo and journal record of my hike. The first good view of the Maryland countryside for the morning was from Lambs Knoll (1,772 feet). All of South Mtn. across Maryland lies between 1,500-2,000 feet with some of the gaps dropping to 1,000 feet, making mostly a ridgewalking Trail.

I descended Lambs Knoll into Fox Gap which was the scene of another fierce Civil War battle fought on South Mtn. Major General Reno and Brigadier General Garland were killed; and Rutherford B. Hayes, our 19th president, was wounded at this battle on September 14, 1862.

By noon I reached the Dahlgren Backpack Camping Area in Turner Gap. I have commended the PATC's efforts for providing outstanding shelters and camping facilities in northern Virginia, and now the state of Maryland is to be commended for providing the outstanding facility in Turners Gap. This is a model other states should consider using to upgrade some of their camping facilities. There were rest rooms and hot showers, many picnic tables and tenting areas, firewood and fireplaces—all of this in a grand setting. I had lunch there and thought how fortunate hikers would be to reach this area after a long, cold, wet hard day.

After lunch and a good rest, I crossed US Alt. 40 at Turners Gap where another part of the Battle of South Mtn. was fought. Nearby is the Old South Mtn. Inn that, according to records, many U. S. presidents used. The AT passes through Washington Monument State Park about two miles north of Turners Gap; and when I reached the entrance to the Park, a sign on the gate indicated that the Park was closed due to storm damage. Hikers, however, could pass through as the AT through it had been cleared. Western Maryland had experienced a major ice storm in March that had caused much damage along the Trail on South Mtn. The Trail clubs of Maryland had done a remarkable job of clearing vast areas of blowdowns along the AT. The road leading to the monument area was obstructed by many fallen trees and limbs. I hiked up to the monument without seeing anyone—not even a hiker.

This monument, built in 1838, was the first one to honor George Washington. The 30-foot high native stone structure stands atop Monument Knob and has a unique design which is the shape of a huge milk bottle or churn. Inside is a spiral staircase with 34 steps leading to the top. I climbed the steps and enjoyed the view over and across Pleasant Valley and the city of Boonsboro. After spending some time on the monument enjoying the panorama and taking photos, I descended it and the Knob and headed for I-70.

The heavy Friday morning traffic was rushing on I-70 under the AT crossover bridge when I left the trailhead continuing my trek across Maryland. The Annapolis Rocks/Black Rocks area was the first that provided views of the Maryland countryside and Greenbrier Lake. There had been a lot of ice storm damage through the Pine Knob and Black Rocks area. Blowdowns from the ice storm were extensive through this area, but the Trail clubs had cleared the AT. I was amazed by the size of some of the trees the storm had taken down. When I hiked into Hemlock Hill Shelter for lunch, I found that many of the large trees around the shelter had also been taken down by the storm, but it, too, had been well cleared by the Trail Club..

After lunch, I hiked across MD 77 and caught up with a northbound hiker (Tim Goulding) and his dog (Zukov) from Indiana who had started at Harpers Ferry and had visions of Maine. We hiked out together at MD 419 in Raven Rock Hollow by mid afternoon finishing for the day, and Tim said he was moving on to the state line.

Before leaving the next morning, Joan fixed a care package (food and treats) for Tim. I told her I would catch up with him before the end of the day. She had visited with him when we hiked out together at Raven Rock Hollow and felt the extra food would give him a lift. The bottom line was that she became attached to him, since he was so close to the age of our son Rod, and felt he needed motherly care. It was 6 1/2 miles from Raven Rock Hollow to the Pennsylvania/Maryland state line and I planned to complete it by mid morning. My climb out of the hollow was through another area that had been devastated by the ice storm. Trees and limbs of all sizes were down and crisscrossed the Trail forming log and brush barriers. The Trail clubs, however, had cleared a corridor through all of this—what a chore this must have been.

I arrived at Pen-Mar Park which is a county park on the PA/MD state line with rest rooms, camping area and a pavilion that offers a good westward view across the Pennsylvania countryside. Pen-Mar (short for Pennsylvania-Maryland) was the site of one of the most famous resort areas in the east from post Civil War times to the 1940's. It provided recreation activities such as a roller coaster, a miniature railroad, restaurants and hotels. The park closed in 1943 when its popularity declined and it was no longer profitable to keep it open. Pen-Mar marked the end of the Maryland section of the AT and another milepost for me—six states down and eight to go. While I was sitting on a picnic table enjoying the view by the pavilion and having a snack, about 30 hikers left the area headed south. They looked fresh and high spirited, and I am sure the climb up on High Rocks, which is the first good one, would be slowing them down.

Before I finished my snack, my attention was directed toward the camping area nearby when I heard a dog bark. I recognized Zukov and then saw Tim taking down his tent. He was getting a late start. He was surprised to see me and more so when I presented him with the care package Joan had sent. This was the beginning of a hiking companionship that lasted until I finished this hike at the Susquehanna River in Duncannon, PA.

We left Pen-Mar about 10:30 crossing the Mason/Dixon line into Pennsylvania. We ate lunch at a picnic table by PA 16 and then continued on to the Deer Lick Run Shelters where we stopped for a snack break. These shelters were new and had been constructed on this site to replace the former Mackie Run Shelter which was in another location. We stopped at Antietam Creek Shelter in the middle of the afternoon to rest and take photos.

From the shelter up to the AT crossing of Old Forge Road in Michaux State Forest, we passed through an area where the ice storm had taken down most of a stand of large White Pines. The damage to this forest was unbelievable. We had to climb over and work our way around the many log and brush barriers in the Trail. The Trail clubs and park personnel had not begun to clear this area yet, and what a major undertaking this would be. When we hiked out at Old Forge Road, Tim decided to stay in the Tumbling Run Shelter near the trailhead.

The next morning I resumed my hike from the trailhead and shortly reached the shelter where Tim had spent the night, and he was packing up to leave. I delivered another care package from Joan and told him I would move on and that he could catch me as I would be taking photos and hiking a couple of blue blaze trails. I ascended to Chimney Rocks getting views and photos of the Waynesboro Reservoir and the PA countryside. After staying at the Rocks for a good while thinking that Tim would come along any time, I moved on.

Through the Chimney Rocks area, there was evidence of the Gypsy Moth damage I had seen back in the Shenandoah; but it had not reached the degree of destruction they had there. I hiked through more areas where there was major storm damage to the forest, particularly near Snowy Mountain Road. What continued to amaze me was the size of the trees that had come down—oaks, pines, Poplars, etc., many with trunk diameters up to 30 inches. These big trees were uprooted pulling the entire root system into the air 10-15 feet. I had been hiking at a slower pace hoping Tim would catch up; but, when I reached the AT crossing of PA 233, he still had not shown up. I decided not to wait there but to continue on to the next spring which was at the Rocky Mountain Shelters. They were located down a blue blaze .3 mile off the main ridge, and by the time I reached them it was lunch time—still no Tim.

After lunch, I began the climb back to the AT and heard my name being called from the ridge—it was Tim. He said he did not want to pass the blue blaze without checking to see if I were there. We hiked out on US 30 at Caledonia State Park in the early afternoon. Tim needed supplies and to do his laundry, so we took him and Zukov to a motel a mile or so west and told him we would pick them up there the next morning. I had purposely planned this to be a short day so we would have time to move our base camp to the Mount Holly Springs, PA, area near the AT crossing of PA 94. This location would provide a good base until I reached the Susquehanna River at Duncannon.

The next morning we drove to the motel, picked up Tim and Zukov and began our hike at the AT crossing near Caledonia State Park. The AT continues to pass through areas with interesting history, and this was no exception. Iron and charcoal were major industries in the early to mid 1800's through this part of Pennsylvania. Caledonia was the site of one of the many iron works extending on up into New England. The one at Caledonia was owned by Thaddeus Stevens, an abolitionist during Civil War times, and was destroyed when Confederate troops marched through what is now US 30 to the Battle of Gettysburg.

Along the AT on South Mtn. in Pennsylvania and on north into New England were many circular flat areas about 25-50 feet in diameter. These were sites where charcoal was made to fire the many iron furnaces along the northern Appalachian range. Through this area, I was also seeing numerous large ant hills, many of which were 4-5 feet in diameter. I am not sure what attracted them to this area as I had not seen them further south. I hiked out in the early afternoon at the Arendtsville-Shippensburg Road on South Mtn. which completed the section planned for the day, and Tim moved on two miles to the next shelter.

For the next day, I planned eighteen miles taking me to the crossing of PA 34 near Mount Holly Springs. I quickly stepped off the two miles and picked up Tim and Zukov at the Toms Run Shelter where they had spent the night. We headed for Pine Grove Furnace State Park where we wanted to spend some time exploring the area. Pine Grove is another one of those areas where I would like to have rolled back time so I could have seen and experienced some of its historic past. Located here was a blast furnace forge and a large settlement containing many homes where people lived who worked in the iron and charcoal industries. Iron and steel which were used in firearm production for the Revolutionary War were produced here and in several furnaces around this area.

After entering the Park, the AT passes the historic Ironmasters Mansion which is restored and is now used as a hostel. If my time schedule had permitted, I would like to have spent a night in this hostel and learned more about the Park and surrounding areas. After spending about an hour in the vicinity of the hostel and the old furnace, we moved out of the Park.

Shortly before noon, we reached the geographic midpoint marker for the AT; or at least this was the midpoint in 1985 when the marker was erected by "Woodchuck," an AT thru-hiker. The marker indicated it was 1069 miles to Mt. Katahdin in Maine and 1069 miles to Springer Mtn., Georgia. This figure, however, changes because of relocations that are made each year. The original midpoint was considered to be on Center Point Knob which is about 12 miles north of this location.

We continued on to near the summit of Piney Mtn. and decided to take the .5-mile blue blaze to a rock outcropping known as Pole Steeple where we had a panorama of the Pine Grove Furnace Valley. This was the finest view we had seen in Pennsylvania so far. A group of rock climbers were testing their skills on the quartzite cliffs beneath the overhanging rocks. Through this section were more of those very large ant hills like those I had seen the day before on the other side of the valley. What is it about this area that attracts them? We hiked out on Pine Grove Furnace Road near PA 34, completing a full and very interesting day. We took Tim and Zukov with us to our camp site where he pitched his tent by our motorhome.

The 14-mile section we hiked the following day crossed PA 94 south of Mount Holly Springs which is a peaceful little town whose buildings on its main street had been restored. We crossed over two ridges which provided us with views of the Boiling Springs and Cumberland Valley area of Pennsylvania. Along these ridges were outcroppings of huge quartzite rock with the AT winding through and around fields of them. Reports are that these rocks date back over 500 million years. The last ridge is known as Center Point Knob, and we stopped by the stone marker which marked the original midpoint of the AT. We took photos, rested and ate lunch before descending the ridge which was the official northern terminus of the Blue Ridge Mountains.

Ahead of us lay the historic village of Boiling Springs and the broad (13.5-mile) Cumberland Valley. We hiked off the ridge and crossed about two miles of farm land before reaching Yellow Breeches Creek. We crossed a stone arched bridge into the village of Boiling Springs where we watched fly fishermen working for trout in the pools in the stream coming from the springs.

The AT passes along the shore of Children's Lake and past the Appalachian Trail Conference's Mid Atlantic Regional Field Office. We stopped there and visited with Frances, the receptionist, who was very friendly and helpful. She gave us a current relocation map of the AT crossing the Cumberland Valley. It had originally crossed the broad valley following public highways and roads and was not an area that hikers looked forward to. I had heard horror stories from hikers who crossed it during hot days in summer.

Before continuing on the AT, we walked up to view the Springs. They were quite impressive—the largest in the state of Pennsylvania—producing a hefty 24 million gallons of water per day. Boiling Springs was another major iron-producing center during the eighteenth century and is listed in the National Register of Historical Places. It is currently a very charming and quiet residential community off the beaten path and certainly worthy of another visit from me. We left Boiling Springs, crossing more farm land, and reached our pickup point for the day on PA 74. Tim and Zukov returned to our campsite with us.

The Cumberland Valley is a very broad agricultural valley with large dairy farms as well as farms producing corn, wheat, and alfalfa. Hiking across it was a nice change from the rocky ridges and crossing the deep valleys. This was flat farm country. Many of the farms were owned and operated by Pennsylvania Dutch with a lot of buildings made of stone. We followed the relocations which took us through farms, woodlands and along streams making it more worthwhile than the original road walk

The AT crosses three major highways in the valley, all within a few miles of each other. The first is the PA Turnpike where we crossed on a macadam road; about a mile further, we crossed US 11; and then about 3.4 mile further was I-81. This was my third and next to the last crossing of I-81. I had crossed it twice in the Shenandoah Valley in southwestern Virginia. After crossing the interstate, the AT went right down through a dairy farm field with a large herd of cattle grazing about. The cattle were curious about us and followed us some distance.

By early afternoon, we reached PA 944 which marks the end of the valley and the beginning of the ascent of Blue Mtn. It took us almost an hour to climb out of the valley to the Darlington Shelter, as it had turned very warm slowing us down considerably. We hiked off the ridge onto PA 850, my pickup point for the day, where we met a northbound hiker. Tim decided he would tent with him about a mile further up the Trail.

The next morning found me on the Trail headed for Duncannon on the Susquehanna River. This would be my final hiking day on this trip. In about half an hour, I caught up with Tim; and he had not broken camp yet. Twenty minutes later we were on the Trail heading up Cove Mtn.—yes, another Cove Mtn.—how many does this make?

The AT from this point on to Duncannon is considered to be a very rocky section. In fact, Trail literature refers to this section as "Rocky I" We stopped briefly at the Thelma Marks Shelter which was .2 mile down a blue blaze. It is an old shelter and was in need of many repairs. We noted that two trees which had been taken down by the storm had come close to wiping it out. No doubt the Trail Club has plans for renovation or possibly rebuilding it in the near future. We continued on over the rocky Trail to Hawk Rock, an excellent overlook, where we ate lunch while enjoying a view of Duncannon and the Susquehanna Valley. We descended Cove Mtn., passed through a rough rocky slide area before reaching the valley and crossed the Sherman Creek Bridge into Duncannon.

Duncannon is another one of those Trail towns which the AT goes right through. It has the services hikers need such as grocery store, telephone, laundry and the "famous" Doyle Hotel where they can get a good night's rest at a reasonable price. We hiked through Duncannon on Market Street (one of its main streets) and crossed the bridge over the Juniata River to the west end of the Clarks Ferry Bridge which crosses the Susquehanna. This completed the hike for the day and for this trip. We left Tim and Zukov on the banks of the Susquehanna where they were going to tent and stay a day or so before moving on to Maine. Joan and I had become quite attached to them during the days we hiked together, and we wished him well on his hike. I do not know if he made it to Maine or not, but we did receive a card that he had written while staying at the Greymoor Monastery near the AT at Garrison, New York.

TOP: A rattlesnake lying across the Appalachian Trail
in the Shenandoah National Park
BOTTOM: Pass Mtn. Hut in the Shenandoah. This shelter
is typical of those along the AT in the Park.

TOP: The Jim and Molly Denton Shelter and area
    (PATC "Hikers' Hilton"), one of the finest shelters
    along the AT.
BOTTOM: The Appalachian Trail Conference Center
    building in Harpers Ferry, West Virginia

TOP: A Lock on the old Chesapeake & Ohio Canal
near Harpers Ferry, West Virginia
BOTTOM: First monument to George Washington
in George Washington State Park in Maryland

TOP: Herb with Tim Goulding and his dog Zukov
    near Caledonia State Park, Pennsylvania
BOTTOM: Twin Shelters—Tumbling Run Shelters
    near Old Forge Road in Pennsylvania

TOP: Pine Grove Iron Furnace in Pine Grove
State Park, Pennsylvania
BOTTOM: The Appalachian Trail half-way marker
near Pine Grove Furnace State Park, PA

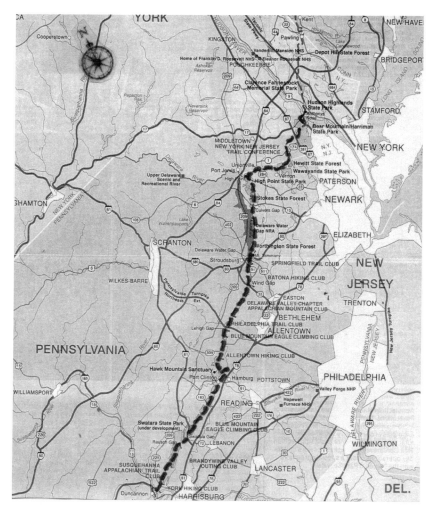

Map detail from Duncannon, PA, to Bear Mountain, NY
(Covered in Chapter eight)
— — — — — Denotes Appalachian Trail Route
Shaded area denotes Delaware Water Gap National
Recreation Area

ROCKS AND MORE ROCKS

*"The AT in Pennsylvania is noted for its rocks—rumor
has it that local hiking clubs sharpen the rocks every
spring in preparation for the hikers."*
—Dan *"Wingfoot"* Bruce

Joan and I returned to the trailhead on the Susquehanna on
September 21, 1993, to continue my hike. Our plans were for a
259-mile hike to Bear Mountain Bridge, New York, where the
AT crosses the Hudson River. We established our first base camp
near Tremont, PA, north of Lebanon.

I left the trailhead at 8:30 and crossed the Clarks Ferry Bridge
on the walkway alongside very heavy traffic. An hour later, I had
crested out on Peters Mtn.—one I would be on for most of the
day. The Trail became very rocky; in fact, the literature had labeled this section "Rocky II." Many areas along the ridge line
reminded me of the Garden Mtn. area in southwestern Virginia,

with rock strata jutting at an upward angle. Some of these areas were rougher than others; but one thing for sure, there were always rocks.

There was considerable fog on the mountain, which prohibited my seeing any of the views listed in the guidebook. I stopped briefly at the Clarks Ferry Shelter and filled my canteen with water. When I reached the Communication Tower Complex on Peters Mtn., the fog remained dense along the ridge line. The temperature, however, was cool, providing comfortable hiking. I ate lunch at the power line crossing of Peters Mtn., which would have provided good views into the valley if the fog had not still clung to the ridge. I stopped for a short while at the Zeager Shelter, which had a dirt floor with bunks around the sides and back, the first I had seen like this. The bunks were so narrow that one would have to lay tight to the walls to prevent rolling out on to the ground. I continued on to the Peters Mtn. Shelter (a very small structure which would fill up with four people), where I met two southbound hikers—one who had hiked to this point from Maine and shared a lot of information with me regarding the White Mountains.

A word about wildlife on Peters Mtn.—there was an abundance of squirrels and deer, and I saw several Ruffed Grouse and heard their "drumming" and also the "*Calc-Calc*" calls of turkeys on two occasions. These are Pennsylvania Game Commission Lands, and the wildlife seem to be doing well.

The fog did not clear, and as I was descending from the ridge, a downpour hit before I could put on my rain gear, leaving me soaked—I put the gear on anyway. It had been foggy and damp all day—so it goes with hiking the AT, reminding me of the hiker's quote: "No rain, No Pain, No Maine." I hiked out in Clarks Valley on PA 325, completing 17 miles for the day.

The hike out of Clarks Valley up Stony Mtn. traversed some interesting and rugged terrain. The Trail follows an old access road ascending the mountain, and it was obvious how this mountain got its name—stones of all sizes were everywhere. There were side spur roads leading off the main road, and I was amazed with the amount of labor it must have required to carve these roads out of such a rugged mountain side remembering that this was done in a day when heavy machinery as we know it today was not available. The area across Stony Mtn. was once a thriving anthracite (hard) coal-producing area, and the AT passes through the ruins of a village where remnants of old foundations are still visible. It is here where the AT traverses a part of St. Anthony's Wilderness, an uninhabited area stretching for 14 miles.

I hiked into Rausch Gap, going through areas of past extensive strip mining and had lunch near an old stone arched railroad bridge. There was evidence of early mining throughout this entire area with the streams showing high concentration of acid from the mine water. Of interest to me was an experimental treatment facility constructed by the Pennsylvania University on Rausch Creek. They had directed water from the stream through a lime treatment system which neutralized the acid from the mine water so the stream could sustain marine life. The water in the stream below the installation certainly showed much better quality. It was clear, and even the stones in the stream bed did not have the rust color that was above the complex. I will be interested to learn how successful this project turns out to be.

I left Rausch Gap, crossing more Pennsylvania Game Lands over Second Mtn. into Swatara Gap, the Trail crossing the Waterville Bridge over Swatara Creek. This is a wrought iron structure built in 1890 by the Berlin Iron Bridge Co., East Berlin, CN. Since it could not meet the demands of modern day transportation, it was to be destroyed but instead was moved to this location and is listed in the National Register of Historic Places. I hiked across it, admiring its structure and completing another 17 miles.

The Waterville Bridge was the trailhead for my next day, and I had planned a shorter hike because my feet were sore from the two previous days pounding on all those jagged Pennsylvania rocks. I began by going under I-81, my fourth and last time crossing this major highway. The day was foggy when I began the ascent of Blue Mtn. out of Swatara Gap, a condition that continued until after I crested out. The weather was unsettled, and rain was in the forecast—another reason I planned a shorter day. I hiked through three miles of a rough section, which continued to remind my feet that I was on PA rocks. Then the AT joined a woods road providing a much smoother surface for about three more miles.

Before reaching PA 501, the AT presented another one of its countless surprises. Standing by the Trail was an American Chestnut tree that was completely loaded with Chestnut burrs (nuts)—a rare sight indeed.

I hiked out onto the highway by 1:45 and saw our little Ford pickup parked across the road with the front of the truck parked toward me. To the rear of the truck on the driver's side stood a man looking toward the cab. When I started across the road, he saw me, turned around, walked to his vehicle and left. Joan and I greeted each other, and I asked her who the man was at the rear of the truck. She replied, "What man?" We both reacted—oh, my gosh—what were his intentions? Maybe good, maybe bad? We were thankful I had come along when I did. From that time on, we set some guidelines: if she got to a trailhead before I did and any vehicles were there, she would drive on and check back later and I would make myself visible and wait for her; if she arrived at the trailhead and no one was there, she would wait; but if someone arrived, she would leave. I also cautioned her to always be aware of the surroundings. This was our policy for the remainder of our hike, and we never had another such incident.

The Trail from PA 501 to PA 183 is only an 8-mile section but one for which I planned a full day. The weather was pleasant for a change, and I wanted to take my time. This section of Blue Mtn. has several historical and natural features. Near the trailhead just off the ridge is (Pilger Ruh), a Pilgrim's Rest spring which was a stop-off point and watering hole for Colonists crossing the mountain. I hiked down to it, read the history on the marker, took some photos and continued on to Round Head—a precipice overlooking the valley. The views of the valley and countryside from the ridge near Round Head were the best I had seen since leaving Duncannon.

A blue blaze leaves the ridge down to the overlook and descends the rocky mountain side in a series of rough rock steps built into the mountain. These steps, known as Showers 500 Steps, were built by Lloyd Showers and at one time were used as a major tourist attraction in the area. I hiked down the steps and marveled at the view of the valley and the efforts required to construct such a stairway. I did not count the steps, but 500 seemed accurate to me; because I had to climb back up them since I could not find the blue blaze loop which I had planned to use to return to the ridge. I spent about two hours, including lunch time, in the Showers Steps area and considered it a very worthwhile side trip.

By 1:00 I reached Hertlein Campsite nestled in a secluded little valley with an excellent water source, good tenting spaces, and a register box—all in a delightful natural setting. A short distance from this campsite were the foundations of two shelters. I do not know whether they had been removed for some reason or whether they had been destroyed. In any event, this was certainly a choice location for them. Before reaching PA 183, I passed a marker near the site of Fort Snyder which was one of several forts built for protection from Indians during the mid 1700's.

The 15-mile section from this trailhead to Port Clinton on the Schuykill River was my next day's hike. My eagerness to get started that morning caused me to forget an important item. I had not hiked 10 minutes when I realized that my hiking staff was left in the truck. I had really become accustomed to it and found it to be very helpful through the countless rough steep areas along the Trail. This was the only time for the remainder of the hike that I did not have the staff with me. The morning went well with the Trail not so rocky for the first nine miles. I met quite a number of people—a bow hunter, a large group of Scouts and several hikers. When I missed the Trail for a short distance, the bow hunter put me back on track. I crossed several more miles of Pennsylvania Game Commission Lands with road accesses at several points along the ridge crest.

The Trail became rocky again before reaching the Phillips Canyon area and continued so on into Port Clinton. On the descent, a vantage point known as Auburn Lookout provided a bird's-eye view of the Schuykill Valley and Port Clinton. The Trail from the lookout into Port Clinton was what Auburn said —"Lookout"— because the descent was a 1,000-foot drop in two miles. I was on my rear part of the time, sliding and grabbing bushes or trees trying to keep my descent under control. I reached Port Clinton at 3:00 PM after a slide-'em, dodge-'em jaunt down the mountain side into the valley. The AT passes through the middle of town past the Port Clinton Hotel, which is a legendary and favorite resting spot for hikers.

I had told Joan I would see her in Port Clinton about 3:00 but unfortunately did not give her a specific location. When I arrived at the street corner near the hotel, she was not there as expected, nor anywhere in town as near as I could tell. I waited and waited— this was not like Joan. She was almost always at the trailhead before I arrived; and, if she weren't, it would not be long before she appeared. I asked at the hotel if there was a parking lot near the trailhead where hikers leave their cars and was told there was one about a quarter-mile south on PA 61. I went to that parking lot thinking she might be there, but she wasn't so I returned to the hotel, becoming quite concerned. Could she have been involved in an accident? Had she become ill? Had something happened at home? All I could do was keep myself visible and wait.

At 4:00, I saw her coming up Highway 61 at a pretty good clip. Looking relieved, she pulled in by the hotel. After a grateful greeting, we exchanged stories about why we had missed each other. She had been waiting at the trailhead parking lot one-half mile south of town, about a quarter-mile further than the one I had checked, since 2:00 and was becoming equally concerned about my whereabouts. She left there after talking with a hiker who had a map of the AT which showed it going through Port Clinton, and then she realized she was probably in the wrong lo-cation. I had told her I would see her in Port Clinton; but there was a trailhead north of town, one south of town and 3/4-mile in between. From this point on, we saw to it that she knew the exact trailhead location for each pick up point before I began, and we never experienced this problem again. Those anxious moments in Port Clinton will not soon be forgotten. Before nightfall, we moved our base camp further east to the Allentown-Lehigh Valley area.

The next day was a very rainy Sunday, so I decided not to hike. Instead, we drove over to the Hawk Mtn. Sanctuary near Eckville and spent some time at this very well-known sanctuary for birds of prey. Near it in Eckville is an AT trailhead which would be my next day's destination, and Joan said she would feel more comfortable if she could see it. She had not yet recovered from the Port Clinton incident, so we decided to locate and check trailheads for the following two days before returning to our base camp.

It was a gloomy Monday morning when I began the 16 miles to the Eckville crossing hoping the climb out of Port Clinton Gap would be nothing like the descent I had made on Saturday. It was steep but on a much better grade. However, when I reached the ridge, the darkening clouds showed signs of rain. I had been hoping for a clear day since, according to the literature, this is a very picturesque section. By mid morning, I reached the site of the Old Windsor Furnace, another early iron and charcoal producing region. A sign near the site read: "Springer Mtn. GA, 1180 miles; Mt. Katahdin, ME, 957 miles"—a long way yet to go.

I climbed out of the area past the Lehigh Valley Astronomical Park which is quite a complex. I wanted to find out more about their activities, but there was no one on duty. Pulpit Rock (1,582 feet) is located near the Park and provides a great panorama of the valley, the River of the Rocks, Hawk Mtn., etc. I was thankful the rain was holding off, as this is one of the most scenic areas I had seen in Pennsylvania. However, fair weather was not to last, as it started to rain shortly after I left Pulpit Rock and continued as I crossed the Pinnacle. According to literature, the view from Pinnacle is one of the best in Pennsylvania, but not on this day, as the whole mountain disappeared in a mist of fog. I descended, in hard rain, along what was probably an old fire tower access to the Eckville Road trailhead completing the hike for the day.

The rain continued for the remainder of the afternoon and part of the night, but by the next morning the storm had moved out. When I reached the ridge crest of Blue Mtn., the AT became another rock scramble. The blue blaze at the crest of the mountain leads back two miles to the Hawk Mtn. Sanctuary where we visited two days before. The AT continued to be very rocky over to the Tri County Corner, and a blue blaze leads to the top of a huge pile of rocks where there is a marker indicating the intersection of Burks, Lehigh and Schuykill Counties. The Trail continued to be very rocky and rugged until I reached the Allentown Shelter where I stopped for lunch and visited with a young couple while I ate. The Trail from the shelter to PA 309 followed an old woods road and provided easy traveling. I hiked out at Blue Mtn. Summit Restaurant, completing my day.

The next day began with cool, crisp, clear weather which was ideal for hiking; and the 10-mile section to Lehigh Furnace Gap is considered one of the most scenic sections of the AT in Pennsylvania. I was looking forward to some great views and photos, as my hiking days in PA so far had been in rain or fog. The first two miles of the Trail followed an old woods road with easy hiking, but that changed rather quickly as I ascended the ridge to an area known as the Cliffs or Knife Edge where the rocks jut into the sky. What a fantastic view this provided. When I reached Bear Rocks—the second great vantage point—I climbed up on the rocks and joined two bird watchers who were studying hawk migration. The view from the rocks was breathtaking with a 360-degree sweep, and I could not have picked a better day to traverse this scenic section.

When I hiked across Bake Oven Knob Road, the parking area was filled with cars, a clue that something special was occurring. The attraction was bird watching from Bake Oven Knob, another outstanding vantage point along this ridge. I had an extended visit with an avid hawk watcher who had binoculars and a camera and had made a number of sightings throughout the morning. The Knob is a very popular spot, not only because of its great panorama, but because of its easy auto access. The AT descent was through another real rock scramble—big ones, little ones and giant ones—until I reached the Bake Oven Knob Shelter. I hiked out at Lehigh Furnace Gap in early afternoon finishing this section and my hike for the day.

The AT crosses a major valley at Lehigh Gap where the Lehigh River crosses the Blue Mtn. Range and flows through Allentown and eventually into the Delaware River. My next day's hike took me along Blue Mtn. over the area where the Pennsylvania Turnpike tunnels through it and then crosses Lehigh Gap and continues on to Little Gap. This was a 10.2-mile section where I had planned to spend more time studying environmental damage done by industrial wastes. When I left Lehigh Furnace Gap in 45-50 degree temperatures, a cold drizzle began.

By the time I reached Lehigh Gap, the weather had cleared, and the east side of the Gap looked like it would be a rocky scramble up out of the valley to the ridge line. It was and, once on the ridge, the view was extraordinary. The guidebook puts it very well when it says, "the area gives impressive, but uninspiring, views of the Railroads and Palmerton industrial home of New Jersey Zinc Company." Trail literature lists words such as moonscape, wasteland, unvegetated area, badlands, desolate—all correctly describing this landscape. The scars left on this mountain from the industrial wastes from the zinc industry are unbelievable.

After cresting out on the ridge overlooking the valley, the Trail traverses through a major field of huge boulders with no vegetation anywhere, not even a blade of grass. Trail literature appropriately refers to this area as "Rocky III." Potable water through here is nonexistent; in fact, signs warn hikers to carry water. In spite of all of this desolation, there was a kind of unnatural beauty to this area, but I would like to have seen it as it used to be. Scars to the landscape extended up the ridge for several miles, and it left me with a feeling of shame that mankind would let this happen. Apparently measures have been taken to correct or eliminate further damage to the environment in the area. It's about time; because it's going to take nature generations, if ever, to heal the damage that has been done.

My goal for the next day was to reach Wind Gap continuing on Blue Mtn. with little elevation change throughout the entire section. The hike out of Little Gap up to the ridge line was quite rocky and rough, and once I was on the ridge line I was on and off of rocks throughout most of the day. The bright blue October weather was striking, providing many photo opportunities from several of the overlooks. This day's hike was rather uneventful and routine, allowing me to complete the 15.3 miles by mid afternoon. This gave Joan and me time to move our base camp to the Stroudsburg-Delaware Water Gap area.

My final day's hike in Pennsylvania was 15.3 miles from Wind Gap to Delaware Water Gap. When I reached the ridge, as usual the rocks were waiting to greet me. Trail literature had correctly labeled this area, "Rocky IV."

As I hiked through these rocky areas, the character of the AT in each state came to mind. From Georgia through Maryland, I had crossed over lofty spruce- and fir-covered peaks and deep valleys and bald mountain areas, along mountain streams, and across broad valleys. Then came Pennsylvania with its rocky-crested Blue Mtn. However, I found more in Pennsylvania than rocks. There was beauty, individuality and continued new sights, sounds and experiences. This is what makes the AT what it truly is—a footpath of diversity.

Wolf Rocks provided outstanding views of the Blue Mtn. Ridge and the Kittatinny Ridge across the Delaware in New Jersey. The Wolf Rocks area was very rocky, but what surprised me was that there was a good camping area nearby. In fact, this was true throughout most of the Blue Mtn. area of Pennsylvania, as I had been seeing good camping areas daily. The problem, however, is water. Hikers would either have to pack extra water or go off the ridge some distance to find a source.

I stopped for lunch at the Kirkridge Shelter which is quite large and built of concrete and stone. The shelter faces the valley and offers a nice view across it. I acquired water from a tap close to the nearby Kirkridge Retreat. When I reached Mt. Minsi, the last mountain in PA, I stopped for a mid-afternoon snack break while enjoying the panorama of Delaware Water Gap. In view were slanted rock stratas of Mt. Tammany across the Gap and the Kittatinny Ridge in New Jersey which the AT follows. There were more impressive views of the Delaware Gap area and the countryside across the river in New Jersey from several locations while descending Mt. Minsi. Since it was a Sunday, the Trail traffic up

Mt. Minsi was quite heavy—I met 20-30 people out for a walk before reaching the trailhead in the Gap. I hiked out at the west end of the I-80 bridge in Delaware Water Gap completing the AT through Pennsylvania.

The Trail crosses the Delaware River on the I-80 bridge, and the heavy early morning work traffic was fanning me with the already chilled air as I crossed the long span. In fact, when the big trucks raced past me, I had to brace myself to keep from being blown off the bridge and was relieved when the crossing was completed. Pennsylvania was behind me now—seven states down and seven to go.

Upon entering New Jersey, I registered at the designated box by the AT at the Delaware Water Gap National Recreation Area (DWGNRA) Visitor Center before ascending out of the valley up to the Kittatinny Ridge. The AT enters the Worthington State Forest after leaving I-80 and remains there for about 7 1/2 miles and then goes into the DWGNRA. The climb out of the valley to the ridge was moderate with signs that showed heavy Trail use. However, the Trail had been very well maintained and continued to be rocky.

By mid morning, I reached the eagerly-anticipated Sunfish Pond Natural Area, which is a National Historic Landmark. This Pond is a 41-acre glacial body of water and is one of the seven Natural Wonders of New Jersey. The sign by the AT indicated that, due to its natural acidic composition, only a few hardy species of fish such as Pumpkinfish, Sunfish and Yellow Perch can survive. I had lucked out by hiking through this beautiful area on a gorgeous October day with the fall foliage starting to show and reflecting in the glassy waters of the pond. I sat on one of the large boulders on the shoreline and got lost in my thoughts in the very tranquil setting. The AT skirts the shoreline for some distance before continuing up the ridge and is very rugged, with a hodgepodge of large boulders which the Trail goes over, around and in between. The Trail was not well marked, and I missed it several times before finding a blaze.

Before leaving the pond, I was greeted by a flock of young wild turkeys accompanied by their mother. I have had many sightings of these great woodland birds along the Trail and am always glad to see them and to know they are becoming more common in many of our eastern forests. When I was growing up, there were no wild turkeys in the forests in our area but today they are plentiful—in fact, so much so that there is an annual hunting season for them.

The Trail through this area reminds me of the one in Pennsylvania. The topography is very similar, and then of course the rocks are still quite prevalent. As I reached the summit of the first high ridge, I began seeing signs of Gypsy Moth damage to the oak trees. At least, this is what I surmised had killed the oaks along this area. From the high ridge, I had a very commanding view of the Delaware River Valley, the Poconos in Pennsylvania to the west, the Kittatinny Ridge to the north and the rural New Jersey countryside to the east. What I had seen along the AT in New Jersey so far was a very pleasant surprise to me. I had never expected this much natural beauty here, as most of my previous traveling in New Jersey had been in the central and eastern sections. I was impressed and I had only begun. The elevation along Kittatinny Ridge seldom exceeds 1,500 feet, but the views continued to be outstanding. On one of the exposed peaks, I talked with more hawk watchers; and, while I was there, several good sightings were made including the Broad-winged, the Red-shouldered, Gashawk and Coopers.

By lunch time, I had entered the DWGNRA part of the Trail and the AT continued to be very rocky. I saw little difference in the rocky Trail here in New Jersey and the one in Pennsylvania. Trail literature had listed this area as "Rocky V"—and, again, I agree. My amazement of the AT in New Jersey continued as I hiked along miles of Trail right along the edge of cliffs. I could look down into the valley and across the countryside for miles; and the bright, clear blue October day enhanced the beauty of the New Jersey landscape. I hiked out at the trailhead on Millbrook-Blairstown Road by early afternoon completing a 14-mile day—my first in New Jersey.

The outstanding October weather was continuing as I began at the trailhead on my second day in New Jersey. I felt invigorated, and the superb weather was promising another day of stimulating outdoor adventure and vistas from the Kittatinny Ridge. I hiked out of the gap up on the ridge to the first overlook and had paused to take in the view of the valleys below when I heard voices up ahead. I hiked up to where the AT crossed through a brushy area to the edge of cliffs similar to the ones from the day before. A few feet from the edge of one of the cliffs was a tent, and seated on the rocks near the edge were two young ladies having their morning coffee and enjoying the view of the valley. I greeted them and told them I hoped neither of them had a sleepwalking problem, and they assured me they did not and that the evening before they had enjoyed the lights of the valley and the stars from their tent opening. They had certainly selected a picturesque tent site.

I continued along the ridge line having unobstructed views all morning of the valleys on both sides. Eleven miles into the hike, I stopped at the Brink Road Shelter for lunch. This shelter had a unique feature that I had not seen anywhere along the Trail up to this point. Unlike the caged shelters in the Smokies and the bear poles in the Shenandoah, a large metal box was provided for hikers to store their food in at night as a protection against bear theft. I am not sure how much of a problem bears have been through this area, as there had not been any signs of their presence so far in New Jersey. I hiked off the ridge into the Culvers Gap trailhead on US 206 completing the hike for the day. Joan and I moved our base camp to a new location in the northeast area of New Jersey near Sussex.

Even though there had been a heavy frost in the valleys the night before, the sunshine was bright and the air was crisp as I began the next day's hike. When I reached the Culvers Gap fire tower, I only climbed up two platforms, as there was fog lying in the valleys somewhat obstructing the view.

Each day I had been noticing a change in the fall foliage—this was October 6 and the colors had just about reached their peak in New Jersey. Few leaves had fallen, making the forests along the ridge and the valleys quite colorful spectacles. Not only was I pleasantly surprised by the landscape in New Jersey, but I was equally impressed with the wildlife. I had been seeing a lot of deer, grouse, grey squirrels, a flock of wild turkeys, many birds including several hawks, and many smaller animals such as mice and chipmunks—and then there were the bear boxes at the shelters—there must have been bears in the area.

The next area providing a nice vista was Sunrise Mtn. (1,653 feet) with a stone shelter affording views on both sides of the ridge and a vantage point for hawk watchers. As I moved on up the ridge, I hiked through more of the old stone fence areas similar to the ones further south. The ridge was very rocky, and the early farmers had to clear the rocks so the land could be made tillable; and even then there seemed to be more rocks than soil. Again, it must have been very hard to eke out a living from such rocky terrain. I arrived at the stone Mashipacong Shelter just in time for lunch. Nearby is the Mashipacong Road that crosses the ridge and goes into the valley. I hiked out at the trailhead on NJ 23 at the High Point State Park Visitor Center, completing another 14-mile day.

The AT passes through High Point State Park, appropriately named because it is the highest point (1,803 feet) in the state of New Jersey. The next day I began at the Visitor Center and hiked about a mile to the wooden observation platform which gives an excellent view of the northeastern part of New Jersey and into New York and Pennsylvania. Visible also from the platform was the High Point Monument which is situated atop the highest knoll in the state and is a memorial to those from New Jersey who fought for our country. After leaving the Park, the AT turns to the southeast closely following the New York/New Jersey state line and crosses the Kittatinny valley. In hiking across the valley, I passed through both productive and nonproductive farm land and a lot of wet boggy areas. The Trail Club had placed hundreds of feet of puncheons across these wet areas. As I moved further across the valley, I could look back and see the High Point Monument projecting into the sky from the ridge in the Park.

After reaching Ferguson Road, the AT pretty much followed the state line to NJ 284 (the Unionville Road) which intersected about a mile from the New York border. After leaving Unionville Road, the AT turns north and crosses into New York forming a "U" and then crosses back into New Jersey. There is a Trail relocation planned for this area which will eliminate the "U."

The valley here is fertile with rich loamy soil extending hundreds of feet in depth caused by glaciation. I passed along the dikes of land where sod farming was practiced—a type I had not seen before. While walking along the dikes, I could see grass in different stages of growth; and, apparently, when it reached a certain stage of development, it was ready to be stripped off and shipped to various points in the east. I would like to have talked to the owner to learn more about this type of farming, but there was no one around. Near the sod farm, the Trail passes through a .4-mile section of wetland known as Vernie Swamp which is spanned by 111 bog bridges as a protection to the environment and to hikers' feet. This was another major effort and expense on the part of the Trail Club and is a great aid to those who cross through this wetland area.

My hike across Pochuck Mtn. was relatively uneventful; however, the old rock fences continued to be a part of the landscape. When I reached Highway 517 in the Vernon Valley, I had about two miles of road-walking since a planned Trail relocation had not been completed. Road-walking the AT never thrills me—I can tolerate short stretches, but two miles is a bit much. While crossing Vernon Valley, I saw many large boulders dotting the pasture fields and other areas—more evidence of glaciation. Emerging onto NJ 94 by mid afternoon, I completed the section across the valleys of northeastern New Jersey.

On my final day in New Jersey, I hiked to the crest of Wawayanda Mtn. in about an hour after a rough hard climb out of the valley. Visibility was not good as I passed a couple of vantage points on the mountain; however, I did witness an impressive sunrise near the summit. By mid morning, the sun was bringing out the bright yellows and reds in the maple foliage and many hues in the woodlands along the Trail—a gorgeous fall day on Wawayanda

Mtn. I stopped for a lunch break on a small footbridge crossing at the upper end of a little lake near the Wawayanda State Park Headquarters. In four more miles, I would be leaving New Jersey, and I reflected upon what a great experience it had been hiking the 74 miles through this state. Its beauty and diversity are impressive. I had feared that the Trail's nearness to urban centers would compromise whatever natural beauty it had and was pleased to find this was not true.

I reached the New York state line by mid day reaching another milestone on my AT hike—I had completed eight states and was starting into the ninth. I ate my lunch on the rock ledges on the state line enjoying the magnificent view over Greenwood Lake which was nestled in forests aflame with color. The sun was bright; the sky was blue; the air was crisp, and I was perched above a sea of color. This was October at its best.

At the state line, the AT turns back to the north on Bearfoot Mtn. and follows the ridge crest paralleling Greenwood Lake, providing many stimulating views over the lake—a very scenic area. As I hiked along this crest, I thought of the sign that was tacked on a tree near the beginning of the AT in Woody Gap, GA, telling hikers not to give up because Rogers Appalachian Cottage was only 1250 miles more. I wondered at the time if I would make it and here I was on the ridge above the cottage. I did not take time to hike off the ridge down to the cottage but talked to many hikers in the days that followed who had and indicated that they enjoyed their stay there. My hike for the day was completed on NY 17A.

Before continuing, we moved our base camp to the Hudson Valley area near Newburg, NY, making the trailheads closer for Joan. The magnificent fall weather continued as I left the trailhead near Greenwood Lake. The AT crosses the extreme southern tip of New York State skirting major population areas, and I wondered how much solitude and wilderness experience the AT would provide in the miles ahead. Would New York match New Jersey's success with having the AT and urban centers coexist so well in such close proximity?

Shortly after leaving the trailhead, I passed over more out-croppings with white stratas and conglomerate compositions. They were jutting upward with some standing almost perpendicular to the ground, and this unusual feature was present for some distance along the Bellvale Mtn. area crossing out of New Jersey along the ridges in southern New York State. Many of these out-croppings provided good overlooks of the New York countryside. Two notable areas were Eastern Pinnacles and Cat Rocks—both showing signs of glacial action with scars imbedded in rocks from the ice sheet. The first road crossing was Lakes Road, and beyond that was Fitzgerald Falls—a nice 25-footer, sadly lacking in water volume on this day. I am sure this falls would be much more noteworthy during periods of high water.

I reached Mombasha High Point (1,280 feet) and, according to literature, the New York City skyline is visible on a clear day from this spot. The day was clear, and there it was—a fantastic view! When I first began hiking the Trail, I associated it with wilderness areas and never conceived that the New York City skyline would be visible or so close—even though it is actually about 80 miles away. This was a major highlight for me while hiking through this section. I had lunch on the summit of Buchanan Mtn. while enjoying the view over Mombasha Lake, Arden Mtn., the Hudson River Valley and many adjacent ridges and valleys. This was a most picturesque area with the splendid weather and fall colors making it a postcard setting. As I crossed Arden Mtn., the views did not rival those of the two previous mountains, but the mountain itself was significant because of the descent onto NY 17. My AT guidebook labeled the area from the summit to the highway as "Agony Grind" and my reply to this designation is, "Congratulations, ATC. Your label was quite accurate." The trek down was quite a knee and ankle jammer.

After leaving the Arden Valley trailhead, the AT enters Harriman State Park which is not only rich in natural beauty but was a major iron-producing area from the early-to mid-1800's. This is also the site of an important bit of AT history, as it was through this Park that the first section was completed in the fall of 1923. As I left the trailhead, I found this section of the AT to be very well maintained and showing heavy use. This did not surprise me due to its close proximity to urban areas of New York and New Jersey. The woods were open with no underbrush, allowing good visibility in all directions from the Trail.

By mid morning, I reached the Lemon Squeezer, a jumble of rocks with the AT threading through a narrow passageway. Some squirming and pulling in of the tummy were required to access it. I descended from the ridge into a valley where I passed many old open pit mining areas, evidence of the early iron industry here. It was interesting to see how successfully nature had reclaimed the area with large trees, particularly hemlock. It did not take on the appearance of a scarred mined area but had a sort of unusual beauty. I stopped by the Fingerboard Shelter for a photo and rest break. The shelter was built of natural stone (a plentiful commodity in this area), had two chimneys and was positioned on a big flat rock. I continued my quest along the AT to check and photograph as many of the shelters as I could and so far had not missed very many.

Near Bear Mtn., I was joined by a thru-hiker whose Trail name was "Bob without Sue" from Baltimore, MD. We climbed the observation tower on Bear Mtn. where we had another good view of the New York City skyline and the Hudson River Valley. We hiked off the mountain and passed through the Trailside Open Air Nature and Geology Museum. It was a major part of Benton MacKaye's dream to introduce nature to urban workers and dwellers. This museum is the lowest point on the entire AT at 124 feet. We completed the hike at the west end of Bear Mtn. Bridge, but Bob and I hiked across the bridge and back for an added bonus and for a closer view of the Hudson River.

TOP: The Bake Oven Knob Rock Scramble
BOTTOM: View along the AT on Blue Mtn. north
   of Lehigh Gap showing the massive damage caused
   by the Zinc smelting industry in the area.

TOP: Mt. Tammany across the Delaware River
   in New Jersey
BOTTOM: Food box for protection from bears
   at the Brinks Road Shelter in New Jersey

TOP: The south entrance to the Lemon Squeezer
 through which the AT passes in Harriman State
 Park, New York
BOTTOM: The AT crosses a rock fence via a style
 in the Kittatinny Valley in northern New Jersey

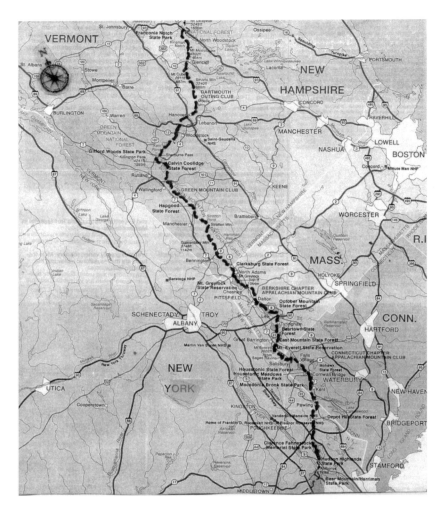

Map detail from Bear Mountain, NY, to Franconia Notch, NH
(Covered in Chapters nine and ten)
— — — — — Denotes Appalachian Trail Route

MARKS FROM THE PAST

"Old stone fences, homestead foundations, old railroad beds and stage roads, charcoal pits and iron furnace sites and scars left by early mining were clues that many others had passed this way before me." —*The Author*

In May, 1994, Joan and I returned to the Hudson River Valley with a goal of hiking from Bear Mtn. Bridge, NY, to North Adams, MA, near the Vermont state line. This would complete New York, Connecticut and Massachusetts. We established our first base camp in the Hudson River Valley near Fishkill, NY. I began at the east end of the Bridge on a beautiful spring morning, reached the summit of Anthony's Nose by mid morning and signed the Trail register in South Mountain Pass.

As the morning sun began to warm the atmosphere, I started noticing an abundance of black flies in the area and hoped they would not become a problem. They were behaving like the ones we used to have in West Virginia, swarming around my face and dive bombing my eyes, ears and nose. I had regrettably forgotten to bring netting and repellent. Shortly after leaving the Pass, one of the pests flew in my ear. (I could not get it out until evening when I was forced to flush my ear canal with a wax removal solution for relief.) Fighting this distraction, I hiked up past Graymoor Monastery (Friars of Atonement) which has for many years been a favorite stopover for thru-hikers. Many praise the warm welcome they receive and the great food they are served during their stay here. I did not stop at the Monastery but did have lunch at the Shrine which was on a rocky point about a mile up the AT. I read some of the prayer notations in the little register there, took some photos and enjoyed the view and the beauty of this very tranquil setting.

In this area, the AT passes through some very historic real estate dating back to Revolutionary War times. As I saw the familiar names (The Old West Point Road, Fort Defiance Hill, Fort Hill, The Old Albany Post Road) on my Trail map and in the guidebook, I remembered these were places I read about in my history book during school days. Through these areas, I passed around and over more of the old stone fences and walls similar to the many I had seen for hundreds of miles down the Trail. The AT follows along old roads which probably were former stage roads or railroad beds and passes through areas where there are stone foundations—probably remnants of homesteads. I often stopped at these sites and wished I knew their historic origins.

Shortly after passing South Highland Road, another Wild Turkey was sighted, leaving the scene about as quickly as he had appeared. I had been seeing places where these birds had scratched away the leaves looking for tidbits on the forest floor. This was the Clarence Fahnestock Memorial State Park, and I am sure that hunting the turkeys was either prohibited or closely regulated. In any event, it was reassuring to see these birds doing well in less than two hours from the largest city in our nation.

I stopped for a snack break on a rocky outflow from a bog pond area near Sunk Mine Road, wondering if the pond were an open pit mine that had since filled in. If that were the case, nature had once again done a remarkable healing job; because this had become a delightful natural spot. After leaving the Sunk Mine Road area, the AT followed a narrow gauge railroad bed, perhaps a conduit for taking out the iron ore that had been mined there.

I was fascinated by an old stone trestle that spanned a small valley and admired the engineering and the amount of labor it must have taken for its construction. The old railroad bed had to be cut through very rocky areas and extensive cribwork completed around some sections of the mountain side where cuts could not be made. This was a remarkable feat for its time.

I crossed NY 301 and ascended the ridge around Canopus Lake. The view from Shenandoah Mtn. was outstanding and one of the best so far through this area. I completed the hike for the day when I reached Ralph's Peak Hikers Cabin (RPH Cabin) near the AT crossing of the Taconic State Parkway.

The following morning I left RPH Cabin in rain; in fact, I delayed starting, thinking the rain might subside. But that was not the case—Mother Nature had other plans. Shortly after leaving the Cabin, the AT crosses the Taconic Parkway (a major commuter highway leading into the Metro New York area); and the crossing is a matter of speed, wit and nerves. The traffic is fast and heavy during morning and evening rush hours requiring hikers to use a stop, look, listen, run and dodge-'em strategy. I crossed at a time of day when the major rush of traffic to the big city was over for the morning. The commuters had reached their places of employment, and the highway would get a break until late afternoon when the rush would reverse itself. The rain continued as I hiked up and along the shoulder of Hasner Mtn.; and I could hear and, at times, see the traffic where the Parkway crossed under I-84. The AT parallels I-84 for a couple of miles, crossing over Stormville Mtn. and then crosses over I-84 on an overpass on Mountain Top Road.

The rain had stopped, but the weather was still unsettled. I decided to aim for the Morgan Stewart Shelter for lunch. While hiking along the ridge toward Mt. Egbert (the next mountain ahead), I could see storm clouds over the Hudson Valley headed in my direction. Would I have time to reach the shelter ahead of it? The clouds turned black with lightning and thunder as I reached the summit of Mt. Egbert. The shelter was .2 mile off the summit, so I ran, trying to beat the storm. I just barely reached the shelter before the force hit. It was a dandy—lightning and thunder almost continuously, the temperature dropping, with hail and strong winds. This was reminiscent of storms I had experienced in North Carolina and Virginia—except for the hail. The hail continued to pound on the shelter and accumulate in front of it until the ground was completely covered. I was thankful I was in a shelter to wait this one out, and the duration of 40 minutes gave me plenty of time to eat lunch. The temperature had dropped to a point where the hail did not melt away and the Trail looked like a snow had fallen. The ground was actually icy as I hiked off the summit. The storm had created a lot of debris from trees, littering the Trail with limbs, twigs and new-growth leaves.

The following morning, Joan and I left our campsite in the Hudson Valley and parked our motorhome near the trailhead at the Appalachian Trail Train Station crossing on NY 22. Here hikers can take a commuter train into New York City from a trailhead if they wish. Joan then took me to the trailhead on NY 55 so I could hike the 7-mile section to the Station.

Of special interest to me through this area was a huge White Oak tree (the largest I had ever seen) that stood by the Trail near the crossing of West Dover Road. Leaving this natural wonder, I traversed hundreds of feet of puncheons across an open wet area in the valley, another remarkable Trail club project. After completing the 7-mile hike, Joan and I moved our motorhome to a base camp near Kent, Connecticut.

The next day was my last one hiking in New York, and my goal for the day was Bulls Bridge near New Milford, CT. After leaving the trailhead, I signed the register at the entrance to the Pawling Nature Preserve, a thousand-acre tract owned by the Nature Conservancy. I ascended Hamersly Ridge and crossed through many boggy areas spanned by more puncheons. The interesting thing about this was that these wet areas were along the ridge and not in the valley as you might expect. This was another result of glaciation—depressions were left along ridge lines trapping water and creating these wet areas. This was a common phenomena along the AT in New England. The elevation along the ridge was between 800-1,000 feet.

By 11:00, I reached Hoyt Road which is on the New York/ Connecticut state line. New York exceeded my expectation of what I thought it might be since the AT passed so close to many urban areas. It had provided me with challenges, diversity, solitude and natural beauty along with areas so rich in history that I could only touch upon in this writing. Like New Jersey, it had passed with flying colors. Nine states down and five to go.

I left Hoyt Road and shortly crossed CT 55, ascended Ten Mile Hill and had a good view overlooking the Ten Mile River Valley and its confluence with the Housatonic River. I descended from the ridge into the valley and down the river about one-half mile to the Ned Anderson Memorial Bridge. The bridge crosses the Ten Mile River where it joins the Housatonic and is quite a structure. It was built especially for the AT and was named in memory of the man who laid out the original Trail route in Connecticut and maintained it for twenty years.

For almost two miles, the AT follows the Housatonic River Gorge to Bulls Bridge, and this section of Trail provides a delightful walk above swiftly cascading pools. The Housatonic is a charming river, indeed, with its crystal clear appearance and a stream bed indicating good quality water. It resembles the mountain trout stream I used to fish in West Virginia, and I had a strong urge to wade right in with a fly rod. The river begins in the state of Vermont, flowing through the Berkshire Hills in western Massachusetts and then through western Connecticut. The ATC guidebook and maps show that the AT parallels the Housatonic River for most of its 50 miles in Connecticut on the ridge crests and along its banks.

Bulls Bridge is a scenic area and is the site of one of the two remaining covered bridges that still carry traffic in the state of Connecticut. After leaving Bulls Bridge, I was expecting a 2.5-mile road walk as was noted in the ATC guidebook but was pleasantly surprised to find that the Trail relocation over

Schaghticoke Mtn. was completed. After a moderate climb up the mountain, I reached the Mt. Algo Shelter for lunch. At various points, the Trail relocation provided picturesque views of the Housatonic River Valley and back over the Ten Mile River section I had hiked through earlier. The shelter is near CT 341, and after lunch I crossed the highway and ascended Caleb's Peak which provided the best view so far in Connecticut. A long stretch of the Valley was visible as well as the village of Kent, CT.

The little village of Kent is nestled on the banks of the Housatonic and is one of many quaint New England communities the AT passes close to in Connecticut. Kent's history is notable and, like Pennsylvania, New Jersey and New York, had a heyday in the iron industry. With the discovery of iron ore in this area during the 18th century, a forge was built at Kent and produced pig iron until coal was discovered in Pennsylvania, making the ironworks obsolete. The ruins of the Old Kent Furnace are nearby along with the Slone-Stanley Museum and its collection of Early American iron and wood tools. Today along CT 7 in the Kent area are beautiful and well-preserved 18th and 19th century homes, reflecting times of prosperity in the valley.

I descended Caleb's Peak (1,160 feet) and reached the top of St. Johns Ledges, where the AT traverses along the edge of the Ledges, a precarious section of Trail. A fall from here would almost certainly be fatal. The ATC guidebook and profile map show the descent from the Ledges as a very difficult one of about 500 feet in .4 mile. A steep and rugged one it was; however, the AMC Trail Club from the White Mountains is to be commended for the engineering of a 90-rock staircase, making the descent easier. I cannot imagine how difficult this section would have been before their work. When I reached the base, rock climbers were making the vertical climb up the cliffs to the Ledges—looked thrilling, but not my game at this point in my life.

That night we had rain, and it continued on into the morning hours when Joan drove me as near as she could to the trailhead. The storm during the night had taken down a tree which fell across the road, blocking vehicle traffic to the trailhead. My day began at the foot of St. Johns Ledges and followed close to the banks of the Housatonic River for about five miles. This is the longest and most scenic river walk along the entire length of the AT. The Trail follows the river road for about a mile until it runs out near where the Old North Kent Bridge once crossed the river. The bridge had been destroyed by a flood in the mid-1930's. The Trail then passed through what had been a spacious stand of Red Pine, some 12-14 inches in diameter. The ATC guidebook noted that these trees had been planted in the 1930's and that they were being affected by a blight. When I passed through them, it looked as though they were about all dead—what a loss. The river walk was a pleasant one in spite of the rain and misty conditions.

I hiked across CT 4, which is less than a mile from Cornwall Bridge, another quaint New England village with an old covered bridge crossing the Housatonic. The rains had swollen Guinea Brook, and a sign warned hikers about crossing when the stream was high. I saw a pine log which had fallen across the water a short distance upstream, and I crossed via the log by scooting across a few inches at a time. The log was too slippery to walk on, and the seat of my pants was wet and dirty when I reached the other side even though I had cleaned and dried the log. After ascending the Breadloaf Mtn. area, I began seeing large stands of White or Paper Birch trees—a sure sign that I was in New England. There were also many circular charcoal pits through this area, similar to those I had seen in Pennsylvania, New Jersey and New York. In fact, there was a charcoal pit every few hundred feet or so throughout this entire section—the greatest number I had seen in such a short distance. I hiked out on West Cornwall Road by mid afternoon completing this section. We moved our base camp from the Kent, CT, region north to the Canaan/Salisbury area, providing us a good location for me to complete Connecticut and part of Massachusetts.

The AT passes through the Housatonic State Forest as it crosses the Sharon Mtn. area. I stopped for a short break at the Pine Swamp Brook Shelter and then climbed to the summit of Mt. Easter (1,400 feet) which is the highest point in the area, but the views were limited. My best view of the morning was from a hang glider ramp which had been constructed on the side of Sharon

Mtn. Below was the broad Housatonic Valley, and to the north the Taconic Range, both of which I would be crossing the following day. I descended into the valley and crossed the Housatonic River on the Ethan Allen Highway (US 7) Bridge. The AT passes Housatonic Valley Regional High School (the first regional high school in New England) and then follows the river for the next two miles. A stand of huge pine trees extended along the river to near the power plant in Falls Village. I really enjoyed the walk through this forest of big trees and wondered how they had escaped the axe and saw of the lumberman.

The AT skirts Falls Village (another peaceful New England community), passes the power plant and crosses the Housatonic on the Old Iron Bridge. It was lunch time, and by the river near the bridge was a park with a picnic table and a good view—just the right place for lunch! I had read and heard about the Great Falls, which was a short distance up river from the bridge, and was anxious to hike past it. There was a lot of water flowing in the river, so I anticipated something spectacular and was not disappointed. They were—awesome yet—with thunder, strong winds, trembling like a little Niagara.

I left the valley and hiked to the summit of Prospect Mtn., where I had a wonderful backwards perspective of the Housatonic Valley I had just crossed. The best view, however, was from an area know as "Rand's View," providing a sweeping panorama of the Taconic Range from Bear Mtn. to Jug End in Massachusetts— my next day's hike. I could also see Mt. Greylock in the far distance. Another feature along this ridge is "Giant's Thumb." a very unusual solitary rock formation beside the AT. I suppose, with a bit of imagination, one could perceive a giant thumb. I continued across the mountain known as Barrack Matiff overlooking Salisbury, CT, descended very steeply to US 44 and crossed Cobble Road to CT 41, completing a 16-mile hike for the day.

The trailhead on CT 41 is less than a mile from Salisbury, CT, a well-known iron-producing center noted for its high quality ore and the production of many types of weapons and implements during the 1800's. I planned a full day from this trailhead across the Taconic Range to Jug End Road near South Egremont, Massachusetts. My Trail literature indicated this was a rugged section with considerable elevation gain, so I thought a 6:45 AM starting time was advisable. The weather was cool and overcast with a breeze, and I took advantage of these conditions by making a rapid climb to Lion's head, the first of several peaks I would be crossing during the day. As I was enjoying the view from the ledges on Lion's Head, a raven alit and gave me his hoarse croak, perhaps saying that I was infringing on his perch. Ravens had been very common all along the high ridges and peaks of the Appalachians.

From here, there was a sweeping view of the Salisbury area, Barrack Matiff (the mountain south of Salisbury) and the valley north of Salisbury including the Twin Lakes region. I could also see the peaks ahead of me that I would be crossing, including Bear Mtn. and Mt. Everett. I reached the summit of Bear Mtn. (2,316 feet) and climbed up on what was left of a stone tower which had been vandalized over the years and reduced from its original height. Its location marks the highest point in Connecticut and provides more vistas over the Salisbury area, north over Mt. Everett, and east over Twin Lakes toward Canaan, CT. There was a strong cold wind blowing across Bear Mtn., and I quickly moved off the peak down a very rocky scramble into Sages Ravine.

At 10:00, I hiked out of Connecticut into Massachusetts. The Trail through Connecticut was well maintained, passing through some picturesque countryside, and the charm of the Housatonic River Valley provided a memorable hiking experience for me. Ten states down and four to go.

Sages Ravine is a remote valley nestled between Bear Mtn., CT, and Race Mtn., MA. It was snack time and what better place for a break than along a rustling brook in this charming ravine. I stopped briefly at Bear Rock Falls on the ascent of Race Mtn. to take some photos across the valley. Bear Rock Falls is a designated campsite with tent platforms, a good water supply and a fantastic view. I continued on to the summit of Race Mtn. (2,365 feet) which offered more outstanding outlooks. This is especially true of the very narrow .3 mile section of the AT that follows the cliff side. One balances right on the edge looking straight down into the valley and into the distance as far as Mt. Greylock. This was an impressive mountain top upon which to spend lunch time, so I ate, enjoying the grandeur of the Berkshires. All day, the weather had been extraordinary, and the vistas along the ridges were at their best. But this view from Race Mtn. was by far the most outstanding I had seen so far along the AT in New England.

I descended into the sag off Race Mtn. and ascended the south slope of Mt. Everett on a very steep rocky Trail with an elevation gain of about 700 feet in .7 of a mile—a fairly strenuous section which could be very dangerous during inclement weather. I reached the summit of Mt. Everett (2,602 feet) and could see why this peak is referred to as the "Dome of the Taconics." From this peak, which is the highest in the Taconic Range and the ninth highest in Massachusetts, one has a grandstand seat. Looking back to the south and east, I could see the southern Taconic Range from Salisbury to Race Mtn. and the Housatonic Valley; the Catskills to the west and Mt. Greylock in the northwestern corner of Massachusetts.

While standing by an abandoned fire tower, I was thinking that the elevation here (2,602 feet) is about 200 feet lower than the elevation at our family farm in West Virginia. Yet, the flora here takes on the appearance of that found in alpine areas. This is in a northern latitude, and climatic conditions are much more harsh here. I hiked off Mt. Everett on a series of step-down ridges for about four miles to an area known as Jug End. The AT then breaks sharply off the mountain, which was a good scramble, into Jug End Road completing a 16.3-mile day. It would have been rewarding to spend two days traversing the Taconic Range allowing more time to explore and enjoy its outstanding natural features.

I left Jug End Road the following morning and started the hike across the Housatonic Valley headed for MA 23 near Great Barrington. It was about five miles across the valley, passing through farm country, residential areas, and requiring a lot of road walking which was not to my liking. At the corner of Lime Kiln and South Egremont Roads was an historic marker indicating the spot of the Battle of Shay's Rebellion of 1787.

I hiked out on US 7 about three miles north of Sheffield, MA. Sheffield was established in 1733, is the oldest town in Berkshire County, and boasts of having two of the best preserved covered bridges in the state. (While we were in the area, Joan and I visited Sheffield and the two bridges.)

I continued from US 7 and crossed the Housatonic River (yet again) and ascended Jane and East Mountains. I stopped for a snack break on some rock ledges on East Mtn. and enjoyed the panorama across the broad Housatonic Valley. Visible also was the profile of the entire 16-mile Taconic Range from Salisbury to Jug End that I had hiked the day before—what a magnificent mountain range. As I ascended several rocky scrambles and crossed East Mtn., I saw more of the charcoal pit areas. I had also seen several while crossing the Taconic Range the day before, indicating how extensive the iron and charcoal industry was in New England during earlier times.

The Tom Leonard Shelter is located on East Mtn. in East Mtn. State Forest near an area know as Ice Gulch. This shelter, built by the Berkshire Chapter of the ATC, is very unique in design. It has a loft area (which would probably sleep six hikers) above an extended front overhang, and has ample space on the main floor for 8-10 hikers, making it possible to sleep 14-16 if necessary. It has a picnic table under the overhang, and nearby a tent platform and a refreshingly cold spring down in Ice Gulch (which is a geologic wonder in itself). I was very impressed with the design of the shelter and thought of only a couple of improvements that could be made. If a few sheets of translucent fiberglass were used on the roof, more light could enter the shelter; and there is ample space under the overhang for benches or shelves which could add cooking space.

After leaving the shelter, the Trail follows along a ledge under a row of cliffs, and below the Trail is Ice Gulch, a rather spectacular crevice across East Mtn. It is a very narrow, rugged gorge; and, as the name implies, I am sure that ice stays in this crevice through late spring and perhaps into early summer.

The trailhead on MA 23 is located about four miles from Great Barrington, where the Housatonic River passes right through the center of town. It was in Great Barrington that William Stanley first successfully demonstrated the use of alternating current in 1886, and it later became one of the first communities in America to acquire electric lighting. William Stanley later founded the company that today is known as The General Electric Company.

The next morning I ascended Blue Hill, dropped into a valley and skirted Benedict Pond. This pond is a product of glaciation and is nestled in a lovely valley. It looked like great fishing habitat, and I wondered how the two fishermen in a small boat on the pond were doing.

After leaving the pond, I hiked through an area where there had been a lot of beaver activity. Noticing a strong smell of sulphur, I thought perhaps it was coming from the water. In addition to the unpleasant smell, in the air were hordes of insects. They were everywhere, the black flies being the greatest nuisance and taking shots at my eyes and ears. I climbed to some ledges above the pond and had the first view of the day back over East Mtn. and the Taconic Range, with Mt. Everett prominent. The Housatonic Valley was also visible.

I hiked to the Mt. Wilcox South Shelter, which was the first of two shelters through this area, and noticed that the porcupines had been doing a considerable bit of gnawing on the wood floor. I had seen this in other shelters, particularly along the front edges of the floor. They have an impulsive craving for salt, and food spills on the shelter floors attract them. Trail literature advises hikers to suspend their boots off the floor to keep the porkies from making a meal out of them, as they are attracted to the salt which comes from perspiration. After leaving the shelter, I passed through more beaver dam areas—some with recent activity.

I continued on to the Mt. Wilcox North Shelter and thought I would stop for a rest and snack break but did not stay long because of the masses of black flies in the area. They just would not leave me alone. I had to keep moving—if I stopped for a moment, so did they—in swarms. The AT passes through a section of

Beartown State Forest, and I stopped for lunch where three stone fences converge marking the corner of the forest. For the first time all morning, the insects did not seem to be as bad. On Cobble Hill near the Tyringham Valley, I had another wild turkey sighting; and, once again, it is rewarding to see them because a habitat that is suitable to them is suitable to a variety of other animal life.

I descended into Tyringham Valley, the site of a very charming and unspoiled community where Shakers had settled in the 19th century. Their life-style was one of simplicity, living pretty much to themselves with farming as their major source of livelihood. Evidence of their old farms still exists—stone fences, foundations, etc., along the AT throughout the area. Located in the valley is the Tyringham Art Gallery which was founded in 1953 and operated out of the "Fairy Tale Gingerbread House" on Maine Road in Tyringham. Joan and I made a visit to this very unique house while we were in the area before moving our base camp to Pittsfield, Massachusetts.

The hike from the trailhead at Tyringham to the Goose Pond area involved a climb out of the valley across Baldy Mtn. and across more wet boggy terrain. These wet sections were producing an abundance of insects, mostly black flies, which had been a problem for the past several days. The only way I could have peace was to keep moving. Regrettably, I still had no netting with me, and the repellent I was using only stayed them for a short while. I placed cotton in my ears to keep the flies out and wore my cap in a way so the bill would give my eyes some protection.

A major feature of the Upper Goose Pond area was a secluded back country pond which at one time was owned by a hunting and fishing club. On the north shore of the pond by the AT was a plaque which read: "Near this site on the shores of Upper Goose Pond stood the Mohhekennuck Club. The Club was incorporated in 1901 and for 72 years served to provide its membership with good fellowship and fond memories. In 1981 the Club conveyed its lands to the National Park Service and provided the Appalachian Mountain Club (AMC) with a gift to assure that these lands would remain a wilderness preserve. July 24, 1982." Near the plaque stood an old chimney which probably was a remnant of the old lodge that once stood there.

I can appreciate the camaraderie that was no doubt experienced here, because my father was a member of a similar club and used to take me hunting each fall. To this day, I remember well and cherish the fellowship that I experienced there.

After leaving the Upper Goose Pond area, I crossed a ridge and descended to the twin bridges that cross the Massachusetts Turnpike. The bridges were built especially for the AT crossing of this very busy highway. One bridge crosses the east lanes to the median, and a second bridge crosses the west lanes to the north side—quite a structure. The AT then crosses US 20 within one-half mile of the Massachusetts Turnpike. From there, it ascends via old logging roads to the summit of Becket Mtn. (2,180 feet) which was the site of a fire tower that provided very limited views. The Trail passes through parts of the October Mountain State Forest which has over 14,000 acres and is the largest state forest in Massachusetts.

I left Becket Mtn., shortly passing lovely Finerty Pond which is nestled down in a little valley. From the summit of Becket Mtn. for the next ten miles, the AT traverses a section with little elevation change, which makes it easy to achieve a high-mileage day. Before reaching the October Mountain Shelter, I passed through an area where beavers had obstructed the Trail for some distance. It is amazing how such little animals can construct dams and totally change the environment in the valley, thereby creating new ecosystems. The flooded trees soon die, and they become skeletons silhouetted across the ponds waiting for the elements to take them down.

When I reached the shelter, I found it be of the same design used for the Tom Leonard Shelter back at Ice Gulch. The shelter was so inviting that I was tempted into taking a snack break and resting a while. I like this design and would like to see more of the same along the AT. It is very practical, offering accommodations for up to 14 hikers—nice job ATC Berkshire Chapter!

When I reached Warner Hill (2,050 feet), I discovered that a portion of the summit area had been burned. I am not sure if there had been a forest fire or if this had been a controlled burn. In any event, Mt. Greylock was in view—waiting like a sentinel. I planned to arrive there in a couple of days. This was my first view of the mountain since leaving Jug End in the Taconics, and now that I was much closer it was looking massive.

I stopped briefly at the Kay Wood Shelter, which was about .2 of a mile off the AT, as I wanted to check out the setting and get a photo. Regretfully, I did not get to meet the lovely lady from Dalton for whom the shelter is named. She was a 1988 thru-hiker, and reports are that she stops by the shelter regularly to visit with hikers while maintaining this section of the Trail. The shelter was situated on a little bench in a nice secluded location.

After leaving Kay Wood Shelter, I followed the Trail relocation into the village of Dalton, Massachusetts. Dalton is noted for the production in its mills of a top grade of paper which is used for U. S. currency. As I hiked down Depot Street, the fragrance coming from huge clusters of lilacs growing along the street filled the air. I was amazed at the overwhelming size of the lilac bushes both there and those I had been seeing through Connecticut and Massachusetts. I completed the 18-mile day's hike at the end of Depot Street.

I returned to the trailhead near MA 8 the following morning to hike the 9-mile section from Dalton to Cheshire, MA. I wanted to spend a full day crossing Mt. Greylock which was the next section beyond Cheshire. I crossed over the Housatonic River for the umpteenth and last time (I think) and had about a 20-minute walk on High Street before leaving Dalton. I passed Gore Pond and discovered that beavers have contributed to raising the water level of the pond by building a dike across the outlet. I signed the register located in a box by the pond and moved on.

Regrettably, when I reached the spectacular overlook known as the Cobble, fog hung over the valley, making it impossible to have the views I had hoped for of Cheshire, the surrounding valley, or Mt. Greylock. The reservoir and part of the community were visible, but Mt. Greylock was completely obscured. I descended the Cobble and crossed the Hoosic (not the Housatonic) through the village of Cheshire. I passed an interesting plaque and memorial across from the post office. The plaque read: "Elder John Leland, eloquent preacher beloved pastor influential patriot Father of Religious Liberty." The plaque was mounted on a cheese press made of concrete, symbolizing the once-thriving cheese industry of the area. John Leland apparently was a very prominent community leader during his time. I hiked through Cheshire to MA 8 completing the section.

There was one more mountain to cross in Massachusetts, and it was the highest in the state at 3,491 feet. I planned a full day to traverse the 14.4-mile section of the AT crossing Mt. Greylock from Cheshire to North Adams (MA 2). Mt. Greylock lies within the Mt. Greylock State Reservation, an 11,450-acre tract of land which contains several additional high peaks.

The weather was very unsettled when I left the trailhead, and I was hopeful it would clear before I reached the summit. Arrangements had been made to have lunch with Joan in the AMC Bascom Lodge on the summit. The lodge is owned by the state but operated by the Appalachian Mountain Club (AMC). It provides food and lodging services for hikers and others interested in enjoying the natural beauty of the mountain. As I was ascending the mountain near where the AT crosses the power line, I found, hanging on a stump, a plastic bag containing three books: a Dictionary for German, a Cantonese conversation book, and a King James Version of the *Holy Bible.* There was no name or any other clues as to who had lost them or left them there. The plastic bag was partially open and had permitted some water to get in causing one corner of the *Bible* to get a little wet. I put the books in my pack and thought I would leave them in the lodge on the summit or inquire whether anyone there would know who they belonged to.

As I moved further up the mountain, the sun came out briefly, and it looked like the weather might clear. But then, to my disappointment, the wind became strong, the air turned quite chilly, and the day became overcast. The temperature continued to drop as I reached higher elevations—another layer of clothing was necessary. It was even beginning to feel as if it might snow. A very heavy shadow moved across the mountain and, as the temperature continued to drop, all the ingredients were there—and snow it did! It started with small round flakes, and the higher I climbed, the more it snowed. Incredibly, would you believe this was May 27 (Memorial Day weekend) and it was snowing. How strange to see the Hobblebush in bloom while snow covers the ground and branches of the spruce trees.

I recalled joking and telling Joan before I left the trailhead at Cheshire that it was probably snowing on the summit of Greylock. Little did I know how true that statement would be. As I approached the summit, the weather conditions were similar to that of a winter storm—strong cold winds with driving snow. Surely Joan would not attempt to drive to the summit to meet me. I met two southbounders who had hiked the entire AT in 1993 except for the Mt. Greylock area. They were completing this section and were dressed like Eskimos. I accepted the fact that I would not be afforded any distant views from the summit, but I was certainly seeing some great winter scenes. I reached the summit at 11:00 and, to my surprise, Joan had just arrived at the parking area and was walking toward the lodge. I really did not think she would attempt the drive; but I was glad she did, as we had a very enjoyable lunch together.

I talked to the staff at Bascom Lodge about the three books I had found, and they indicated that no inquiries had been received. I decided to keep them and watch the lost-and-found in the *Trailway News*. Before leaving the summit, I cautioned Joan to wait in the lodge for about three hours in hopes that the weather would clear and to use care in descending the mountain. I hiked up to the 100-foot granite War Memorial which was erected in 1932 honoring Massachusetts residents who sacrificed their lives in times of past wars. It is located on the highest point, and I took several photos before beginning the descent into North Adams.

In less than an hour the weather had cleared, providing views into the valleys and into Vermont. The weather had made an abrupt turn around—the sky had cleared, the sun was bright and I could look back and see the summit of Mt. Greylock as the clouds moved out. It was hard to believe that the weather had made such a drastic change in such a short time.

I hiked down to the Wilbur Clearing Shelter, about 1/4 mile off the AT, for a snack and photo break. After leaving the shelter, I had the best view of the day from a precipice on Prospect Ridge overlooking the valley, Williamstown, into Vermont and the Taconic Range. The AT made a very steep two-mile descent to the trailhead in North Adams. Before reaching the trailhead, I had a nice surprise. Joan had parked the truck and walked down Prospect Street where the AT comes in and up the Trail about a mile to meet me, and we walked out together. I had completed another link in my Appalachian Trail adventure continuing along the ridges and through the valleys into New England.

I unloaded my pack, and we sat and talked for a while. I told Joan I had truly been blessed physically, mentally and spiritually to have been able to hike these wondrous ridges and valleys and to enjoy nature at its very best. I had been given the opportunity to see and experience nature in its various moods, each of which was special in its own right.

This section of Trail from Bear Mtn., NY, to North Adams, MA, through charming New England landscapes had inspired me, making this a most memorable part of my hike north. As an added bonus, I was now 186.4 miles closer to my goal—Mt. Katahdin, Maine.

Joan said that since the weather had cleared, the views from the summit of Mt. Greylock were breathtaking when she left. We decided to drive back over the summit en route to Pittsfield. She was right—the storm had cleared the atmosphere, and the views into northwestern Massachusetts and areas of New York and Vermont were outstanding. Mt. Greylock is truly the grandstand of the Berkshires.

TOP: Morgan Stewart Memorial Shelter on Egbert Mtn.
BOTTOM: Huge White Oak tree near Pawling, NY.

TOP: Puncheons crossing a marshy area near Pawling, NY
BOTTOM: The Housatonic River at Bulls Bridge, CN

Giant Thumb Rock formation on Racoon
Hill near Salisbury, Connecticut

TOP: Old covered bridge crossing the Housatonic
River in West Cornwall, Connecticut
BOTTOM: Beaver pond in Beartown State Forest, MA,
one of scores along the AT through New England

10

RIDGE TOP ENCOUNTERS

"I felt as if atop the world, with a sort of planetary feeling..." —Benton MacKaye

In preparation to continue my hike, I had to replace some of my equipment that was showing extensive wear. I exchanged my Camp Trails pack for a new Kelty, went to a lightweight tent (a North Face Tadpole), and purchased a new pair of Vasque boots to replace my old ones whose soles had seen better days. I also purchased a new L. L. Bean medium-weight sleeping bag, rated to 20 degrees.

In early September, 1994, Joan and I returned to North Adams for a planned fall hike from the trailhead there to Franconia Notch, New Hampshire. This was a 217-mile section traversing the Green Mountains of Vermont to near Rutland and then turning east crossing the Connecticut River Valley into New Hampshire. We established our first base camp near Arlington, VT, a small community off US 7 north of Bennington and spent a part of our arrival day locating trailheads along the AT in southern Vermont.

I began my hike late in the morning, planning to reach the Seth Warner Shelter near the Massachusetts/Vermont state line. Carrying my big pack with a considerable amount of equipment including three cameras, I had planned a slow pace out of the valley, because I knew I needed some conditioning time even though I had been working out at home in preparation for the hike.

I ascended from the valley to a rocky area along the ridge line with views back across the Hoosic Valley, North Adams and Williamstown, including Mt. Greylock. I passed Eph's Lookout (2,254 feet), named for Ephriam Williams, who was the founder of Williams College in Williamstown. From this vantage point, there was another good view of the valley in the Williamstown area. Being lunch time, I took advantage of this setting to relax, eat and enjoy the panorama from the overlook.

After lunch, I continued along the ridge to the Massachusetts/Vermont line, marking another milestone—eleven states down and three to go. I was also starting the section of Trail traversing the ridges which lie within the Green Mountain National Forest. At the state line is the southern terminus of the Long Trail, a scenic hiking trail starting here and following the Green Mountain Range for 263 miles to the Canadian border. The AT follows the Long Trail for approximately 97 miles to Sherburne Pass near Rutland, VT, where it swings east to the Connecticut River.

When I hiked into the Seth Warner Shelter and camping area where I planned to spend the night, one hiker was there ahead of me—a southbounder named Jason from Concord, NH. I was going to pitch my tent but changed my mind when two tough-looking locals with a large dog came to camp for the night. They had a chain saw, a can of gas, unkempt bed rolls and a bag of supplies. I should have shouldered my pack and moved on up the Trail, but instead I decided to stay in the shelter with Jason. I had not checked my map carefully enough to realize that there was a mountain access road nearby, and I knew from previous experience that shelters near road accesses along the AT were frequently used and abused by locals. If hikers were around, they would often be harassed.

As the afternoon moved into the evening hours, the chain saw and loud talk started. Jason and I prepared our evening meal, put things away and retired to our sleeping bags after dark. In the meantime, the noise continued from the camping area. Shortly, the two characters came over to the shelter with the dog and said, "Let's get the guys up that are in the shelter." I did not like the atmosphere and thought we were in for some trouble. I also thought about the movie, "Deliverance," and hoped this would not become a similar scene. They were drinking and (I think) doing drugs and seemed to hold a grudge against the National Park Service and possibly hikers as well. We heard them say, "This is our land, too. We have just as much right to be here as hikers do. If it rains tonight, we will be coming to the shelter, and you can just scoot over." We had not provoked any of these statements, and we attempted to remain calm, making no remarks and taking no actions that would incite them any further.

No doubt their mission was to harass us. Since this did not seem to work, they left after a while, returning to their campsite. I could hear their noises, outbursts and their barking dog throughout the night and did not rest well. I told Jason that I would be leaving early the next morning and advised him to do the same. At 5:00 AM, our noisy neighbors again revved up their chain saw, renewing the harassment. Just at the break of day, I was on the Trail, wishing I had moved on another few miles the day before and tented in a more peaceful location. This is the major reason that the Park Service and Trail clubs are relocating these near-road shelters to more distant and remote sites. Had the situation become more critical, I could have used the pepper spray I carry for protection from dogs. (Firearms are not permitted to be carried along the AT.)

Since I had not had breakfast yet, I stopped at a power line crossing about two miles from the shelter. This had given me time to really work up a good appetite. Before I finished eating, I could hear thunder rumbling in the distance, indicating rain was in the making. Less than a mile later, the rain started and came down hard, continuing until I reached the Congdon Shelter where I had lunch with three other hikers.

After lunch, the weather cleared and I moved on to Harmon Hill (2,325 feet) where there were good views ahead of Bald and Glastenbury Mountains and the city of Bennington, VT, with the obelisk Battle Monument in the distance. On the rough arduous descent from Harmon Hill, I was caught in another storm before I could put on my rain gear. This descent was quite similar to the one off Arden Mtn. (Agony Grind) in New York State, both of which left a lasting impression on my leg joints. In fact, Harmon Hill could be appropriately named Agony Grind II. I hiked out at the AT crossing on VT 9, which is about five miles from Bennington.

Joan and I had spent some time in Bennington before I began the hike through this section. We climbed up the Battle Monument which I could see from Harmon Hill, visited the Old First Church and the adjacent Old Burying Ground where five Vermont Governors and poet Robert Frost are buried.

The section of Trail from VT 9 (Bennington-Brattleboro Highway) to the next trailhead on the West Wardsboro Road was 22.5 miles, so I planned for another overnighter. When I began, there was a group of Harvard students at the trailhead, completing their freshman outdoor education environmental experience. They had spent the night in the Melville Nauheim Shelter, which was about 1.5 miles up the Trail. This was the first of many college groups I would meet at various points along the AT through Vermont, New Hampshire and Maine.

I ascended Maple Hill to Split Rock, which is just what the name implies—a large boulder that has been split apart, with the AT passing between the two halves and providing an interesting bit of geology. My first good view for the day was from Porcupine Ridge (2,815 feet), where I took several photos of the ridges and valleys in the Bennington area. Since entering Vermont, the AT showed signs of heavy use, yet the NPS and the Green Mountain Club have kept it well maintained. I am sure the convergence of the two trails has greatly increased hiker traffic.

When I crossed over the Little Pond Mtn. area, I had good views of Little Pond and Glastenbury Mtn.—my destination for the day. I passed five ladies who had spent the night in the Glastenbury (Goddard) Shelter. They reported that it had been very cold during the night, and I anticipated my new sleeping bag would soon be put to the test. I arrived at the shelter in mid afternoon—what a magnificent structure and what a view! I was grateful I had arrived early, so I would have the rest of the day to enjoy this. The weather was outstanding with an atmosphere that had been cleared by storms the previous day. There was no one at the shelter and, at least for the moment, I had this stately mountain to myself.

The Goddard Shelter is a beautiful rustic log structure that would probably sleep 15-20 hikers. It faces to the southwest with an outstanding view of Mt. Greylock and the Bennington-Arlington Valley area and even further south into the Berkshires, with the Taconics to the west. This was truly a front porch view, surpassing any I had seen on the AT for some time. I just sat on the porch, leaning against my pack marveling at this scene. The shelter was surrounded by spruce and Mountain Ash, and nearby was an excellent piped spring. It seemed as if all of this had been waiting there just for me—Mother Nature had opened her arms to reward me again for the hard climbs and stormy times.

The shelter was spic and span—not a particle of dirt or trash anywhere. I knew who to credit—those southbound ladies I met earlier in the day who had stayed here the night before. Since the weather was so agreeable, I hiked up to the tower, climbed it and took photos of the 360-degree view afforded from there. To the north I could see Mt. Equinox and Stratton Mtn., and to the south and west were the ranges I saw from the shelter. After dinner, I returned to the tower and took some panoramic photos at sunset. I was joined by a young couple later in the afternoon who spent the night in their tent near the shelter, and just before dark three young men hiked up from Highway 9 and stayed in the shelter with me. It was a cool night on Glastenbury Mtn., with a temperature around 40 degrees, but I was snug in my new sleeping bag.

When I left the shelter the following morning, the mountain top was socked in with fog, so I was thankful I had taken my photos the afternoon and evening before. The summit of Glastenbury is covered with an impressive stand of spruce and plush fern gardens. After leaving the mountain, I passed through areas where extensive Trail work had been completed, especially through the wet boggy sections. Huge flat rocks were placed to form walkways through these bogs, allowing easier access for hikers and less impact on the environment. A sign on a tree caught my attention. It read: "Katahdin—559 miles, Springer 1595 miles"—my goal was getting closer but still a lot of miles to go.

Upon reaching Kelley Strand Road, I noticed the truck belonging to the couple that spent the night near the shelter. It was parked by the trailhead where they told me it would be, and I left a note on the windshield with my name and address on it so they could send me information regarding a small wood stove they were using at the Goddard Shelter. They cooked their evening meal using only twigs they had gathered around the campsite—I was impressed. Regrettably, I never heard from them. Perhaps the note blew off the windshield.

Before reaching Arlington-West Wardsboro Road, I saw my first moose track. I had received reports from people in the area that there had been sightings, another sure sign that I was in New England. When I reached the trailhead, I had completed four hiking days since leaving North Adams and was really enjoying the Green Mountains. The Trail was generally well maintained and passed through many boreal bogs and areas with a lot of beaver activity. Much of the Trail passed through heavily forested areas with views only along the high ridges and peaks. Notable was Glastenbury (3,748 feet), which is the highest peak in southern Vermont; and now ahead was the Stratton Mtn. area—my next day's hike.

Stratton Mtn. is a well-known winter sports area in southern Vermont with several ski trails leading off its northern slopes. Even though the AT shares the 3,936-foot summit of Stratton Mtn. with the ski facility, it is not visible from the AT but can be reached by a spur trail.

A cool crisp wind was blowing across the ridges when I left the trailhead to begin my ascent of Stratton Mtn. I crossed over two areas with rocky ledges that had views back over Glastenbury Mtn. and the Taconics. As I ascended higher, the wind changed from cool to cold. By the time I reached the summit, a very cold strong wind was whistling through the steel structure of the fire tower. I ascended the tower, rising above the tops of the spruce trees for a fantastic view; however, the wind just about blew me off. These conditions encouraged me not to stay there long. According to Trail literature, Benton MacKaye conceived the idea of an Appalachian Trail while sitting in a tree on top of Stratton Mtn. On the descent of Stratton, I stopped at an overlook and had a sweeping panorama of Stratton Pond, which according to statistics is the largest pond on the AT and the most heavily-used area. I descended to the east shore of the pond but with regret did not take the time to follow the loop trail around it which ran for probably close to two miles. I am certain making the loop would have been very rewarding, as the beauty of this pond is unsurpassed.

I paused for lunch after crossing the footbridge over the Winhall River, then entered the 14,300-acre Lye Brook wilderness area. I stopped briefly at the Spruce Peak Shelter—the first I had seen that was enclosed. It had a sliding front door, double-decker bunks, a wood-burning stove inside and would probably sleep 12 hikers with ease. After leaving the shelter, I stopped at the overlook on Spruce Peak which offered another view of the valley and mountain ranges and then descended into the valley where VT 11 and 30 cross the Green Mountains.

Before beginning the hike on the next section, we moved our base camp north to the Rutland, VT, area. I also took the next day off due to rain, and we needed to shop, do laundry, etc.

The rain and fog had cleared when I left the trailhead on the ascent of Bromley Mtn. I had planned a 17.3-mile day which would take me across four major peaks: Bromley Mtn. (3,260 feet), Styles Peak (3,394 feet), Peru Peak (3,429 feet) and Baker Peak (2,850 feet). Trail literature noted this section as very scenic, and I was grateful for the balmy weather I had been blessed with to traverse this area.

In a little over an hour, I was on the summit of Bromley Mtn. enjoying the sweeping view from the observation deck near the summit station of the chair lift. Bromley is another mountain with a number of ski trails leading down from the summit. At the base of the mountain is the ski lodge which is visible from several locations on the mountain. From the observation deck, the ski trails on the north slope of Stratton Mtn. (which I had crossed earlier) were clearly visible, as were Style Peak and Peru Peak to the north. The deck provided an outstanding 360-degree view of the Green Mountains and valleys in southern Vermont.

I left the summit of Bromley and stopped briefly in the gap at the Mad Tom Shelter. It was another enclosed design, similar to Spruce Peak Shelter. These enclosed shelters provide more protection from storms and cold weather than the ones with the open fronts. I had been in open-front shelters during stormy weather when the rain blew right in, and on a cold night it is like sleeping with a big door open. After leaving the shelter, I entered the Peru Peak Wilderness Area and ascended to the summit of Styles Peak. Part of the summit had a rocky exposure surrounded by spruce and Mountain Ash, and the Mountain Ash trees were in full fruit with red berries aglow in the bright morning sun. I had been seeing Mountain Ash almost daily along the ridges, but their brilliance on this peak was unequaled. The fruit is inedible to humans but is a favorite of birds.

I left the Styles Peak area and crossed over many wet boggy areas on puncheons which were common along the AT in the Green Mountains. I crossed over spruce-covered Peru Peak and descended past the Peru Peak Shelter to Griffith Lake. Yes, this body of water was listed as a lake and not a pond, and I am not sure why because I always thought a pond was smaller than a lake. Case in point here is Stratton Pond, which is larger than Griffith Lake. I will adjust to this terminology as I move on into Maine, as it will become more and more common.

Griffith Lake was a visual gem. While skirting its shoreline, I noticed that the foliage was starting to show some color, especially the maples; and I was looking forward to watching nature's great transformation into autumn take place in the days ahead. Around Griffith Lake was a long stretch of ecologically well-designed puncheon walkway spanning an expanse of wet areas. Again, the Park Service and Trail club had gone to a lot of effort and expense to reduce the hiker impact through another fragile area and to provide a comfortable walk out of the mud and water.

Baker Peak is the lowest of the four through this area; and after leaving Griffith Lake, I began its ascent. My guidebook noted that the final climb to the summit would be a rock scramble up a rugged series of ledges. This is just what it was—I was down on my knees crawling up the ledgy backbone of the mountain. A blue blaze trail was provided that would be a safer alternative during times of inclement weather to bypass the summit. Even though the altitude is lower than adjacent peaks, the view from its summit is one of the best along the AT in the Green Mountains.

I descended Baker Peak to the Big Branch area which looked more like a small river or a large creek. Where I grew up, a "branch" was a small stream or tributary of a creek—confusing terminology again. Big Branch was a beautiful stream with the AT following it for some distance and then crossing Big Branch suspension bridge, which was an impressive structure. In about a mile, I reached the Danby-Landgrove Road, completing the section and my hike for the day.

It started to rain almost immediately when I left the trailhead the next morning, and that meant rain gear—poncho and pack cover. I stopped at the Lula Tye Shelter to escape the persistent rain for a while and visited with a gentleman from Scotland. I finally left although it was still raining and stopped to converse with the caretaker at Little Rock Pond, another placid pond encircled by conifers and birches. This was one of several locations

I had passed in the Green Mountains where a caretaker was in residence. The caretaker's presence here and elsewhere along the Trail is another continuing effort by the Trail Club and the NFS to help minimize the impact on the environment.

After leaving Little Rock Pond, I crossed White Rocks Mtn. through another lush green stand of spruce and fern gardens and thought how appropriate the name Green Mountains is for this range. I was surprised at how rough some of the section was since the guide and profile map did not reflect this. The Trail was not particularly difficult but was quite rocky along the ridges with more wet boggy areas, some of which were in need of bridge-work.

The Trail crossing of VT 140 followed Bear Mtn. Road for quite some distance on the ascent of Button Hill, and I have a feeling that much of the Trail will be relocated in the near future. Perhaps this explains the lack of maintenance. After leaving Button Hill, I descended quite steeply into Clarendon Gorge of Mill River. The AT crosses a suspension bridge over the rugged gorge that was created by the river cutting through the bedrock. The bridge was built to provide a safe crossing of the gorge; and, according to the sign on the bridge, it stands as a memorial to Robert Braugmann, a thru-hiker who drowned here in 1969.

Joan met me at the VT 103 trailhead near Clarendon Gorge and brought the insoles I had left out of my boots. We had a snack together and hiked back down to the suspension bridge so she could view the gorge.

The climb from the trailhead up Beacon Hill was a rock scramble through a rough notch between cliffs. Because of fog and unsettled weather conditions, I could just faintly make out the Rutland airport from its rocky ledges. On this day's hike, I wanted to complete the section to a trailhead on Upper Cold River Road which is at the south base of Killington Peak. Near the summit of Beacon Hill, I passed more old rock fences encircling large rocky areas cleared of trees and possibly used for pasture land in the past. After crossing Cold River Road, I passed through a region that was densely covered with small spruce trees. The trees were so close together beside the AT that passage through them gave the feeling of walking through a tunnel. I reached the trail-head by mid afternoon and planned to hike Killington and Pico the next day.

Killington Peak (4,235 feet) is in the Coolidge Range of the Green Mountains and is the highest peak the AT crosses in Vermont and the highest since Virginia. Long before hiking the AT, I knew Killington was famous for its skiing but did not realize that the AT passed over it until I started my hike. Ever since the last 4,000-footer in Virginia, I began looking forward to Killington; and now I was at the trailhead on Upper Cold River Road, ready and excited about climbing it. This was a familiar anxious feeling I always experience when about to climb one of the major peaks along the AT.

The weather was cool with a nice breeze resulting in good climbing conditions; however, we noticed when driving to the trailhead that the upper elevation of Killington was in fog. The forecast was favorable with clearing as the day progressed, and I hoped it would be accurate. Shortly after leaving the trailhead, I passed the Governor Clement Shelter which was built of stone in 1929 (my birth year) and named for a former governor of Vermont, Percival Clement. A lone hiker had spent the night there and was still encased in the cocoon of her sleeping bag as I passed. I say "her" because she caught up with me later in the day on the north shoulder of Killington and told me she had spent the night at that shelter.

As I ascended to the subalpine forest of spruce and fir near Consultation Point, the sun had burned the fog away. It looked like the forecast of favorable weather would be accurate. The AT flanks the southern and western slopes of Killington Peak, never passing directly over the summit. I hiked around this area to Cooper Lodge (an enclosed shelter) which is .2 mile off the summit and took the blue blaze trail from the lodge to Killington Peak. The blue blaze was another straight-up rock scramble to the peak, but well worth the effort. The weather was perfect for yielding a remarkable view.

From this lofty perch, the grandeur of southern New England stretched for miles in every direction: the Green Mountains from Glastenbury north, the Taconics and Adirondack Ranges in New York, and the distant White Mountains in New Hampshire. Again, the poem flashed back, "Great Wide Beautiful Wonderful World." I had read that it was from this peak in 1763 that Rev. Samuel Peters and his picnicking party christened the region "Verd Mont" (Green Mountain in French) with champagne they had brought for refreshments—hence, the name for the state of Vermont.

On the summit of Killington is the ski complex anchoring the skiing industry king of the mountain. Before leaving the summit, I was joined by two mountain bikers who had ridden up from the Sherburne Pass area via one of the ski trails. They told me that mountain biking has become a very popular off-ski-season activity here. The wind was strong and cold on the summit, so I descended the blue blaze to Cooper Lodge. This is not a lodge as our customary terminology implies but is an old enclosed stone shelter used by hikers and others. It will sleep approximately 12 and has the front enclosed with clear plastic where windows apparently once were. The shelter showed heavy use and considerable abuse, due in part, I am certain, to its proximity to the summit.

I left the shelter and crossed the eastern flank of Pico Peak to Pico Camp, which was yet another enclosed cabin similar in design to the others I had encountered. From this point, a blue blaze trail leads to the summit of Pico Peak, another major skiing center. From Pico Camp, I could see the ski trails descending Killington into the valley and would see them for many miles along the AT moving toward New Hampshire. I hiked into an open power line area where there was a good view of Sherburne Pass and the range of mountains that lay ahead toward the Connecticut River and New Hampshire. I met a number of hikers before reaching Sherburne Pass and was overtaken by the young lady who had spent the night in the Governor Clement Shelter. I descended into the Pass where US 4 crosses the Green Mountains and where Joan was waiting. We had planned to move our base camp east toward the Connecticut River.

We moved to White River Junction near the Connecticut River Valley for my final hiking segment through Vermont and into New Hampshire. The AT profile map of the 40-mile section from the Pass to the Connecticut River shows a continuous series of ups and downs with the peaks ranging in elevation from 1,500 to 2,000 feet.

Shortly after leaving Sherburne Pass, I reached the Maine junction Trail marker which is where the AT and the Long Trail split with the AT turning east toward Maine and the Long Trail continuing north to Canada. The sign here also marked the distance to Katahdin as 468 miles—I was getting closer but still a lot of miles to go and many mountains and valleys to cross. The AT soon passed through Gifford Woods State Park and skirted Kent Pond with the fall foliage reflecting on its mirrorlike surface. The maples and other deciduous varieties of trees were starting to show their brilliance with fall coloration likely to climax within a week.

From Kent Pond, I crossed the Ottauquechee River Valley and ascended a very steep unnamed mountain. There were occasional worthwhile views from vistas along an old logging road back toward Pico and Killington with their outstanding ski trails. I had been seeing and hearing a variety of wildlife through Vermont including Ruffed Grouse, red squirrels (no grey squirrels yet), hawks, many song birds, signs of porcupines, moose tracks but no sightings, no wild turkey yet, but lots of small wildlife including mice, chipmunks and turtles. Much of the AT through this area has been or is in the process of being relocated. My *1992 Seventh Edition ATC Guidebook* profile maps were not reflecting these changes, so I was discovering features along the Trail that were not noted.

I stopped for a morning snack break at the next shelter (Stony Brook) and visited with a hiker who had spent the night there. We discussed the major timber cutting operation that was active in the area and wondered what affect it would have on the AT and any possible relocations. After leaving Stony Brook, I continued ascending ridges and descending into valleys, now consistent with the up-and-down pattern shown on the profile map. Views were limited because of the lack of overlook points. However, the view from The Lookout gave a hazy glimpse into the White Mountains. A college professor from Troy, New York, joined me at The Lookout, and we had lunch together further up the Trail. By mid afternoon, I reached the Winturri Shelter, a nice little log eight-sleeper with a red roof that alerted me to its location from some distance away. There was a large stack of wood near the shelter for hikers to use, a thoughtful touch on someone's part.

The AT intersected Old Town Road, which at one time was a crossover when this was a farming community. I passed more of the old stone fences and had an occasional view across the valley of idle fields partially overgrown with brush. Southeast from one of these vantage points in the distance was Mt. Ascutney—the largest monadnock (an isolated hill rising from a plain) in New England and the site of a ski resort and conference center. The AT does not pass over Mt. Ascutney but the mountain is visible from the AT for many miles. Before hiking out on VT 12, I spotted two deer—the first in Vermont—and shortly afterward I met Joan who had hiked up the Trail to meet me, making a great ending for my 18-mile day.

The VT 12 AT trailhead is about 4.5 miles north of Woodstock, another very charming Vermont town, with a population of around 1,000—many more during tourist season. Woodstock has many attractions: skiing, a covered bridge, Rockefeller Estate and the Vermont Raptor Center. The surrounding countryside is a mecca for raising and training horses, all of this nestled in a picturesque Vermont valley setting.

From the trailhead, I continued the routine of valley to peak, passing through open woodlands containing many of the stately white birches for which New England is famous. I began noticing unfamiliar blazes painted on trees along the Trail and then realized that the AT from VT 12 into New Hampshire was in the Dartmouth Outing Club (DOC) maintenance jurisdiction. Originally, they had painted black and orange stripes once known as "tiger paws" on trees, marking the section of the AT for which they were responsible. That practice had been discontinued, and the standard white blaze is currently used. However, many of the old blazes were still visible. As I continued east toward White River, the up-and-down pitch continued with the AT going straight up to the peak and straight down to the other side with little Trail grading or switchbacks. The peaks were not high, but the workout was continual, providing little recovery time.

After crossing Pomfret-South Promfret Road, I passed more rock fences; and these caught my attention immediately. Of all the miles of them I had seen along the AT, none had been as precisely built as these. They were not only in straight lines, but each rock had been selected to fit into its own spot leaving the least amount of space between it and the next, like pieces in a jigsaw puzzle. Many of these were built with the precision that you see in a modern home fireplace and chimney, with the walls near vertical. In passing through this area, I thought of Robert Frost's poem "Mending Fences" and wondered if any of these had ever been mended. If so, the work had been completed with utmost care. Wouldn't this have been a sight to see back in early Vermont days when these hills were first cleared and the rock fences made geometric designs over the landscape. I hiked out at the trailhead on VT 14 in West Hartford on the White River later than planned. The Trail was rougher and more strenuous than I had anticipated and, with the gorgeous fall day, I consciously took more time to enjoy its splendor.

I began the next day's hike at the trailhead, passed through the small community of West Hartford, crossed under I-89 and began the ascent of Griggs Mtn. It was only nine miles to the Connecticut River which would complete the state of Vermont. Near the crest of the mountain were land features that I had been noticing and wondering about since leaving VT12. They were unusual in that the land was very irregular with many depressions on the forest floor. It looked as though the land had been put to some specific use that caused the depressions. I was puzzled about this and wondered about their origin, as there was no reference made about it in my Trail literature. Maybe they were natural features— if so, this was an unusual phenomenon meriting notation.

The Happy Hill Shelter is the only one in this area and, according to the plaque there, was constructed in 1918 and is the oldest on the entire AT. The shelter is actually an enclosed cabin with bunks and a large floor where hikers could spread out with a big fireplace in the middle of the structure. After leaving the cabin, I descended into Norwich, another Vermont town of about 1,000 population. Unexpectedly, while descending Elm Street into the main part of town, two deer were standing on the edge of one of the resident's yards. I thought this was interesting because, of the four deer sightings I had in Vermont, half of them were in town. For the next 2.5 miles, I would be road walking—through Norwich on streets, crossing the Connecticut River on a highway and hiking through the Streets of Hanover.

I hiked through Norwich, passed under I-91 and reached the Connecticut River by noon, completing the last section of AT in Vermont. I had reached another milestone—twelve states down and two to go. I enjoyed the walk through Vermont—its landscapes of Green Mountains and tranquil valleys left me greatly inspired. Ahead lay New Hampshire and the White Mountains. A 1987 thru-hiker made the statement, "When you get to Hanover, you've done 80% of the miles, but you still have 50% of the work left." I would find later that this statement was fairly accurate; however, at this point, completing 12 states and over 1,700 miles was an accomplishment which filled me with both pride and reverence.

I crossed the Connecticut River bridge and entered the town of Hanover, New Hampshire. The AT passes through many towns along its 2,100-plus-mile course but none like Hanover. All the other towns were small, quiet and peaceful; but Hanover is a town of over 6,000 population not including the students of its renowned Dartmouth College, an Ivy League school which was founded in 1769. The town was bustling with activity as I hiked up West Wheelock Street to the corner of North Main with my pack and walking stick. I blended in quite well with the college students milling to and fro. No one seemed to take notice that I was a hiker; after all, hikers pass through town regularly and many of them have small packs on their backs. I did not take a great deal of time to look around while in town because I was anxious to move on and get back to a more natural AT setting.

I had made arrangements with Joan for a lunch rendezvous at a gas station on VT 120 east of town. As she was driving through Hanover, she was able to pick me out amidst the many students along the streets and later met me at the gas station where we sat on the tailgate of the truck, ate lunch and talked.

After lunch, I left the highway and skirted a playing field into the woods where I was confronted with a sign that had a "No mountain bike" symbol placed there by the DOC. I thought this was appropriate, because earlier in the day a mountain biker approached suddenly from the rear, startling me. Alas, he was past and gone before I had a chance to tell him that the AT is a foot-path-only Trail and not intended for any other means of transportation.

I took the .2-mile blue blaze to the Velvet Rocks Shelter, the first in New Hampshire. It was a small log six-sleeper nestled among some large rocks. Since entering the DOC's area of maintenance jurisdiction back in Vermont, the signs marking various locations—shelters, springs, trails, etc.—had been outstanding; and the DOC is to be commended.

I descended and crossed over a wetland area on a well-engineered and constructed walkway, which I am sure was built by the DOC. The walkway offered the hiker a vantage point of the wetland that would not have been possible otherwise, yet the distraction and impact on the environment was minimized. I hiked across Trescott Road and passed more of the old stone walls and fences. It seems they were used in early New Hampshire days as well. I completed my hike for the day at the Etna-Hanover Center Road trailhead which was about 7 miles into New Hampshire.

The next day would begin my journey into the foothills of the White Mountains. I had seen the distant ridge lines of the Whites from various vantage points as far down the AT as Killington. Now I was getting closer, and the upcoming peaks should bring them into clearer focus. I had never been through the Whites and really did not know much about them beyond location. Joan and I had traveled through the Gorham, New Hampshire, area a few years before but never visited or spent any time in the mountains. During my many hikes on the AT from Georgia to this point, I had talked with scores of hikers who had been through the Whites, and their comments had given me mixed feelings. They certainly had increased my desire and excitement about hiking through them, yet, at the same time, down deep I felt some apprehension. Some statements they made were: "You think this area is rough, you ain't seen anything yet." "Wait 'till you get to the Whites." "When I went through the Whites, I had a feeling I was on top of the world." "The weather was so brutal when I hiked the Whites that I couldn't see anything." "All I wanted to do was get out of there as quickly as possible." "Be prepared for bad weather because you're likely to get it." Now I had arrived in the foothills and had some time to think about this challenging range and to prepare myself both mentally and physically for the test ahead.

I continued my hike across Three Mile Road and ascended and crossed both the south and north peaks of Moose Mtn. (2,290 feet). The trees were dripping from a recent rain, and the wet overhanging brush was washing and rewashing my pant legs as I brushed past. The AT definitely needed some attention through this area as weeds and underbrush had the AT completely hidden in some places. Both peaks were socked in with fog so there were no views from either, but I held out hope that things would clear before my next vantage point. Before descending into the valley, I reached a rock outcropping where the fog cleared briefly, and I had a quick view of Holts Ledge, the next peak I would be crossing. Was this a sign that the weather was clearing? I hoped so, because the peaks were getting higher as I was approaching the Whites, and the AT was passing through what promised to be very picturesque terrain.

When crossing the valley, I passed through more boggy areas below a beaver dam and found it impossible to get through without getting my feet wet and muddy. This is an area that desperately needs a walkway because hikers, in searching for a dryer passage across, were leaving the AT and causing needless damage to the surrounding area.

I ascended out of the valley to Holt's Ledge and was greeted by some clearing and occasional sunshine. The view from the ledge into the valley included the fairly large Goose Pond. On this ledge, the endangered Peregrine falcon had been successfully reintroduced, and scattered signs alert visitors to respect and protect the nesting area. The top of the Dartmouth Skiway is located near the ledge bringing more visitors here.

I descended into Lyme-Dorchester Road where Joan was waiting to pick me up, but I decided to hike the new AT relocation to the next trailhead near the base of Smarts Mtn. Before I reached the trailhead, I passed an official AT concrete post mile marker indicating 1,770 miles to Springer Mtn. and 412 miles to Katahdin. I was reducing the number of miles left, but those mountains up ahead were beginning to look more and more massive.

The weather was unsettled when I left the trailhead the next morning. A drizzly rain had fallen during the night, with dreary conditions extending into the morning hours. I planned a 14-mile day crossing Smarts Mtn. and Mt. Cube, both of which were in the 3,000-3,200-foot range, and I was hoping to have my first good close-up view of the Whites. My previous glimpses from further south were distant with a considerable amount of haze in the atmosphere reducing the clarity. When I reached the first series of open ledges on Smarts Mtn., I moved into fog and realized then that a view from the summit would not be possible on this morning. It was quite a rock scramble to the summit over open ledges; and I was sure there would be good vantage points to the south, had the fog not obscured everything. The fog was less dense on the summit, but there was a heavy fog line a few hundred feet down the mountain. I climbed up to the second platform on the fire tower and saw that climbing further would be useless. All that was visible were the spruce trees standing like ghosts in the fog, their images fading away in the grey mist.

I descended the tower, took a snack break at the fire warden's old cabin and then hiked off the mountain to the bridge over Jacobs Brook. As I crossed the bridge, I looked down into the cascading waters swirling around huge boulders and was grateful for the easy picturesque passage the bridge provided. Crossing this stream prior to the construction of the bridge would not only have been a challenge but a risky undertaking.

Within 1 1/2 miles of the bridge, I hiked the .3-mile blue blaze to the Hexacuba Shelter with its unique hexagonal design with three of its six sides closed in. It had a large center support projecting from the floor to its gazebo-style roof. When I first saw it from the Trail, I thought it looked like a low squatting gazebo. It was designed and built by the DOC in 1990, and I understand there is a matching privy nearby; but I was so interested in the shelter construction that I forgot to check it out.

As I began the ascent of Mt. Cube, the weather started to clear. From a rocky ledge part way up the mountain, I had a view of the striking fall foliage in the Jacob Brook Valley. Even the fire tower on Smarts Mtn. across the valley, which I had left cloaked in fog hours earlier, was becoming visible. The view I missed on Smarts Mtn. was more than made up for on Mt. Cube. The Trail literature indicated that the view from Smarts Mtn. was one of the best through this area, but I don't know how it could be any better than the one from Mt. Cube. To the south and west was the vast Connecticut River Valley and the Smarts Mtn. area with Mt. Ascutney, VT, in the distance. To the north awaiting my arrival were the high peaks of the Whites with massive Moosilauke (the first big one) beckoning me. Moosilauke would be my first major climb in the Whites and the first time I would be ascending above tree line with the AT passing directly over its summit.

It was about 16 miles from the Mt. Cube summit to the summit of the giant. As I viewed Moosilauke, I felt a surge of adrenaline and that little uneasy feeling in the pit of my stomach. However, I still had another day's hike before reaching its base. While descending Mt. Cube, more Ruffed Grouse took flight from the Trail side, and I was amazed at seeing these great woodland birds in this subalpine environment. The grouse had been spotted in every state I hiked through thus far. I was also seeing the little red squirrels and a grey squirrel now and then. My hike for the day ended on NH 25A near Warren. Joan picked me up and we moved our base camp to Warren, NH, for my final segment of this trip.

Because of rain and fog during the night with unsettling conditions lasting into the morning hours, it was 10:30 AM before I began my day's hike. In fact, the weather was so dismal I considered taking an R & R day but changed my mind and decided to keep moving on. I was hoping the unsettled conditions over the last several days would moderate allowing me better and clearer hiking through the Moosilauke region of the Whites.

The fall foliage was reaching its peak in the foothills of the Whites, and the breezes along the ridges were bringing down some leaves. The fog and lack of sunshine were prohibiting the spectrum of colors from radiating across the landscape. I reached the AT crossing of Highway 25C where a major power line crosses the area. Due to the extreme fog, I missed the Trail blaze thinking it followed the power line and had to do some backtracking. During such challenging conditions as this, I had learned to be extra alert for the white blazes and not to go very far if I did not see one. I have missed the Trail many times but never for very long. In areas where the AT was poorly blazed, I would often stop and look for blazes in the other direction to confirm that I was on the Trail.

Once back on the Trail and moving, the inevitable happened— it started to rain, and rain it did as I ascended a very appropriately named peak. I chuckled as I read the marker on the summit through the haze and raindrops—"Mt. Mist elevation 2,230 feet." I descended to an overlook with Wachipauka Pond barely visible through the mist below. However, the weather can change with startling abruptness in these mountains; and within minutes, while I was standing at the overlook, the mist and fog around the pond just seemed to melt away. I was blessed with a breathtaking view of the pond below encircled by a wreath of trees in full color, speckled with bits of spruce green. By the overlook was another humorous sign: "Wachepauka Pond—beware of tourists." This overlook is heavily visited because of its proximity to NH 25 at Glencliff, NH. From this vantage point, I had hoped also to have a close-up view of Mt. Moosilauke, but the majority of the mountain continued to be engulfed in heavy fog. When I reached the trailhead on NH 25 where Joan was waiting, I told her I was going to hike to the Sanitarium Road trailhead which was about another 1.5 miles closer to the base of Mt. Moosilauke. She agreed to pick me up there.

As a supplemental aid in hiking through the Whites, I acquired a copy of the *AMC White Mountain Guide 25th Edition* which gave complete information about the area and trails. For several days prior to my reaching the Whites, I had been studying the guide very carefully with special emphasis on the areas through which the AT would be passing. Both here and throughout other AT literature, repeated references were made about mountain safety and the extremes of weather in the Whites. The weather extremes can and do occur during the summer months according to the Guide and can become winter-like with hurricane force winds. But this was late September, moving from summer into early fall. Surely, I thought, this would be the exception rather than the rule this time of year. Perhaps the Guide was being a little overly cautious.—How wrong my skepticism! I was in for a rude awakening.

For the next two days I did not hike because the weather remained rainy, foggy and quite cool. I was waiting and hoping for a clear shot at Moosilauke, which had not been visible because of fog for several days. We used the two days to resupply, rest, catch up on laundry and review my hiking plan for the rest of the trip.

In studying my plan, I decided to use a north-to-south hike over the mountain with the trailhead located on NH 112 in Kinsman Notch, the first of several deep valleys the AT crosses through New Hampshire into Maine. The Trail on the north side of the mountain follows a very treacherous section along Beaver Brook with steep ascents over cliffs and ledges. I felt there would be more photo opportunities ascending rather than descending this very picturesque area and also that it would be safer going up rather than down the wet slippery areas. This was the second time since leaving Springer that I would be hiking north to south.

On our way to the trailhead at Kinsman Notch, we noticed that the mass of Moosilauke quickly disappeared into a foggy embrace. Conditions did not appear any more favorable than the day before, but I decided it was a go anyway. As I left the trailhead, I looked up the rough ravine of Beaver Brook to the fog line and wondered what lay hidden on its high ridges and 4,802-foot summit above tree line. The elevation at Kinsman Notch is 1,870 feet, and the distance to the summit is 3.2 miles, making a 3,000-foot elevation gain in three miles or 1,000 feet per mile—a rigorous climb. Before starting the ascent of the Beaver Brook Trail, I looked for but was unable to find the Beaver Brook Shelter near NH 112 that was listed in the guidebook. A very chilly breeze was blowing down the Brook as I ascended the steep rocky ledges. That uneasy feeling just seemed to hang with me about the weather. I had been watching the forecast with intense interest, and it indicated there would be clearing later in the day with a possibility of showers in the mountains during the morning hours.

When I reached the fog line, the chilly breeze changed to a cold wind with a fine mist hitting my face. As I climbed higher up the steel hoops and steps built into the rocks, the mist changed to a fine round snow; and the wind became cold and strong. Beaver Brook is a very picturesque cascading stream plunging over a series of waterfalls and flumes into the valley below. When I reached the blue blaze leading off the AT to the Beaver Brook Shelter, the snow was accumulating on the branches of the spruce and fir trees. The shelter had been built in 1993 replacing the one that had been at the base of the mountain near Kinsman Notch. The close proximity to NH 112 probably had prompted the AMC to rebuild the structure further up the mountain.

After a snack break at the shelter, I continued my ascent. The higher I climbed, the colder it became, with more snow and stronger winds. Within two hours, I had hiked from the colorful foliage of the hardwoods in the valley to the snow-covered spruce and fir on the mountain, which gave the appearance of a winter wonderland. When I reached the junction of the Beaver Brook Trail and the Benton Trail, I noticed a fresh footprint in the snow leading up the Trail through the scrubby spruce toward the summit. The wind was brutally driving the snow into my face with the force of BB shot, and visibility was almost zero. I reached tree line and noticed that the footprints led on toward the first rock cairn (pile of rocks marking the AT) which was just barely visible. The wind was blowing with such force that I could hardly stand without leaning into it to keep my balance.

Suddenly, a figure in a brightly-colored ski outfit approached me from the first rock cairn; and without even a greeting said, "Don't even THINK about going up there. The wind is FIERCE and DANGEROUS." He said he had only gone a couple hundred feet or so and had to turn back. We hiked back down the AT together to the Trail junction (about one-half mile) where the trees gave us some protection. He said he was "off of this mountain" and would not be making another attempt and that I had better do the same. I ate a snack and put on another layer of clothing which was all I had and decided I would wait a while and then consider making another attempt. If I aborted the hike, I would have to repeat what I had accomplished to this point. As near as I could determine, the distance across the summit from tree line to tree line was about 3/4 mile. I decided to give it a try and if it got too bad, I could turn back.

While I was waiting, two hikers came up the Benton Trail which is another route to the summit from the valley. I advised them of the conditions near the summit, and they said they had no intention of going any further than this point. The weather did not seem to moderate any—on the contrary, it seemed to be getting worse; so if I were going to attempt the crossing, I knew I had better get moving. I hiked back up to tree line on the ice- and snow-covered Trail. The sounds and sight of the storm raging across the mountain almost prompted me to turn back.

If I could reach the first cairn and seek protection on its lee side, then I would go to the next cairn and so forth across the summit. This was the strategy I used, always maintaining a low profile to keep from falling or being blown down on the ice-covered rocks from the hurricane force winds. When I reached the summit, I found a sign on a post amidst the boulders from the foundation of the once-present summit house. Thick ice and snow made the information thereon unreadable. I managed to kick a rock loose from the Trail and used it to scrape the ice and snow off the sign. My hands almost froze trying to clear it enough so it could be read. Once I got my direction from the sign, I moved as rapidly as possible across the summit on the Glencliff Trail.

It took me about one-half hour to make the crossing from tree line to tree line. This was without doubt the worst weather situation I had ever experienced in my lifetime. There were moments when I doubted whether I could make it across because of the brutal force of the wind and the cold. It seemed like an eternity before I reached the trees and protection from the storm on the south side of the summit. I dropped down, exhausted with my back resting against a spruce and thought about the warnings given in the Trail literature about the weather in these mountains and the dangers of injuries and hypothermia. I realized then that this probably was not a very smart thing to have attempted. Maybe I was just lucky, or maybe my "Guardian Angel" was with me. One thing for sure, this experience made a believer out of me regarding the danger and hazard warnings given in the Trail guides and provided me with a greater respect for the weather and the mountains themselves. After hiking off the mountain that day, I found out that the wind speed on Mt. Washington was 88 MPH, and no doubt the wind speed on Moosilauke exceeded 65 MPH.

On my descent, I met several hikers who were going up the mountain and I cautioned them about crossing the summit. Only one, a thru-hiker, indicated he was going to attempt the crossing. It was amazing how rapidly the temperature increased as I descended. Before reaching the trailhead at Glencliff, the sun had burned through the cloud cover opening up the view of the valley. I looked back toward the mountain and could see the snow line on the spruce trees, but the summit was still obscured, indicating that the storm was still raging.

When I reached Sanitarium Road, Joan had not yet arrived. While sitting on a foot bridge by the roadside, I received a thrilling and unexpected treat. A large bull moose walked out of the forest on to the highway near the AT crossing. I smiled with irony because I had been seeing their hoof prints along the AT for days in true wilderness locations, and the first sighting was here on the highway near a small community. Joan came along shortly while the moose was still in the road, and she had a chance to see him also. The sighting was quite timely and appropriate because, after all, I had just hiked over <u>MOOS</u>ilauke.

One of the first things Joan said to me was that she was glad I had such a great day to climb the mountain. That was the understatement of the year! It had been a beautiful fall day at the campground where she was relaxing! Our contrasting perspectives go to prove how dramatically climatic conditions can change from valleys to mountain tops. Joan said it was a good thing she had no idea until it was over what was happening on that summit.

The AT follows a very rugged course through the White Mountains, a section considered the most scenic along the entire Appalachian chain. Trail literature and guides advise hikers not to plan for high-mileage days so that the segments are more manageable and the great natural beauty that abounds can be more fully enjoyed. Beginning at Kinsman Notch, NH, and continuing to Grafton Notch, ME, the AT is under Appalachian Mountain Club maintenance jurisdiction. The AT follows segments of older established trails still bearing their original names. However, the AT maintains its official 2" by 6" white blaze marking.

I planned for an overnighter in the next section from Kinsman Notch to Franconia Notch which would be the final segment on this trip. Near Kinsman Notch is Lost River which is a narrow gorge with the stream plunging over, around and many times under massive boulders which have tumbled into the valley. A walkway provides access to this marvelous geological wonder, containing many cascades and waterfalls. Access to the gorge can also be made via a blue blaze from the AT.

I climbed out of the Notch on the Kinsman Ridge Trail and continued over a series of ridges to Mt. Wolf (3,478 feet). From an outcrop on Mt. Wolf, I had my first panoramic view of the Pemigewasset River Valley and the North Woodstock and Lincoln, NH, areas. Across the river was the impressive snow-capped Franconia Ridge, a section the AT traverses and that I would be hiking on my next trip. The snow on Franconia Ridge was the result of the storm I experienced while crossing Mt. Moosilauke the day before, and it reminded me of how unpredictable and violent the weather can be in the mountains even in early fall. I descended Mt. Wolf into the Eliza Brook Shelter where I planned to spend the night. Later that afternoon, I was joined by five other hikers who tented near the shelter, and we all had a great evening of fellowship.

Before leaving the shelter the next morning, I reviewed the Trail guide and profile map for my hike from Eliza Brook across South and North Kinsman to Franconia Notch. From the description given in the guide (as well as reports from hikers), I knew the ascent of South Kinsman Mtn. would be a challenge. After crossing the brook, the AT follows the banks of the stream, passing some beautiful cascades for about a mile before beginning the ascent of South Kinsman. Harrington Pond is about half way up the mountain in distance but certainly not in time. Phrases used in the Trail literature describing its climb— "steep pitch" "hikers with heavy packs allow extra time" "they've got to be kidding"— are accurate. Now, I could add some of my own like "a four-by-four dig-in over a mile-long rock scramble." This was the most challenging section I had climbed for a while and would rate it about a 10 on my difficulty scale.

The weather had been cool and partly overcast when I left Eliza Brook. By the time I reached the summit (4,369 feet), it was cold, foggy and very windy and the spruce and fir were covered with hoarfrost. Was it going to snow again? Well, it did after I crossed the col (a depression in the summit line of a chain of mountains) to the summit of North Kinsman. The snow was brief, with partial clearing occurring before I left the summit. A window opened in the clouds and mist and exposed a remarkable view of the White Mountain landscape. I had a breathtaking view across Franconia Notch of the snow-covered Franconia Ridge beginning with Mt. Flume and Mt. Liberty to the south, moving up the ridge to Mt. Haystack, Mt. Lincoln and the highest—Mt. Lafayette. Beneath me and to the northwest was a good view of Lonesome Lake and the Cannon Mtn. This was without a doubt the best view I had seen of the White Mountains, appropriately named because they were white-capped.

I descended past Kinsman Pond down the Fishin' Jimmy Trail, and it started to snow again, continuing until I arrived at the Lonesome Lake AMC Mountain Hut which is the first of several along the AT in the White Mountains. The huts in the Whites are large lodge-type facilities offering food and shelter for from 30 upward to 100 guests. These huts were built and are operated by the AMC through a special use permit from the USFS and are strategically located throughout the White Mountains. Being an AMC member, I stopped to check the facility and to visit with the Hut Croo (pronounced and meaning the same as "crew"). It was an excellent facility with a picturesque location on Lonesome Lake, and I was impressed and decided that I would stay in some of them on my next hike through the Whites into Maine.

I left the hut and descended into Franconia Notch via the Cascade Brook Trail. I had met many hikers since entering the White Mountain National Forest near Glencliff, as there are many trails other than the AT, some heavily used.

Before reaching US 3, I met again two thru-hikers Joan and I had talked to a couple of days earlier at the Flume Visitor Center. One was "The Pathfinder" and the other was "The Banjo Man." Can you imagine that strapped to his pack was—yes, a banjo. I told him I hoped both he and his banjo made it safely down the rock scramble off South Kinsman, as they were headed for Eliza Brook that day.

I crossed under US 3 in Franconia Notch where the AT joins the bike path leading to the Flume parking lot. About one-quarter mile from the parking area, I had a pleasant surprise, for Joan had walked up the bike path to meet me. We hiked out together, completing the 217-mile segment of the AT from North Adams, MA, to Franconia Notch, NH. My hike through the Green Mountains and valleys of Vermont had been memorable and inspirational, and the grandeur of the Whites challenged my return.

TOP: Goddard Shelter on Glastenbury Mtn, Vermont
BOTTOM: Griffith Lake along the AT/Long Trail, VT

TOP: Maine Junction near Sherburne Pass, VT, where the
    AT and the Long Trail split. The AT swings east toward
    NH and the Long Trail continues north to Canada.
BOTTOM: Hexacuba Shelter between Sharps Mtn. and
    Mt. Cube in New Hampshire

TOP: The AT crosses the wet areas on this walkway
   north of Hanover, New Hampshire
BOTTOM: Rock cairns marking the AT across Mt.
   Moosilauke, NH. This photo was taken during a
   snow storm.

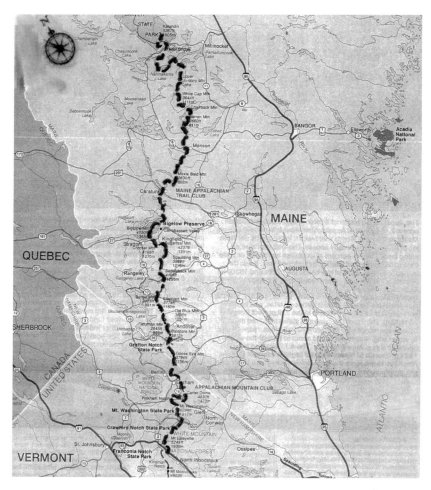

Map Detail from Franconia Notch, NH, to Mt. Katahdin, ME
(Covered in Chapters eleven through sixteen)
— — — — — Denotes Appalachian Trail Route

11

THE MAJESTIC WHITES

"The White Mountains and particularly the Presidential Range are majestic and even awful, when contemplated in a proper mood."
                                                        —Nathaniel Hawthorne

Franconia Notch is one of the outstanding wonders of the White Mountains. This deep picturesque valley has attracted millions of people through the years to enjoy its unique features. Among these visitors were noted American writers such as Henry David Thoreau (who passed through the Notch in 1839 and marveled at its beauty), Nathaniel Hawthorne (who wrote about the Old Man on the Mountain, a geologic marvel in the Notch) and poet Robert Frost (whose home was at Franconia from 1915 to 1920). I am sure that many lines in these famous writers' works were inspired by this great natural landscape.

Prior to beginning the hike at Franconia Notch, Joan and I spent a couple of days visiting a few of the Notch's many marvels—The Old Man on the Mountain, a 40-foot stone profile of a man's face formed by rock ledges on Cannon Mtn.; the Flume, an 800-foot gorge with 80- to 90-foot granite walls; and the Basin, a 20-foot diameter pothole cut into the stream bed rock by water and sand over thousands of years. For the first section of the hike, we established our base camp near Twin Mountain, NH, and I prepared for three days for the first trek from Franconia Notch to Crawford Notch.

So here I was in Franconia Notch, NH—the date was August 10, 1995—the beginning of the last stretch of my AT adventure. It was 370 miles to my goal, Mt. Katahdin in the north central Maine wilderness, and I had planned 39 hiking days. If all went well, I expected to climb Katahdin on September 26, or with luck on September 25. My schedule was tight and I knew it. First, I had reservations to stay in three of the AMC Huts while traversing the White Mountains. Second, my niece and her husband were scheduled to meet me near Gorham, NH, on August 20 to hike the Mahoosucs with me. Third, our son Rod would be joining me at Monson, ME, on September 15 for the thrust through the "100-Mile Maine Wilderness," and last, our other two children, Melinda and Dave, would be joining us at Katahdin Stream Campground at the base of Katahdin on September 25 to hike the mountain. I did not allow for lost hiking days due to inclement weather but thought, if necessary, I could make adjustments using some R & R days I had built into the plan. Yes, this was a tight hiking schedule involving many commitments and mainly stemming on two factors: the weather and me!

I had spent weeks at a fitness center back home in Ohio conditioning for this hike, but the climb out of Franconia to near the ridge line at Liberty Spring told me that the preparation was insufficient. It usually takes me several days to get loosened up. The Franconia section is considered a rather rugged leg with a significant amount of elevation gain and loss, so I planned extra time to Crawford Notch. I stopped at the Liberty Springs campsite and visited with the caretaker, who informed me I would find no water for the next eight miles—my planned destination for the day. I had a good hearty drink and filled both my canteens in anticipation of a long day of climbing. I reached the junction of the Franconia Ridge Trail by late morning and would be following the Trail to Mt. Lafayette. Weatherwise, I could not have picked a better day. The atmosphere was very clear, and the temperature had been cool all morning; but, as I progressed up the ridge, it became warmer.

The warm temperature, my heavy pack and insufficient conditioning were slowing me down more than expected. My plan was to reach Lafayette by early afternoon, but the climb up the ridge was taking longer than anticipated. Also, I was making many stops to take in the views and to snap photographs. The first peak along the ridge is Mt. Haystack (4,760 feet), and from this point on across Mt. Lafayette the AT is above tree line. The views from this ridge are breathtaking. The entire Franconia Notch region is visible as are the Cannon and Kinsman Mountains across the Notch. I was on North Kinsman during my last hike when I viewed this area under snow cover. The next peak along the ridge is Mt. Lincoln (5,089 feet) and the view gets even better.

I met many people along the ridges, most of whom were day-hikers, including several groups and individuals taking pictures at each view point along the ridge. Franconia Ridge is a very popular attraction, and the AT along the entire ridge shows heavy use. The AMC and/or NPS had installed low rock fences along each side of the Trail in an effort to guide hikers in times of foggy conditions and to prevent the very fragile alpine plants along the high ridges from being trampled.

It was mid afternoon before I reached the summit of Mt. Lafayette which stands 5,249 feet and within a few feet of the elevation on Mt. Katahdin. There were at least 25 people on the summit, and I had met many more descending. I thought it remarkable how many people had made the ambitious climb and was struck by the different age groups represented—seniors, middle-age, young adults and yes, even children. The New Englanders really love their mountains and the network of trails leading through them and to their summits. In spite of the crowded summit, the view was remarkable. Notable was the sweep down the narrow jagged backbone of Franconia Ridge with the AT zigzagging along its crest over Mt. Haystack, Mt. Lincoln and across a narrow col up on Mt. Lafayette where I was standing. To the north, I visually followed the AT as it crossed the north summit of Lafayette and descended out of sight over the distant ridge.

The weather had turned quite warm as I continued across the north peak of Mt. Lafayette and enjoyed one of the best views to date in the White Mountains. By the time I reached the col between Mt. Lafayette and Mt. Garfield, I had consumed most of my water. My plan was to hike to the Garfield Ridge Campsite, but I still had to climb Mt. Garfield and make a long descent into the camping area, and I needed water. Luckily, before beginning the ascent of Garfield, I found a small spring (which was not listed in my guide, nor was it mentioned by the caretaker at Liberty Spring) so I could get a much needed drink and fill one of my canteens. The water flow from the spring was slow so it took a while.

It was late afternoon before I reached the summit of Mt. Garfield, and I was starting to feel the effects of the many strenuous climbs of the day. I was thankful for the little spring that provided me with the added water supply. I always made a point to keep a close watch on my water needs and the supplies available, but this had been a particularly long and difficult section. The rise in temperature had also increased my water consumption. From the summit, I could look back and see the entire length of the Franconia Ridge I had just hiked from Mt. Liberty to Mt. Lafayette—what a remarkable ridge and sight. The steep rough descent from the summit to the campsite just about wiped out my already-fatigued body.

Using my pump and filter, I retrieved my evening water supply from a stream before reaching the campsite, eliminating the necessity of a return trip. I chose to stay in the shelter because it had only one occupant, and I was just too tired to bother pitching the tent. The lone hiker was from Israel and was anxious for company. We spent the evening exchanging information about each of our countries, and I shared many of my experiences on the AT. We were both in our sleeping bags early for a much-needed night's rest.

My next day's hike began with a one-half mile very steep, rugged descent of the remainder of Mt. Garfield to the junction of the Franconia Brook Trail. Ascending this section would have been another challenge. By mid morning I reached the Galehead Hut, the second AMC-operated Hut I had passed in the White Mountains. I stopped for a visit with a member of the hut croo, had a couple of fruit drinks, filled my canteen with water and began the ascent of South Twin Mtn. Hiking traffic continued to be heavy. Some were thru-hikers passing me and racing for Katahdin. I ate my lunch on the summit of South Twin Mtn. (4,902 feet) while admiring the surrounding skyline. After lunch, I descended a short distance and had my first sighting of Spruce Grouse—a pair of marvelous coniferous forest birds that showed little fear of me. There would be many other sightings of these birds along the spruce- and fir-covered ridges of New Hampshire and into the mountains of Maine.

I had a reservation to spend the night at the AMC Zealand Falls Hut with dinner served at 6:00 PM sharp, and I certainly did not want to miss dinner. By 4:45, I arrived at the junction of the Zeacliff Trail, a shortcut down into Zealand Notch cutting off the loop around Zealand Falls. This shortcut was for hikers not planning to make the loop or stay in the hut—but I was staying there and it was about 1 1/2 miles downhill to the hut. I would have to hustle to reach it for dinner. My arrival time was 5:40, giving me a little time to register and prepare for the meal.

While getting ready to eat, I recognized a hiker/worker helping the croo serve the meal. After some memory searching, I remembered him as "The Marathon Man," a hiker I had met at the Davenport Gap Shelter in the Great Smoky Mountains. He was working in the hut with serving and cleanup in exchange for his meal and night's lodging. Many thru-hikers do this while passing through the Whites to keep their expenses to a minimum.

The stay at Zealand Falls was my first hut experience on the AT and a very pleasant one. I was given a warm welcome, had a fabulous meal (all that I could possibly eat), good fellowship and entertainment during the evening and a comfortable bunk for a good night's rest. The breakfast was also hearty (hot oatmeal, eggs and bacon, homemade bread) and included all the coffee and juice I could drink, replacing those liquids I had lost during the last couple of days. I enjoyed the amenities provided at the Zealand Falls Hut and was impressed with its setting beside a striking waterfall.

Crawford Notch was my goal for the next day, and as I set off, the AT descended through Zealand Notch, following the old logging railroad grade beside Whitewall Brook. The sides of the Notch are steep with large rock fields where many giant boulders have tumbled from the mountainside into the old railroad bed and some into the valley below. According to records, this area was heavily timbered during the late 1800's; and the logs were taken out over this old railroad bed. This was followed by a series of forest fires that destroyed the slash and whatever timbers that remained, leaving the exposed and scarred areas found in Zealand Notch and several adjacent peaks. I descended into Crawford Notch, completing what is said to be the longest uninterrupted wilderness section in New Hampshire and Vermont in 2 1/2 days, but wished I could have taken four days because of its superb rugged beauty.

It was 7:45 AM when Joan dropped me off at the little parking lot off US 302 in Crawford Notch to begin my next section, and a very special section it was—the Presidential Range of the White Mountains. As I stood and read the Webster Cliff sign near Saco River, listing the distance to and elevation statistics of the peaks in the southern Presidential Range, that excited yet uneasy feeling came over me. It was the same feeling I had since early on the AT and the one I had before ascending Moosilauke. The brutal storm on the summit of Moosilauke flashed through my mind, as well as the warnings given in the Trail literature regarding the hazards of the range.

This was the Presidential Range—the highest north of the Smoky Mountains in North Carolina. About 12 miles of its ridge crest is alpine terrain above tree line and is subject to rapid and extreme changes in weather. Near the center of this range is Mt. Washington (6,288 feet), claiming a reputation for the worst weather and considered the most dangerous small mountain in the world. Not only are the weather extremes of concern to hikers, but the terrain is extremely rugged with enormous elevation gains from either a north or south approach. According to Ken Kimball, research ecologist for the AMC, there are only about 13 square miles of alpine terrain east of the Mississippi River, and nearly 8 square miles of it are in the Presidentials in New Hampshire.

Here I stood at the foot of the range, ready to tackle this giant; and I was desperately hoping my physical and mental faculties were up to it. My first big hurdle was to ascend out of the Notch up the steep rugged Webster Cliff Trail to the top of Webster Cliffs, forming the east wall of Crawford Notch. It was a hard slow climb to the summit of Mt. Webster (3,910 feet), the first of the six peaks in the southern Presidentials. The ascent along the open ledges of Webster Cliffs provided a panorama of Crawford Notch and the Franconia Range. From the Cliffs, I could see the Willey House and the Willey Slide in and across the Notch. All the members of the Willey family were killed when part of the wall of the Notch slid away in 1826. I continued my ascent of the precipitous cone of Mt. Jackson, and it was on this climb that my trusted hiking staff almost became a casualty. It slipped from my hand and was stopped by a small rock before taking flight into open space over Crawford Notch. Phew!—that was a close one! The cherished staff had been with me since the Shenandoah.

Mt. Jackson (4,050 feet) is the second peak in the southern Presidentials. From its cone, I could look up the range to the Big One—Mt. Washington. While I was eating my lunch on Mt. Jackson, a northbound thru-hiker ("Lone Scout") came by. We had an enjoyable visit and were later joined by the Hutmaster from the AMC Mizpah Hut, which was about 2 miles up the AT and where I would be tenting for the night.

After leaving the summit, I crossed over a newly-constructed puncheon walkway through a tranquil alpine meadow and paused in silent tribute to the AMC and the NPS for the care taken in preserving this special area. By 3:00 PM, I arrived at the Mizpah Hut (the third Hut along the AT) and made arrangements for a tent site for the night. I was assigned to site #4 which was located in a delightful spruce forest. This area, known as Nauman Tentsite, is located near the Hut and is the only tenting area along the AT through the Presidentials.

During the evening, I was visited by a snowshoe rabbit (or Varying Hare), a common sight throughout these northern mountain slopes, yet the first I had seen so far. The weather was clear for the entire day with sunshine and a cool breeze blowing across the ridges, and the stars were sparkling when I retired to my tent. I awakened about 3:00 AM to the pitter-patter of rain on my tent, and I sighed with the realization that I would be packing a wet tent up the ridges all day.

When I peeked out of my tent in the morning, water was dripping from the spruce; and the forest was socked in with fog—it did not look to be a favorable hiking day. Fortunately, I was not planning to hike far, since I had reservations for the night at the Lakes of the Clouds AMC Hut, about five miles up the range. After breaking camp, I ascended in fog to the summit of Mt. Pierce (4,310 feet), the third peak in the southern Presidentials. A misty rain and fog continued to hover around me. I put on my pack cover and a new Gortex rain suit, purchased specifically for such wet, cold, windy weather. I had learned a dear lesson about the extremes in weather in these mountains and the need for proper clothing.

About one-half mile from the summit, a cold hard rain started, driven by high winds. I wondered if I were in for another Moosilauke here in the middle of August. Fortunately, as I ascended higher, the rain and wind subsided. Regrettably, a fog moved in that was so dense I could see only a few feet ahead. These conditions prevailed as I hiked over the summits of Mt. Eisenhower (4,761 feet) and Mt. Franklin (5,004 feet) and along the ridge line to the Lakes of the Clouds Hut.

The dense fog continued and I could not see the Hut until within about 75 feet of it. The Lakes of the Clouds Hut is the fourth along the AT; and, again, I received a warm welcome by the croo. It is a custom of the huts that hikers get one drink (juice, lemonade, coffee, etc.) on the house, and each additional one is at the hiker's expense. I quickly obliged and purchased two extras. I registered and was assigned to Room #1, which would be shared with other guests who arrived later that afternoon. I found places to hang my clothing for drying, but there was no place inside to spread out the tent. Outside conditions certainly were not favorable, so I just left the tent in its bag and hoped for better conditions later.

During the remainder of the afternoon, I visited with croo members and guests, ate some of their great homemade bread and soup and rested. There was nothing to do outside, for the fog continued to firmly embrace the mountain. The Lakes of the Clouds Hut, accommodating up to 90 guests, is located above tree line in a col between Mt. Monroe and Mt. Washington. Additionally, it features a basement room (known to hikers as "The Dungeon"), which is also available to backpackers and is open year-round. Lakes of the Clouds is the largest one in the high hut system and is heavily used because of its close proximity to the summit of Mt. Washington.

Guests continued to arrive until the maximum of 90 was reached, and promptly at 6:00 PM a hearty dinner was served, including all of the coffee, juices and water one could want. I just never could seem to get enough liquids. Again, the dinner was followed by an evening of entertainment and fellowship with guests from more than a dozen states.

One interesting diversion was a demonstration given by the hut croo on the use of their pack frame. Since there are no auto road accesses to the huts, supplies have to be packed in and out. One of the duties of the hut croo is to secure the supplies to a heavy wood pack frame and transport them over the steep rocky trail to the hut from the valley below. Supplies are also carried from the hut to the valley. It was reported that individual members of the croo have packed up to 150 pounds over the terrain—quite an impressive feat.

The Hut accommodations were not hard to get used to in comparison to my little tent or the cold open shelters where I had spent so many nights. The hut was the best system for my hiking in the White Mountains. Otherwise, each night I would have had to descend the ridge, camp somewhere below tree line and then hike back up to the ridge line to continue on my way. Tenting was not permitted above tree line because of weather extremes and protection of the fragile ecosystems.

After a restful night and a breakfast fit for a hiker (or anyone else for that matter), I was ready for another day. I had anticipated this day many times along the AT—I would be crossing over Mt. Washington. When I looked out of the hut, my heart gave a heavy thump, because the weather had not improved. In fact, I could scarcely see which direction the AT headed from the hut. I was aware that Mt. Washington is in clouds about 60% of the time, and it appeared as though my hike over it would fall to the law of averages. After passing the two small lakes near the hut, a sign appeared through the dense grey mist. I was unable to read it until I was within a few feet. "THE AREA AHEAD HAS THE WORST WEATHER IN AMERICA. MANY HAVE DIED THERE FROM EXPOSURE, EVEN IN THE SUMMER. TURN BACK NOW IF THE WEATHER IS BAD. "I thought, "Oh boy! Here we go with the weather again, but it's not too cold and the wind isn't too strong…but then this is at the base of the cone— the summit is another 1,200 feet up. Oh boy!" I considered that I was better equipped than when I crossed Moosilauke, and I felt confident that my clothing was adequate for the challenge.

I ascended the cone on Crawford Path which I had been following since Mt. Pierce. As usual, the higher I climbed, the colder and stronger the wind. Part way up the cone, I passed a wooden cross lurking in the rocks marking the spot (as a grim reminder of how unforgiving the mountain can be) where a hiker had perished in a storm. According to the history of the mountain, dozens have died because they misjudged its weather extremes and the difficulty of negotiating its rugged terrain. I stopped for a break and to take a picture of the cross through the fog.

Shortly, a member of the hut croo from Lakes of the Clouds came along ascending the AT behind me. His pack was laden with what he said were records from the hut. He never told me how much weight he was carrying, but he had a load! In this case, he was making the trek to the summit of Mt. Washington where the nearest access road was.

To my surprise, the temperature seemed to remain the same; however, the wind speed increased significantly. When I crested, I could not believe it as the weather was much better than I had anticipated even though there was a dense fog with a strong wind. There are a number of buildings on the summit including the Adams Building which houses a Post Office, food service, the observatory and the Mt. Washington Museum. The oldest building on the summit is the Tip Top House, an old hotel built in the mid-1800's. There are other buildings not open to the public. I went to the Adams Building and checked the wind speed (40 MPH) and the temperature (52 degrees Fahrenheit). I had definitely hit Mt. Washington on one of those 60% cloud-cover days, but the weather was better than it might have been. I would be back later on a clear day to fully enjoy the spectacle of this great mountain. I was surprised to see so many people on the summit during these weather conditions. Most had come up on the Cog Railroad, had driven or had taken the Stage vans up the Auto Road. I got the usual curious looks and questions such as: "Did you carry that pack up here in this weather? How heavy is your pack? How far are you going?"

I stayed for a short while and descended the Gulfside Trail which would take me across the northern Presidentials to the Madison Springs Hut—my destination for the day. Foggy conditions continued on my descent crossing the Mt. Washington Cog Railroad tracks and into a col between Mt. Washington and Mt. Clay (the first peak in the northern Presidentials). By the time I reached the col, the fog was clearing from the lower peaks and valleys. The view into an area known as the Great Gulf Wilderness, a deep ravine between Mt. Washington and the peaks of the northern Presidentials, was magnificent—what a sight! The clouds still held a firm grip on the cone of Mt. Washington as I looked back from an area known as Monticello Lawn near Mt. Jefferson.

It was lunch time, and I found a high perch on a large boulder where I could eat and enjoy this fascinating landscape. As I looked across these rugged ridges and valleys, I thought of Nathaniel Hawthorne's description of this magnificent range when he wrote: "The White Mountains and particularly the Presidential Range are majestic and even awful, when contemplated in a proper mood, yet their breadth of base and the long ridges which support them, give the idea of immense bulk rather than height."

Before leaving my lofty perch, I glanced back toward Mt. Washington and, lo and behold, the mountain had completely cleared, exposing a man-made skyline of buildings and towers, with smoke billowing from the old steam engine on the Cog Railroad. The Mt. Washington Auto Road was also visible, winding and switchbacking its 8-mile course from the summit into the valley. I could even see flashes from the sun reflecting on car windshields as they descended the Auto Road.

I continued my hike through immense rock fields to an area known as Thunderhead Junction near the summit of Mt. Adams (5,798 feet) and was impressed with the massive 10-foot rock cairn at the Junction. On my descent of the flank of Mt. Adams, I was astounded by the Craiggy King Ravine to the north extending into the valley and the sharp-pointed Mt. Madison ahead projecting from the mountain crest like the Great Pyramid of Egypt. I had never seen such rocky terrain—all of the areas above tree line looked more like the Rocky Mountains than the White Mountains. The AT meandered over, around and through large fields of jumbled boulders of all sizes.

What continued to amaze me were the hundreds of people I met along the AT while crossing the range. Most of these were day-hikers and not very well-equipped for the rugged terrain and changing weather environment. Many were wearing tennis-type shoes with no ankle support whatsoever, and I am surprised there are not more injuries in terrain like this.

I arrived at the Madison Springs AMC Hut (where I had reservations for the night) at 4:30. I had carried a wet tent across most of the range, and this gave me enough time before dinner to spread it out to dry on the rocks nearby. The 50-capacity hut filled up with guests before the 6:00 meal. Again, everyone was served excellent food and drink along with great entertainment. Dawn broke bright and clear the following morning, as the hut croo gave everyone a phenomenal send-off breakfast.

After ascending the sharp-pointed summit of Mt. Madison, I had an outstanding panorama of Mt. Washington, the Great Gulf Wilderness and the northern Presidential Range. Also visible was the long Osgood Ridge which was lined with rock cairns, diminishing in size until they were out of sight. This was the route the AT would follow from the mountain summit into the valley. I descended the long rocky backbone of Osgood Ridge following the cairns to the tree line and eventually reached the Osgood Tenting Area in the Great Gulf Wilderness Valley. There was a significant temperature increase in the valley; in fact, it reached the mid-70's. About a mile before reaching the Mt. Washington Auto Road, I could tell I was near it because I could smell overheated brakes from the vehicles making the long steep descent. I crossed the road and descended into Pinkham Notch to the AMC Visitor Center where Joan was waiting for me. I was elated at having completed one of the most rugged and picturesque sections along the entire AT and could now put to rest the uneasy feeling I had about it. I would not have missed, for anything in the world, the experience of traversing this magnificent range—its beauty and grandeur is etched in my memory forever.

I had lugged my big Kelty pack through the Presidentials, but for the next 20-mile section crossing the Carter-Moriah Range of the Whites from Pinkham Notch to the Androscoggin River, I planned to carry my small pack and make an overnight stay at the AMC Carter Notch Hut. Reviewing my guidebook and profile map showed the section to be no breeze by any standards. Even though the peaks do not compare in elevation to the Presidentials, there are twelve peaks over 4,000 feet, plus the deep spectacular Carter Notch. In addition, there is a 2,000-foot (in two miles) climb up Wildcat Ridge out of Pinkham Notch, with many of the ascents over exposed rock ledges. The guidebook recommends three days to traverse this section, but I wanted to try it in two.

The climb out of the Notch was quite steep and rugged with ascents over some of the ledges on steps. This could be very treacherous, especially during times of wet snow or icy conditions. However, the ledges did provide outstanding panoramas of the entire Pinkham Notch, Ellis River area and the Presidential Range across the Notch. After reaching Wildcat Ridge (4,041 feet), I passed the Gondola Terminal building for the Wildcat Ridge ski trails, the only ski facility the AT passes through in the White Mountains. I stopped for a break on the observation deck and visited with some tourists. They had ridden the tram car to the summit to be at the finish line for a group of marathon runners who were finishing their race there that morning. I did not wait for the finish but continued up Wildcat Ridge, meeting many hikers going in both directions—men and women from young adults to seniors. I continued to be amazed that there were so many people along the Trail in these mountains. In parts of Virginia, I hiked for as long as three or four days without seeing a person.

I continued on up the ridge, crossing over what is referred to as the Wildcat Kitten (peaks E, D, C, and B). All of them range in elevation from 4,000 to over 4,400 feet and have beautiful, lush, spruce-covered summits, quite a contrast from the rocky treeless summits of the Presidentials. The last and highest is Wildcat Mtn., (4,422 feet). From an open ledge, I could look 1,000 feet down directly into Carter Notch upon the rooftops of the Carter Notch Hut facility and the two small lakes nearby. This was an ideal setting for lunch, so I took advantage and enjoyed the view of Carter Dome Mtn. and the Carter-Moriah Range across the Notch, terrain I would be hiking the following day.

After registering, I spent the rest of the afternoon exploring this marvelous area. There are two Carter Ponds surrounded by a mixed forest on three sides and the 1,000-foot vertical cliffs of Wildcat Mtn. on the other. A jumble of large boulders near the hut provide a rugged wilderness setting. The hut croo was very congenial and provided meals and services of the same quality I had received in the previous huts.

The Trail beckoned me immediately after breakfast the following morning. I did not even stay for the after-meal entertainment, because I had a rugged 15 miles ahead and company arriving in the afternoon at our base camp near Gorham. We had made arrangements for my niece and her husband (Jeanne and Charlie Moses—Jeanne is my brother Osbra's daughter) to join me in hiking the Mahoosuc Range (my next section), extending from Gorham, NH, to Grafton Notch, ME. I wanted to try to hike out before their expected late afternoon arrival. After leaving the hut, I passed the two tranquil lakes nestled down in the Notch and vowed to return to this secluded valley after completing my hike.

The ascent of Carter Dome was my first challenge and the highest of the eight peaks I would cross during the day. From an open ledge, I had an outstanding southern view of Carter Notch and the cliffs of the north wall of Wildcat Mtn. It was from this vantage point on a later hike that Charlie and I watched a helicopter land on the roof of the Carter Notch Hut on a resupply mission. It took one hour to climb out of the Notch to the rounded summit of Carter Dome (4,832 feet). The spruce-covered summit has one vantage point where the views are reasonably good, but the best was yet to come.

The summit of Mt. Hight (4,675 feet) is one mile further along the AT, and "The Wonderful World" poem flashed to mind and is certainly in order here. The summit is open, and the view ranks with the best—to the west across Pinkham Notch was the complete majestic Presidential Range with Mt. Washington rising above all, flanked by its subordinates; to the south was the king of this range—Carter Dome; to the north was the Carter Range to Mt. Moriah; and to the east was the Wild River area and Maine. Providing a 360-degree panorama, this mountain top impressed me so much that I would return a year later for another visit to the area.

After leaving Mt. Hight, I ascended and crossed South Carter (4,458 feet), Mt. Lithe (4,584 feet) and North Carter (4,530 feet), which were mostly spruce-covered plush green with masses of ferns, but with limited views. The descent from North Carter Mtn.

to Stony Brook was a joint pounder and a challenge to wits and nerves. This section demanded extreme caution. So it goes with the AT—variety is what the Trail offers. There are rough, rougher, and still rougher areas like this one. And there would be more sections ahead, posing even greater challenge.

After a lunch break at the AMC Imp Shelter at the foot of North Carter Mtn., I began the ascent of Mt. Moriah. The AT crosses up and over many exposed rock ledges from which I had more spectacular vistas of the northern Presidentials, including Mt. Adams and Mt. Madison. Visible also were Carter peak which I had just crossed and Carter Dome further south. From near the summit of Mt. Moriah (4,049 feet), the AT follows along many more hundreds of feet of puncheon walkway installed by the NPS and AMC to help maintain the pristine beauty of these high ridges. The delicate mosses and ferns on the forest floor grow right up to the edges of these walkways and have been spared the damage caused in so many areas along the AT from heavy hiker traffic.

The AT follows the Carter-Moriah Trail from Carter Notch to where it joins the Rattle River Trail on the shoulder of Middle Moriah Mtn. There were a lot of fresh moose tracks near the Junction Trail to Rattle River, but these great animals apparently preferred to stay under cover of the forest while I passed. I had been seeing their tracks in several locations through the Whites but had not had a moose sighting since Moosilauke. I descended Mt. Moriah to the Rattle River and stopped briefly at the shelter for a snack and a short rest.

Soon after leaving the shelter, I had a very pleasant surprise— Charlie had hiked up the AT from the trailhead near Gorham to meet me. He and Jeanne had arrived earlier than we expected. After a warm greeting, he gave me a good cold drink of water he had brought for me and—best of all—he said, "Chief" (he always calls me Chief), "give me your pack. I'm carrying it out for you. I need to practice for the Mahoosuc's." How could I refuse him? After all, he had hiked up the AT to greet me and bring me a cold drink. Besides, I had had a long hard day, and I needed the break. We hiked out at the trailhead on US 2 by 5:15 completing the Carter-Moriah Range.

I hiked this range in two days but, as I have said so many times along the AT, I wished I had taken more time. Its twelve 4,000-plus footers—some with open rocky pinnacles and some with plush green coniferous trees—along with the deep wild rugged Carter Notch, were challenging and impressive. In fact, I was so impressed that I returned a year later and brought Jeanne and Charlie with me to rehike some of the section.

TOP: Franconia Ridge in the White Mountains of
New Hampshire as viewed from Mt. Wolf
BOTTOM: The AT meandering along Franconia Ridge
as viewed from the summit of Mt. Lafayette with Mt.
Liberty and Mt. Flume in the distance

TOP: Herb's tent and backpack on platform at
Nauman Tentsite near Mizpah AMC Hut
BOTTOM: Mt. Madison in the northern Presidentials.
Note the Madison Springs Hut in the col.

TOP: The Presidential Range of the White Mountains
as viewed from Mt. Hight.
BOTTOM: The Grey Jay, or Canada Jay, sometimes
known as "Camp Robber," on Middle Carter Mtn.

12

THE TOUGHEST MILE AND BEYOND

"Scholars claim the earth is round but I'm convinced its
up and down." — Bill Leffler ("The Poet")
(From a shelter register on his AT thru-hike)

Originally, I had made arrangements with Charlie and Jeanne to hike part of the Presidentials with me, but their work schedules conflicted with the time I would be passing through them. The only time their schedules and mine coincided was when I would be going through the Mahoosuc's, and this caused me some concern. I had read literature, studied the maps and sent them copies of all the information I had about the area. I knew it would be a very difficult section and wanted them to be properly informed and prepared, yet, I tried to be careful not to discourage them. We had talked on several occasions, and I advised them about proper conditioning and equipment selection. They seemed confident that their equipment was adequate and that their regular exercise and conditioning programs had prepared them.

I took the next day to rest, resupply and review the hiking plan of the Mahoosuc's with Charlie and Jeanne. She said this hike meant a lot to her because her Dad, Osbra, had wanted her to hike with him but she was never able to work it into her schedule and had regrets about this. She felt that hiking with me would help in the healing process.

The AT traverses the rugged northeast-southwest Mahoosuc Range extending from the Androscoggin River near Gorham, NH, to Grafton Notch, ME, and is a 31-mile section. Due to its roughness and major elevation changes, the ATC Guidebook recommended planning 3-5 days. I had planned four, and this was acceptable to them. I spaced the hike with two shorter days at the end of the section where the AT traverses the infamous Mahoosuc Notch. I had long been aware of and heard horror stories about this landmark with a reputation for challenge.

Our base camp was located about three miles from the trailhead near the Shelburne Birches along Rt. 2 east of Gorham. As we ascended Mt. Hayes (the first mountain) out of the Androscoggin Valley, that anxious feeling continued to plague me about Charlie and Jeanne hiking this section with me. Neither of them had ever hiked anywhere on the AT, and I would rather they had their first exposure on an easier section further south, perhaps in Virginia. It was great having them hike with me and I very much wanted them to enjoy their initial AT experience, hoping they would perhaps want to join me again in the future to hike other sections or trails.

I was far enough along in my hike that I was in good physical condition. The White Mountains had seen to that, so the ascent of Mt. Hayes (2,555 feet) was a relatively easy climb for me. I had backed off my usual pace to give them some conditioning time. They completed the ascent capably, but Jeanne (who was prone to foot problems) was keeping a close check on her feet. Our first day's hike of about 12 miles into the Gentian Pond Campsite went fairly well; however, Jeanne started developing some foot problems. I had advised them before beginning the section to try to keep their pack weights to a minimum, especially so in Jeanne's case due to this medical problem.

We pitched our tents on adjacent platforms and enjoyed a hot meal and evening of fellowship. I reviewed with them the next day's hiking plan, literature on the section and the Trail profile map. I told them to be prepared for a pretty strenuous day, because the most difficult sections lay ahead of us. We all retired rather early; and as I lay listening to the brisk wind that had picked up and was whipping our tents, I hoped the weather would remain favorable and that everything would go well. It was hard for me to shake the feeling of concern, because I felt a sense of responsibility for whatever might come to pass.

We were on the Trail early the following morning, facing a more rugged section of Trail, and this was a special day for all of us. It was Charlie and Jeanne's 20th wedding anniversary, and it was the day I would be crossing into Maine—my fourteenth and last state on the AT. We all had a fairly good night's rest and were moving along quite well toward the Maine/New Hampshire state line. As we crossed over the summit of Mt. Success (3,565 feet), we hiked into fog and wet conditions; but the sun quickly burned through the heavy overcast and fine weather promised a great hiking day.

Near the summit of the mountain, we were overtaken by a 72-year-old thru-hiker whose name was Bill Leffler ("The Poet") from Lima, Ohio. He had started at the Tyringham Valley in Massachusetts in July, a point he had hiked to the previous year, and was planning to complete the Trail in late September. He said he would hike on to the state line and wait for us there so we could take his picture at the state marker.

Jeanne developed more problems with her feet on the descent of Mt. Success; and to complicate matters, Charlie sprained his knee while climbing down a rock drop-off near the junction of the Mt. Success Trail. When we arrived at the state line, "The Poet" was waiting for us to take his picture as promised. We decided to take a lunch and rest break. Jeanne attempted to get her feet doctored up while Charlie was trying to get the stiffness worked out of his knee. During the morning, we had talked with a couple of southbounders who said there was a large group of college students ahead of us near Goose Eye Mtn. headed for the Full Goose Shelter to camp for the night. This was our planned destination for the day, and we wondered if there would be any space left for us. "The Poet" said he would move on to the shelter, which was also his goal for the day, and that he would see us there.

With my concern about Charlie and Jeanne's physical problems, I had not had a chance until after lunch to reflect on my hike through New Hampshire. I was in Maine now—another milestone—and reality started to impact on me. This was my last state and where the journey would end. Maine is the state where the northern terminus of the AT is—Mt. Katahdin. At last—it had been so long since Georgia! The sign at the NH/ME state line indicated that Mt. Katahdin was 276 miles away. The distance was sounding more and more manageable. New Hampshire was behind me now, but it had left me with memories I would never forget. The White Mountains were truly majestic. Their ruggedness and grandeur had provided me with a hiking experience unlike any I had so far on the AT. My uneasiness about hiking through them was relieved. I had learned to respect their moods and temperaments and to use good judgment in crossing their lofty peaks.

Charlie had developed a noticeable limp, and Jeanne's foot problems continued as we crossed Mt. Carlo and began the Goose Eye section. Their hiking pace had been greatly reduced, and my level of concern steadily increased. It was mid afternoon, we still had to cross three mountains known as the Gooses (West Peak, East Peak and North Peak), and the terrain was rugged. The last hundred feet or so up West Peak (3,860 feet) was on a rickety ladder over a cliff that gave me concern for my personal safety, and even more for Jeanne and Charlie. Relieved, we all made it up the ladder okay and then stretched out on the rocks of the open summit to rest, snack, get a drink and enjoy a breathtaking view of the wild and rugged Mahoosuc Range. This range of mountains is ranked among the most difficult along the entire AT, and we were starting into the most strenuous segment.

After our break, we descended into a low sag and climbed the exposed rock face of East Peak (3,794 feet). By the time we reached the summit, Jeanne and Charlie were having a lot of pain and had to slow their pace significantly. One mountain and two miles lay between the three of us and Full Goose Campsite. We had met about 20 northbound hikers headed for that location, and we had no idea how many southbounders were headed there as well. We considered that we might be forced to establish our own campsite somewhere in the vicinity, as it appeared we might arrive late to find a full camp. We made a decision that I should hike ahead to the camp and stake a claim to a spot before all of the sites were taken—even then, we feared that none would be available. As I set off, I wondered if Jeanne and Charlie would be able to make the last two miles. I thought if the camp were full, I would set up a site nearby and return for my hiking companions if they did not arrive within a reasonable time.

When I reached the shelter, I did find a full camp. The Full Goose Shelter was bursting at the seams with the college group, and tents were set up on every level spot in the area and on every tent platform except one. But then came that Trail Magic again. "The Poet," who had set his tent on one of the platforms, called me over and said, "That empty platform is yours to share with Jeanne and Charlie." He had placed his pack on it to hold it for us and told the college kids who kept asking about it that we were hiking with him. I told him I was grateful and that it was a kind gesture on his part, since the college group had left no spaces for thru-hikers. He replied that he knew Charlie and Jeanne needed a level place to sleep and that he was concerned about them. Our feelings were certainly mutual. I quickly set up my tent, spread out my mattress and sleeping bag, went to the spring for our night's water supply and heated some water to have soup and hot drinks ready for them.

I was hoping they would arrive by the time the water was hot. They would certainly be exhausted and hot food would be in order. I kept waiting, but they never arrived. Finally, I told "The Poet" I would give them another 15 minutes and if they did not arrive, I was going in search of them. An hour after I reached camp, with darkness approaching rapidly, Jeanne and Charlie were still not in. I grabbed my flashlight and told "The Poet" I was going to look for them. Without my pack, I moved along rapidly out of the col and began the ascent of Goose Eye Mtn. I was thinking all the time, "Oh boy, what have I done now?" I felt totally responsible for putting them in a situation like this, where their safety may be in jeopardy.

I called Charlie's name every hundred feet or so as I climbed the Mountain. Receiving no response, I began to think perhaps they had not gone very far from where I left them, about two miles from camp. It was getting later, the sun had sunk below the horizon, and the shadow of the mountain was darkening the woods. I was determined to keep going back and calling until I found them, even if darkness overtook me. A lot was going through my mind—we were in the middle of the Mahoosuc Range. What if their injuries prohibited them from walking? What about the hike through the difficult Mahoosuc Notch? Would they be able to meet its challenge? Every hundred feet or so, I called "Charlie! C-H-A-R-L-I-E!" Finally, I heard a faint reply from up the mountain, almost out of hearing. I said, "Thank God," and speeded up my pace to a run.

When we reconnected, I was extremely grateful to find that they were relatively okay and still moving, even if their pace was slow. They had been about ready to pitch their tent by the Trail for the night, but were having trouble finding a spot that was level enough. I told them that our campsite was prepared and that we must move along as rapidly as possible, so total darkness would not catch us. I took Jeanne's pack and sent her on ahead, telling her we had about a mile to camp, that my tent was set up with the bed already made, and for her to lie down when she got there. We arrived just as it was getting dark, and Charlie and I set up their tent right by mine while Jeanne was caring for her sore feet.

A good hot meal, lots of water and our fellowship together seemed to heal the struggles and hardships of the day. We sat there together reflecting over our day's hike across the rugged, yet beautiful, range and were thankful that Trail Magic was alive and well. They had made it through okay. I said, "Happy Anniversary, Guys," and Jeanne replied, "Thanks, Uncle Herb. This is one we will never forget." We then retired to our tents for a peaceful and well-earned night's rest.

The next morning, Charlie and Jeanne's physical problems seemed to show marked improvement, and I was glad because this day's hike would make major demands on joints, muscles and willpower. We would cross the Mahoosuc Notch, said to be the most difficult mile on the entire AT. As if this were not enough, the climb out of the Notch up what is known as Mahoosuc Arm was rumored to consume any energy one might have left. As we were leaving the shelter, we were approached by some of the college students who had spent the night there. They had read some of the horror stories written in the shelter journal by some who had previously hiked the Notch and asked, "Aren't you afraid to go in that awful place?" We told them we were not afraid to tackle it, and that if others had made it we could, too. Our hiking friend, "The Poet," had left earlier and told us he would see us later in the day at the Speck Pond Campsite, our next camp location.

We left the shelter, hiked across Fulling Mills Mtn. and descended into the west end of Mahoosuc Notch. The AT traverses through this one-mile glacially-carved valley, filled with a jumble of huge boulders that have tumbled from the sheer cliffs on each side. This rugged natural phenomenon is listed in the National Registry of Natural Landmarks and is an area I had long looked forward to seeing and hiking through.

I had read comments made by previous well-known thru-hikers about the Notch in the book, *Hiking the Appalachian Trail, Volume One* by James R. Hare. Dorothy Laker (1957 thru-hiker) writes: "This famous Notch which might be called Nightmare Alley was a channel between two steep walls jammed with giant boulders tossed one on top of the other. It was a very strenuous part of the Trail, very time-consuming, very dangerous and very hard on gear and the seat of the pants. I had a horrible time, absolutely awful. At one point, I lay down on the rocks and cried. I took hours to go the one mile through the Notch."

Howard E. Bassett (1968 thru-hiker) writes: "This certainly was the roughest and most dangerous section of the entire Appalachian Trail. One mishap here—but I tried not to think of what could happen. You won't find many spots like this and believe me it is no place for a novice to hike." Elmer L. Onstatt (1968-1969 thru-hiker) writes: "For me the Mahoosuc Notch was the most time-consuming mile on the entire Appalachian Trail. I spent 3 hours going through it under good weather conditions."

So here we were, at the west gateway to this new AT challenge. I asked Charlie and Jeanne if they were ready for this test of stamina, and they assured me they were. Our journey through the Notch went very well, with only a couple of scrapes. Jeanne took the middle position, with me leading and Charlie bringing up the rear. That way, we could assist her from the front and back. She is not very tall, and the 6-10-foot drop-offs from the huge boulders posed a greater difficulty for her.

Near the middle of the Notch, we saw a southbound hiker approaching. As he got closer, we realized it was "The Poet." We thought he was coming back to check on Charlie and Jeanne, as he had shown much concern for them the day before. He asked us, "Are you going in the right direction?" I immediately realized he had become disoriented in the maze of rock boulders and was headed back south. I assured him that we were heading north, and he joined us to complete the scramble the rest of the way through the Notch. We felt good that we came along when we did, eliminating a lot of unnecessary rough hiking for him. We were thus able to return the favor he did for us the day before.

We made the trip through in two hours and twenty minutes— not bad! I commended Charlie and Jeanne on how well they had done, and Jeanne said it was "scary" and the most difficult physical challenge she had ever completed. We took an extended break at the east end of the Notch, reflecting on its rugged beauty and our journey through it.

Now we faced the second major hurdle in this valley—the climb up the almost vertical 1,500-foot Mahoosuc Arm. It took us almost two hours to make the ascent out of the Notch to the summit of the Arm and, in my estimation, this climb was as difficult as the journey through the Notch. Charlie and Jeanne did remarkably well on this rugged climb, as well.

The weather on the summit was cold, with a heavy overcast and strong wind blowing. These conditions continued until we arrived at the Speck Pond Campsite, and then a cold drizzle started. "The Poet" had hiked ahead of us after resting on Mahoosuc Arm and had pitched his tent on a platform near ours. The drizzle changed to a more general steady pelting rain, with the strong cold wind blowing across the pad and around our tents.

Speck Pond, a beautiful remote tarn nestled between Mahoosuc Arm Mtn. and Old Speck Mtn. with an elevation of about 3,400 feet, is one of the highest in the state of Maine. What a lovely spot for a campsite, but the cold dreary weather prohibited our exploring the area. We were confined to our tents for the remainder of the afternoon and evening.

This was our last night out together, so we combined our food resources for a great evening meal. Jeanne prepared a large serving of chicken herb rice, and we all sat Indian style in a circle in their tent. We reflected on our hike through this rugged range and were thankful we could share this experience together. They said they had underestimated the difficulty of the Mahoosucs and that their conditioning was not commensurate with the physical demands required in this section. I assured them they had done remarkably well, considering that seasoned hikers tell of the struggles they had in this range. They said they were determined to meet the challenge of this hike by successfully completing it, and that out of their struggle had come a rededication and even tighter bond in their relationship to each other. Jeanne also said that this hike had helped her fulfill a need that she had missed with her father, to hike on the Appalachian Trail. My reply was that— yes, this is that "Trail Magic" that happens along this great footpath.

The next day was our last hiking day together on this trip, and we were up early, packing wet gear from the night's rain. My pack thermometer measured 38 degrees Fahrenheit, and there was a strong cold wind blowing across Speck Pond, whipping the spruce trees back and forth. We had one mountain to cross—Old

Speck (4,180 feet), the highest in the Mahoosuc Range. We ascended to an alpine meadow below the summit of Old Speck where we hit fog, a cold mist and strong winds. On a clear day, the summit of Old Speck would have been visible from this alpine area, but today all we could see was where the mountain disappeared into a swirling mass of grey mist.

We donned our rain gear to help break the force of the wind and began the ascent of Old Speck Cone. I placed Jeanne close behind me with Charlie directly behind her, because I knew we had exposed rocky ledges to climb. I wanted us in close formation in case the force of the wind caused her to lose footing. The higher we climbed, the more fierce the wind. It seemed as though the full force of it was hitting us directly, and we had no cover. I was beginning to have flashbacks from Moosilauke, and I was stunned by how violent the weather had become. I told Charlie and Jeanne to hang on, that the distance over the summit was short, then we could drop into the cover of the trees out of the brutal wind. Once over the summit and into the trees, we plopped down, nearly exhausted. It had taken most of our strength just to stay upright.

After catching our breath, I asked, "What did you think of that climb, Guys?" Jeanne's reply was one I had heard before, "That was scary." I would have to agree—things did get serious there for a while, but I told them it was all downhill from this point into Grafton Notch—all 3.5 steep miles of it.

Before we finished our break, we were joined by "The Poet" who said he would hike out with us and from there go into Bethel for supplies. I told him Joan was picking us up in Grafton Notch and that we would drive him into Bethel. After descending about half way down the mountain, Jeanne started to have problems with her feet again. The long downhill was doing a number on her toes. We stopped for lunch at the junction of the Eyebrow Trail and shared our lunch with "The Poet," who had exhausted his food supply.

While we were eating lunch, I said to "The Poet" that he must have been given that Trail name because of some poetic talents. Might he have some lines to share with us? He said that he did and recited the following (which he acknowledged came from a shelter journal): "Scholars claim the Earth is round, but I'm convinced it's up and down." That brought a chuckle from all of us.

Jeanne doctored her feet and we moved on. I told them to take their time while I hiked out to meet Joan, who I suspected would be there waiting for us. Shortly after I reached Grafton Notch, "The Poet" arrived. He very quickly took off his pack and asked if I would keep an eye on it. He was going back to get Jeanne's pack, as she was having major problems. I told him to give her time, that I was sure she would want to finish the hike carrying her own pack, but he insisted that he was going anyway. About fifteen minutes later, as predicted, here came all three of them, including Jeanne with her pack. She and Charlie were elated— they had completed the Mahoosuc Range from Gorham to Grafton Notch, and they assured me they would be back and better prepared the next time. They shared many of their leftover supplies with "The Poet," as he needed to resupply for his trek on north. We drove him into Bethel where he planned to rest a day or two, purchase more supplies and continue his hike to Katahdin.

Before leaving him, I told him I would be along later on my journey on the AT and that I would probably see him again along the way. During the following several weeks, I watched shelter journals, talked to hikers, but never saw or heard from him again on the Trail. However, I have since learned that he completed his hike on September 20.

It sure was great to have had Charlie and Jeanne hike a part of the AT with me, despite a lot of anxious moments regarding their health and safety. They had certainly risen to the occasion and were so moved by this hike and the mountains of Maine and New Hampshire that they would return the following year in top form to hike with me on some of the outstanding peaks, including Mt. Washington.

After taking an R & R day to resupply and recover from the stresses of the Mahoosucs and the Whites, I returned to Grafton Notch to continue my journey. This Notch is another one of those spectacular deep valleys characteristic of the White Mountains and the mountains of western Maine. The area where the AT crosses the Notch is within the Grafton Notch State Park, where impressive 1,000-foot cliffs make this another outstanding natural wonder for hikers along the AT as well as for travelers driving through on ME 26. The 278-mile section of the AT from Grafton Notch to Mt. Katahdin is under the Maine Appalachian Trail Club (MATC) maintenance jurisdiction.

It was another cloudy cool morning when I left Grafton Notch on my climb up Baldpate Mtn. This was MATC territory, and I was impressed with the Trail condition out of the Notch and more so when I reached the Baldpate Shelter, a relatively new, very well-constructed and maintained facility. I visited with two lady hikers who had spent the night in the shelter and had a long talk with one whose name was Karen Robinson ("Trail Snail"). She gave me a lot of information about the AT in Maine and areas along the AT that the MATC had upgraded or planned to in the near future. I left with the impression that the MATC was a very active and committed Trail Club.

When I approached the summit of the West Peak of the Baldpates, I started to reach the fog line and realized that both the West and East Peaks would probably be under fog cover. This was disappointing, because the literature had noted that great views of the Mahoosucs and western Maine mountains and valleys were visible from these peaks, especially from the East Peak. On the summit of West Peak, looking through the fog across the col, I could barely see the lower exposed granite ledges of the East Peak. I crossed the col and climbed up the open ledges through the cloud layers, and it gave me the sensation of being out in space; but I could see nothing. I reached the top ledges on the summit of East Peak (3,820 feet) and could see only two or three grey forms of rock cairns marking the AT path across its flat open summit. I was very impressed with the beauty and the alpine environment on this mountain, even in the fog.

My stay on the mountain was brief due to the weather, so I descended the steep open granite face on the east side of the mountain to tree line. The east face was similar to its west face with its steep smooth granite ledges, which were easier to descend by sliding on the seat of my pants. I hiked into a deep ravine known as Frye Notch and had lunch near the shelter.

After lunch, I climbed out of the Notch over Surplus Mtn. and descended for about 3 1/2 miles to another geological wonder—Dunn Notch. This is a deep narrow gorge where the West Branch of the Ellis River plunges over a high waterfall into the boulder-strewn ravine. Had I had more time, I would have hiked down into it for a better view of the waterfalls and cascades. After crossing Ellis River above the high falls, the AT follows the rim of the gorge for some distance where sections of it can be viewed from overlooks. About one-half mile from the last overlook, I reached East B Hill Road, completing the day's hike.

There was a feel of autumn in the air when I left the trailhead to hike the Wyman Mtn. section near the village of Andover, Maine. The weeds along the AT were showing shades of brown and yellow, indicating that their life cycles were completed, and the cool crisp air gave the Maine woods a sweet smell of freshness. One of the great pleasures I have had while hiking through New Hampshire and here in Maine is witnessing the pristine beauty of the northern forest and landscape. The collective beauty—of its wetlands, its back country lakes and ponds lined with spruce and hardwood reflecting in the crystal clear water, its sphagnum bogs with their complex ecosystems, its spruce- and fir-covered peaks—is glorious.

After leaving East B Hill Road, I passed Surplus Pond. Each time I pass one of these bodies of water, I pause to sniff the freshness in the air, pan across the peaceful waters and find a place to sit and daydream. They are absolute delights. I ascended to the summit of Wyman Mtn. and sighted more Spruce Grouse. I had been seeing these birds nearly every day, and I noticed that they behaved like the chickens we used to have on the farm—they seemed so tame you could almost pick them up. I had been seeing another bird that also showed little fear of me—the Grey Jay or Canada Jay, which is similar in size to its relative, the Blue Jay. I had seen several pairs of them, and they literally would light on a tree branch at arm's length as I passed by. My sightings of these marvelous birds had been at higher elevations in coniferous forests.

I had lunch at the Hall Mtn. Shelter, located just over the crest of Wyman Mtn., and then descended very steeply into the deep Sawyer Notch. Before reaching Sawyer Brook, which is at the floor of the Notch, I met a southbound hiker ("Mr. Miserable") who was finishing up a few segments of the AT that he lacked to complete the entire length. He gave me information about the Crocker and Saddleback Ranges that I would be hiking over in a couple of days, advising that I allow about four days to hike the area due to its rugged terrain.

Sawyer Notch is a 1,100-foot deep valley, and the AT follows a near vertical course up Moody Mtn. If that is not enough, when you get to the top of Moody, you are faced with the same back down into Black Brook Notch. Moody Mtn.—or as hikers refer to it, The Unnecessary Mountain—has several features hikers do not like: straight up, straight down, no views and yellow jackets. The accuracy of this statement was not contested by me. On the positive side, it did give me a good workout.

South Arm Road in Black Brook Notch was the trailhead pick up point; and when I hiked out, Joan was waiting for me. I took off my pack and my shoes and we were sitting on the tailgate of the truck talking (as we had often done) when a southbound hiker came off the hill into the road looking like he was about ready to call it a day. His name was Todd Schaffer ("The Outlaw") from Medina, Ohio (not far from our home). He told us his goal for the day was the Hall Mtn. Shelter where I had my lunch, about 3 1/2 miles from this trailhead. He said he was not sure if he were up to any more mileage that day. I said, "Todd, if this will help you decide, you have Moody Mtn. to cross. From here to the summit is 1 1/2 miles straight up. You have one mile straight down to Sawyer Notch and one mile straight back up to the shelter. Now, you have other options. You could camp here by Black Brook, you could hike 3 1/2 miles to Hall Mtn., or Joan said you could load your pack and yourself into the back of our truck and spend the night with us at our campsite. I will be back here in the morning to continue north, and you can come along and continue south." (It is characteristic of Joan to have a soft spot and extend a hand to hikers.) It only took him a couple of minutes to decide to go with us.

Todd got in the truck with his pack, and I told him we would be stopping in Andover (population, 470) at Addie's Place to buy one of her pies that I had heard so much about from other hikers. Joan and I had stopped there the day before, but it was Sunday—the one day she is closed. We did stop with Todd—out of luck again—she had sold all of her pies. She apologized and asked if we would sign her register which she keeps for all hikers who pass through.

On the following morning, Joan took us to the trailhead, where Todd continued southbound and I began my northbound hike through the Bemis Range. The state of Maine was experiencing a drought, and we were advised that this was the driest it had been in 25 years. I had been noticing that smaller streams along the AT which I am certain ordinarily have water in them had dry beds, and many of the bog areas were either dry or barely moist. This was probably why I had not been seeing moose. I suspect they had sought out a more favorable habitat, such as back country ponds, lakes and marshy areas. I took care to carry enough water to reach the Bemis Mtn. Shelter about nine miles on, because I was sure most of the water sources had dried up along the Range.

The weather was clear, but there was a good bit of haze when I reached Old Blue (3,600 feet), the first and highest peak in the Range. Even though the haze greatly reduced the visibility, I could see the Baldpates back to the west. South Arm Lake to the northwest and Elephant Mtn. The summit of Old Blue was very interesting, mostly covered with smooth granite ledges, large boulders and scrub spruce struggling for nourishment from the scant soil between them. I left the summit, crossed the col and ascended to an open ledge on Elephant Mtn.

I saw evidence of strip cutting of trees in some of the valleys and could hear chain saws in the distance. This was the first time I had seen any evidence of timber cutting in Maine; and even then, it was at some distance. The Maine woods are vast—18 million acres. I was surprised to learn that 90% of Maine's total land area is covered with forest, most of which is privately owned. Paper and wood products are Maine's most important industry. I would see more and more evidence of this as I moved north often in the form of haul roads that the AT crosses from time to time.

I began my descent of the Bemis Range by crossing over three successive peaks with each peak getting progressively lower. I found this area to be most fascinating, consisting of vast expanses of those smooth granite ledges which I had seen in many regions to the south. However, the difference here was the immensity of these areas and the distance that the AT followed these long smooth rock surfaces. The Trail descended from one long ledge to another for almost four miles, with rock cairns strategically placed on the ledges to keep the hiker on course during inclement weather. The scrub spruce formed a green dot pattern on the landscape in their quest for life in this rocky and ledgy environment. I was surprised to see two garter snakes sunning on one of the ledges and thought they must be taking advantage of the few short sunny periods that were left before cold weather would set in and they would be going into hibernation.

As I was descending the ledgy peaks of Bemis Mtn., I could see a mammoth lake with one of those tongue-twisting names common in Maine—Mooselookmeguntic Lake. Now, is that a mouthful or what? I am not sure of the Indian translation, but somewhere in the literature I read that maybe in English it means, "that is the way a moose looks." Many of the places with Indian names became part of my vocabulary as I hiked through Maine and approached Katahdin. Most were derived from the Abenaki Indian tribes, early inhabitants of this area.

Before reaching the next trailhead on ME 17, I talked with a group of MATC Trail volunteers doing extensive work through the area. I commended them for the very fine condition of the Trail as well as the shelters, Trail blazes, signs, etc. Joan was waiting for me at a roadside pull-off near the trailhead, enjoying the view over the vast Mooselookmeguntic Lake. We then drove into Rangeley, Maine for a pizza dinner, climaxing a great day.

The haze cleared by the next morning, providing a sharp clear view back over the Bemis Range. The mountains had received a little shower of rain which was by no means enough, but it did make the woods smell fresh and clean. A fairly easy day's hike lay ahead over a series of connecting ridges between the Bemis Range and the Saddleback Range. There were no major climbs or descents, but I did pass some more of those beautiful northern forest ponds: Moxie Pond, Sabbath Day, Long Pond and Little Swift River Pond, to name a few. Each had its own unique beauty, nestled in the pristine settings of the north woods. Speaking of the north woods, they are truly magic. They seem to want to keep me there; and when I leave them, they keep beckoning me back.

This area also had an abundance of sphagnum bogs with moose tracks scattered throughout, and the terrain here had remained wet through Maine's very dry period. Despite all the apparent moose activity, I did not see a one while hiking through the section. Before descending into Sandy River where ME 4 crosses, I had an outstanding view of the Saddleback Range, where I would begin my next day's hike.

My small pack had been sufficient for several days now since the trailheads were about a day's hike apart, but that would change the next day, as the distance from trailhead to trailhead lengthened, requiring overnighters and my bigger pack. After Joan picked me up, we moved our base camp to Farmington, Maine, where it would remain until I hiked into Caratunk—about 67 miles.

The next section from Sandy River (ME 4) to ME 27 near Stratton crosses the Saddleback Range, Spalding Mtn. and Crocker Mtn. This is considered the most difficult 30-mile section in the state of Maine. Due to the total elevation gain of 9,600 feet and rugged terrain, I planned four days for this section. I had talked to many thru-hikers who had previously crossed it, and while saying three days was possible advised taking four. The AT crosses over four peaks which are at or above 4,000 feet and three peaks which are over 3,000 feet. In addition, there is a 3-mile section which is above tree line and a potential problem during times of inclement weather.

After leaving the trailhead, I hiked to the Piazza Rock Shelter area and took a blue blaze trail up to Piazza Rock. This interesting rock formation is a huge granite slab that juts out into space from the side of the mountain and rests on an immense boulder. The old log shelter there was still intact and functional, while nearby was another, recently built by the MATC. There was also a new and quite unique privy near the shelters. Its custom features included a roof with translucent panels which made it very light inside, a two-seater design and an unusual greeting on the door that said, "Your Move." There was also a nice tenting area in the vicinity. The MATC is to be congratulated for the planning and work that made this an outstanding rest stop for hikers. On my ascent of Saddleback, I passed two back country ponds—Ethel and Eddy, and both looked like great habitat for moose. There were tracks there but still no sightings.

There was another rain shower in the mountains, doing nothing more than dampening the brush and weeds along the AT. Due to the severe lack of rain in Maine, the Governor had issued a "Red Alert" meaning there was to be no outside burning, such as campfires.

I reached an overlook about half way up Saddleback and could see that the mountain summit had disappeared in fog. Would I be crossing another fogged-in mountain top? If so, I would miss one of the finest views along the AT in Maine. The literature indicated that Mt. Katahdin, 105 miles away, is visible on a clear day and appears as a tiny bump on the horizon to the northeast.

Before reaching tree line, I passed through an area with many blowdowns, enabling me to see the clouds being rapidly blown across the top of the mountain. Maybe it would clear by the time I reached the summit. When I moved above tree line, the wind was rapidly taking one cloud bank after another across the mountain with intermittent sunshine appearing. These openings offered fantastic views of the mountains and valleys of western Maine. The force of the wind was unbelievable—almost equal to what I experienced on Moosilauke but without snow, cold and ice. Before reaching the summit, I met a southbounder ("Flip Flop"). He said there was a group of college students at the Poplar Ridge Shelter, making it rather crowded. I told him that was my destination for the day and that I would be tenting and it would not be a problem for me.

When I reached the summit (4,116 feet), the wind was so fierce I could barely stand. I quickly snapped some photos and moved off the summit into the col between Saddleback and a mountain called The Horn. I ascended The Horn in winds that were unreal. When I reached its summit (4,023 feet), I sought shelter behind a rock cairn to take photos and record my notes, but the wind was so strong that it interfered with the audio on my recorder.

The alpine environment on these two summits was the finest I had seen anywhere along the AT. The view was outstanding with a panorama of western Maine lying beneath me. Could I see Katahdin? I was not sure, although there were some dimples on the horizon in that direction. In view or not, Katahdin was out there— a little over 100 miles as the crow flies, about 210 miles as the hiker walks. If all went well, I would be arriving there in about three weeks.

I crossed another col and ascended Saddleback, Jr. (3,640 feet), offering still more sweeping views of the western Maine mountains and valleys. Poplar Ridge Shelter and Camping Area was overflowing, as "Flip Flop" had predicted. I did, however, find a small space for my little tent across the stream from the shelter. During the evening, I visited with the college freshmen occupying the shelter and told them the campfire they had built was illegal since the Governor had issued a "Red Alert." They quickly extinguished it without question.

The next morning the students were up early and moved out northbound ahead of me, but I caught up with them in the deep valley at Orbeton Stream. Before beginning my climb up Spalding Mtn., I visited with their leader ("Red Squirrel"). After crossing the stream, I ascended two long steep log ladders around a cliff and marveled at the engineering and work it took to put them there. Without the ladders, a rope may have been necessary to make the climb over the cliffs. I reached the summit of Lone Mtn. (3,280 feet) by late morning, and this was only about two miles short of my day's planned destination, Spalding Mtn. Shelter.

I had been making very good time, so much so that I was considering continuing on into the section planned for the next day. If I could pick up a day by combining the two days' hike into one, I would have in reserve a spare day that may be needed later. The more I thought about this, the more it seemed the thing to do. By the time I reached the shelter, my mind was made up—it was a go, even though I would be getting in late. I ate a quick lunch and was off. Spalding Mtn. lay ahead, and there was part of Sugarloaf to cross. In addition, I faced a very steep rugged descent of Sugarloaf Mtn. into the Caribou Valley, and finally about another 1 1/2 miles up Crocker to the Crocker Cirque Campground. My hiking pace would really have to be increased, as it was September and the days were getting shorter. If darkness caught me, I would just have to stop and camp because my flashlight had given out the night before at the Poplar Ridge Campsite. But I was determined—Crocker Cirque, here I come.

I moved along briskly, ascending Spalding Mtn. which provided a great view of Sugarloaf Mtn. Then I descended to the commemorative plaque located in the saddle between Spalding and Sugarloaf. The plaque has historic significance, marking this as a special spot on the Trail. It reads: "Maine CCC in honor of the men of the Civilian Conservation Corps who from 1935 to 1939 contributed greatly to the completion of the Appalachian Trail in Maine and who on August 14, 1937, near this spot completed the final link of the entire 2054 miles. Trail dedicated August 14, 1987, by the Volunteers of the Appalachian Trail Club." (I quoted the plaque just as it was written and later discovered a discrepancy in the dates. The "1935 to 1939" possibly should have read "1935 to 1937" since the CCC completed the final link of the AT here in 1937.)

I reached the junction of the Sugarloaf Mtn. Trail, a blue blaze leading to the summit of Sugarloaf. I had considered hiking up to the summit and spending the night in the ski building there as many thru-hikers do, but that would not have saved me a day. Prior to 1974, the AT crossed over the summit of Sugarloaf (4,237 feet), the second highest point along the AT in Maine. Because of ski development, it was relocated to the north slopes of the mountain. As with Killington, Stratton and Bromley in Vermont, skiing is king here. I began my descent of the north shoulder of Sugarloaf, moving along at a good pace into the Caribou Valley.

TOP: Jeanne and Charlie in the infamous Mahoosuc
   Notch of western Maine
BOTTOM: Herb, Bill Leffler ("The Poet") and
   Jeanne near Grafton Notch, Maine

Photo by Charlie Moses

TOP: A Birch growing over a huge boulder near
    Grafton Notch
BOTTOM: East Peak of Baldpate Mtn., Maine

TOP: The "Pygmy Ladder" near summit of East
Peak of Baldpate Mtn.—"one rung too short"
BOTTOM: Bemis Bountain (2nd Peak) 2923 ft.

TOP: Is this a fancy John or what? Photo taken
at Piazza Rock Shelter near Rangely, Maine
BOTTOM: View to the northeast over "The
Horn" from Saddleback Mountain, Maine

13

THE INJURY

*"Utter wilderness" was the description given of the AT
through Maine during the 1930's by Myron Avery,
ATC Chairman, 1931-1952, who was the major force
in making the AT possible through this wilderness.*
                                            —The Author

The descent into the Caribou Valley was a rock scramble about equal in difficulty to any area I had experienced along the Trail with, perhaps, the exception of the Mahoosuc Notch. In fact, on a scale of one to ten with ten being the most difficult, I had rated this one-mile stretch a nine plus.

While descending, I thought how hard I had been pushing on this hike since leaving Franconia Notch, New Hampshire, on August 10, 1995. Also, I had more time commitments ahead. Our son, Rodney, was going to join me at Monson, Maine (the beginning of the "100-Mile Wilderness"), on September 15 for the final segment to Katahdin. In addition, our son, David, and daughter,

Melinda, would meet us at Katahdin Stream Campground at the base of Mt. Katahdin on September 26 and hike the mountain with us to finish the hike. All three of our children had made special arrangements with their places of employment and families to be with me when I finished the Trail. It was, therefore, imperative that I meet them at the appointed times and places.

The distance from the north shoulder of Sugarloaf Mtn. to Monson is about 81 miles and about 193 miles to Mt. Katahdin. I had made it to this point on schedule although I had been pushing it and could make Monson to meet Rodney on time if all went well. I did, however, want a couple of days after hiking out at Monson to rest and prepare supplies for the "100-Mile Wilderness."

If I could maintain this schedule, Rod and I would have 10 days to hike the Wilderness so we could climb Mt. Katahdin on September 26. If we could hike through the area in nine days, finishing September 24, we would have a two-day choice to hike Katahdin, as the weather can dictate when the mountain can or cannot be climbed. In any event, we had to hike Katahdin by September 26, because David had to return home the next day, and I wanted them all to climb the mountain with me. The weather in north central Maine in late September can change very quickly, especially at high elevations, thus affecting hiking speed and distance or at worst a loss of hiking days. This could be especially critical when hiking the "100-Mile Wilderness" when our pack weight would be at maximum, as we would have to carry 10-days' supply of food and other necessities.

My plan from the beginning in hiking the Appalachian Trail was to do it at a comfortable pace allowing time to observe and study wildlife, flora, fauna, geology, and history along the Trail and to enjoy to the fullest its natural beauty. It was never my intent to be a marathoner or to compete for time and distance, although many find challenge and satisfaction in hiking the Trail this way. To use a quote from Benton MacKaye, "Some people like to record how speedily they can traverse the length of the Trail, but I would give a prize for the one who took the longest time."

Many things affect hiking speed and distance: the terrain, trail conditions, elevation gain and loss, weather, equipment, health (physical condition), personal feelings, and injury to mention the more important ones. I had experienced all of these at one time or another during my hike over the years, but they did not affect my goals to a great degree since I was doing it in sections. This was to change on this descent of Sugarloaf Mtn. into the Carrabassett River.

I had pushed my hiking schedule to a point that I had gained one day on the section of the Trail between ME 4 and ME 27. The hike had gone well; and I had not experienced any health problems or injuries, even though I had some expected weight loss. The Whites, Carter-Moriah and Mahoosucs, along with my husky Kelty pack had proven more of a challenge than anticipated.

Before I reached the South Branch of the Carrabassett River, I developed discomfort in my right heel. I had to work around and slide down a number of extremely rough rocky scrambles, and it was one of these maneuvers that overstressed my heel. It was not until after crossing the river that I began to notice something was wrong, because I was having pain when I put weight on my heel.

It was one mile to the Crocker Cirque camping area which I limped into just before dusk. It is located in a unique glacial depression at the base of the South Peak of Crocker Mtn. The Trail from ME 4 across the Saddleback Range, Spalding Mtn. and Sugarloaf was impressive and is considered to be one of the most outstanding in the western mountains of Maine. Its rugged ascents and descents to and from some peaks above tree line had presented a real challenge. I had hiked through this section in two days and might have been pushing too hard.

Since the two tent pads there were already occupied and were large enough for two, a young couple from Portland, Maine, invited me to share theirs. They said that they return to this area each year to stay a day or two, as this was one of their favorite spots to spend some time with nature. This was understandable because of its tranquil setting.

By 8:00 AM the next morning, I was on the ascent of the South Peak of Crocker Mtn. My heel was sensitive, and I was favoring it with a limp but thought it was a sprain that could be worked out. I did not know it then, but this was an injury that would not get better but plague me for the rest of my hike and for months to follow.

The hike over the South and North Peaks of Crocker was completed with little difficulty, but at a much slower pace. The weather continued to be warm and dry. It had for the most part, been excellent since leaving Franconia Notch except for a couple of days of inclement weather on some of the higher peaks.

The pain in my heel flared up on the descent of Crocker Mtn. on to ME 27, and it was slowing me down significantly because each step brought pain. I was one day ahead of schedule and had made arrangements with Joan to pick me up at the AT crossing of ME 27—she would not be there until the next day.

About half way down Crocker, I stopped for a lunch break and to rest my heel. There was no need to hurry because I knew, upon reaching the highway, I would either have to hitch a ride or hike to the nearest phone to call Joan and then wait. But a coincidence was about to take place.

After lunch and the rest break, I continued my descent and shortly met two ladies (Judy Cyr and Margaret Colman) from Maine, who were spending the weekend at the Sugarloaf Resort and were out for the day on Crocker Mtn. I hiked down to the highway with them and had some difficulty keeping up because of the pain in my heel.

By the time we neared the highway, we had become acquainted, and they volunteered to give me a lift to the nearest phone which was at Sugarloaf—what a streak of luck! Just before we got within sight of the highway, I told them I wanted to sponge off a little and change clothes and that I would be along shortly. They said they would wait for me at their car.

I hiked out to the parking area by the highway, unloaded my pack, put it in their car and was in the process of taking my camera and recorder cases off when I glanced across the highway. To my surprise, Joan was pulling off the highway at the Trail crossing; and I said, "That's my wife Joan—she is not supposed to be here today—she is 24 hours early." The ladies replied, "Well, the truck does have Ohio license plates." They thought I was kidding. I had told them she was not scheduled to be there until the next day. What a great surprise!

Our timing was perfect. If either of us had been a minute or so earlier or later, we would have missed each other. A minute earlier and I would not have been off the Trail yet, and a minute later and I would have been in the ladies' car headed for a telephone. It was as though there was a guiding force for both of us that brought us together at this unscheduled rendezvous.

Joan's explanation for coming to the trailhead a day ahead of schedule seemed more than just a coincidence. As I noted earlier, there was a severe drought in Maine with fire danger in the Maine woods reaching a critical state. There had been about 200 small forest fires that had been reported as possible arson. When the fire department was dispatched to go north of Farmington in the direction of the area I was hiking through, Joan became concerned, thinking the fire or fires may be in my general locale. She then decided to drive north toward the area where I was; but, after driving a few miles, she found out the fires were not anywhere near. She did not stop, however, but kept driving north as though there was some power guiding her. The trailhead was 44 miles from Farmington. She drove 29 miles, almost turned around to go back, but then decided she would drive on to locate the trailhead where she would pick me up the following day.

We returned to our base camp at Farmington, and I took the next day off but did not say anything to Joan about the problem I had developed with my heel. Perhaps resting and a day off my feet would remedy the problem. I did not know the extent of the injury but thought it was possibly a sprain or bruise caused by overstressing it.

The Bigelow Mtn. Range was the next major hurdle facing me, and this was another group of mountains I had been looking forward to crossing for many weeks. It consists of peaks ranging in elevation from 3,000 to over 4,000 feet with the higher peaks above tree line. This is considered to be a fairly difficult section due to significant elevation gain and loss and a net climb of about 6,000 feet over rough steep terrain. I had hoped for fair weather and that my physical condition would be commensurate to the demands this section would require.

After the day's rest at Farmington, I began the Bigelow section and realized before reaching Horns Pond on the mountain that my heel was going to give me problems. The day's rest had helped, but the pain had returned and seemed to be more intense. This was only the beginning, and my hiking pace was slow. It was at this point that I really started to become concerned and wondered if I had more than just a sprain or bruise and should have had it checked by a doctor. I could not afford to be off the Trail for any length of time if Katahdin was to be reached by September 26.

The Bigelow Range is not only beautiful and rugged but has some interesting history. It was through this area that Benedict Arnold's forces passed during Revolutionary War times en route to Quebec City. The Range was named after one of Arnold's officers—a General Bigelow who was sent to the mountain summit to see if he could see Quebec City. The range lies completely within the Bigelow State Preserve, an area established through a long struggle between would-be developers and various conservation groups who wanted the mountain to remain a wilderness area. I am glad the conservation groups won, as this is one of the finest mountain ranges in Maine.

While taking a rest and snack break at the Horns Pond camping area, I tried to ease the pain in my heel by massaging it and adding padding to the inside of my boot. It was almost noon when I reached the summit of the South Horn and had hoped that by this time I would have reached the West Peak which was two miles further. At this rate, a camp would have to be established at Bigelow Col, a camping area between West Peak and Avery Peak which would make an 8 1/4-mile day—not the miles I had anticipated. I hiked from South Horn to the summit of West Peak where there was a group of college freshmen from Harvard. They were doing their freshman outdoor environment experience and was another group among many I had met along the way. Less than one-half mile from Bigelow Col, my heel seemed to be doing better. It was only 2:00 PM. so I decided to cross over Avery Peak and try for Safford Notch campsite—another two miles.

When I crossed Bigelow Mtn., the weather was crisp and clear. The views were absolutely outstanding; and upon reaching Avery Peak (East Peak), I had the mountain top to myself. It is always a delight for me when reaching these high summits to have nothing between me and the sky. I stood in awe absorbing the breathtaking beauty from this 4,088-foot stately peak, a fragile alpine area above tree line.

Bigelow Mtn. was a favorite area of Myron H. Avery, a native of Maine and a diligent worker, developer and promoter of the Appalachian Trail. He was the third Appalachian Trail Conference Chairman and served in that capacity for seven consecutive terms from 1931-1952. Avery was honored by an act of the Maine Legislature to name the East Peak of Bigelow—Myron H. Avery Peak. After reading the honorary plaque on a large boulder near the summit, I gazed across the Maine wilderness and understood why he loved this mountain.

A major part of the landscape below Avery Peak was the expanse of the man-made Flagstaff Lake. I had read a brief account of the history of the Lake and looked for signs of the community of Flagstaff that lies submerged beneath its waters. A dam had been built across the Dead River during the 1940's to provide a lake and power source for electric power in New England. As the water levels rose when the dam gates were closed, a once-thriving community sank beneath its waters. While gazing down into the lake and panning its shoreline, I wondered about the struggles these people must have had to try to save their town. I vowed to learn more about the rise and fall of this community by reading the account given in Fessenden S. Blanchard's book, *Ghost Towns of New England*.

Bigelow Mtn. had really left a lasting impression on me. As I panned the view once more before beginning my descent, John Burroughs' lines came to mind, "I come here to find myself—it's so easy to get lost in the world." The mountain had recharged me physically and spiritually, and the pain in my heel seemed to have lessened as I descended into Safford Notch. The descent was steep, and the Trail meandered around an arrangement of huge boulders scattered at random, some the size of a two-story house. The Bigelows were a rugged area requiring extra time, and I was pleased to have reached Safford Notch earlier than anticipated.

The campsite was unoccupied, so I pitched my tent on a platform close to the spring, obtained my night's supply of water and prepared an evening meal of beef Stroganoff. I did not eat well, as I had no appetite. I shared a major part of my meal with a northbound thru-hiker ("Blind Faith") who came in late and set his tent up near mine. We would see each other often as we hiked north toward Katahdin.

There was a snappy chill in the air the next morning as I ascended Little Bigelow with Long Falls Dam Road as my destination. I felt an urgent need to contact our family physician regarding my heel, as the pain continued to plague me. It was only 8 1/2 miles to the pick up point; and, at my slow pace, it would probably take me six hours to get there.

There was a haze in the atmosphere as I stood looking across the valleys and the part of the Bigelow Range I had hiked the day before. To the north lay Flagstaff Lake with its blue waters meandering around necks of land extending into the lake all around its shoreline, and back to the south stood Sugarloaf with its ski trails zigzagging down the mountainside. Katahdin was not visible, but it was out there and I was hoping my heel would improve enough for me to finish the hike.

The temperature increased as I descended Little Bigelow toward the Little Bigelow Shelter. Along the open rocky ledges, the warm sun brought out the "clicking" grasshoppers, which I thought quite interesting. They looked the same as the species I had been accustomed to further south; but as they took flight, they made an unfamiliar clicking sound. I enjoyed watching and listening to them and knew their activity would be short-lived due to the approaching cold weather.

Before reaching the Little Bigelow Shelter, a thrashing sound came from the brush just off the Trail. Expecting a moose to cross the path by the noise it was making, I was astounded when a black bear bolted out into the Trail a few feet in front of me, surprising both of us. I had seen many bear signs along the Trail but had no sighting since hiking through the Shenandoah. The bear left the scene as quickly as he had appeared.

Even though I had been expecting to see a lot of moose, so far I had only two sightings—one at the base of Mt. Moosilauke and one near the Crocker Cirque campsite on South Crocker Mtn. The weather had been so dry that many of the wet boggy areas along the Trail had dried up forcing the moose, who normally feed there, to seek better feeding grounds further away from the Trail.

After making more stops than usual to rest my heel, adjust my boots and shift the padding to try to ease some of the pain, I reached Long Falls Dam Road. It had taken me seven hours to hike 8 1/2 miles—once again, not good time. Joan was waiting for me at the trailhead, and what a relief to get off my feet. On the way into Farmington, I discussed my heel pain with her and told her that the next section of the Trail to the Kennebec River crossing at Caratunk should be relatively easy and that I would try to reach that point before calling our physician. There was only one low mountain to cross, and the rest of the Trail would pass through the flat Carry Pond country of Maine. This would relieve some of the stress on my heel, as the rough downhills were giving me the most problems.

The hike through the Carry Pond region was a welcome change from the previous terrain. After crossing Roundtop Mtn., a low one compared to the Bigelows, the Trail flattened out crossing several brooks and skirting the shorelines of West Carry, Middle Carry and East Carry Ponds. It also passed Pierce Pond where there is a campsite and shelter about 3 miles from the Kennebec River. These are charming ponds as were so many of the others I had passed along the AT in Maine.

What continued to surprise me, however, was that these were called ponds. Many of them were quite large, and it seemed they should meet lake status; but then the deep valleys in New Hampshire and Maine were referred to as Notches rather than valleys. I found the difference in terminology along the AT interesting. These ponds would have been called lakes where I grew up.

This is a delightful section with interesting local and national history. Around the Carry Ponds, a part of the AT follows a section of the Old Arnold Trail that was used by Benedict Arnold's forces en route to Canada. I thought how difficult it must have been for his forces to negotiate some of the wide bushy bogs in this region. In that day, there was no trail with puncheons and bridges over the wet areas for them to follow; and to complicate it even more, the weather conditions were bad when they passed through here.

Making good time for the day, I reached the Pierce Pond Shelter and Campsite early. The shelter is located in a tranquil setting overlooking Pierce Pond, and I decided to stay in it rather than set up a tent. The sunset across Pierce Pond was spectacular, and I was able to capture some of it on film. During the evening, the loons announced their presence, my first time to hear them since reaching Maine. Their calls echoed back and forth across the Pond throughout the crisp starlit night, assuring me that this was truly a wilderness area—what a peaceful place!

The Trail descending from Pierce Pond along the cascading Pierce Pond Stream to the crossing of the Kennebec River is about 3 1/2 miles. Ferry service across the River is provided to hikers by the ATC and the MATC. When I hiked through, the ferry service was on a schedule from 10:00 AM to 5:00 PM, so there was no need to hurry, because I knew the crossing could not be made until 10:00. The Kennebec River, until recent years, was considered to be one of the last major obstacles for hikers along the AT before Mt. Katahdin. It is about 70 yards wide where the Trail crosses, and the water depth and currents are very treacherous because of releases of water from an upstream dam which is used for hydro-electric power.

I had read accounts of and talked to many hikers about the hazards of making this crossing; and it was not until after 1987 when, for safety sake, a reliable ferry service was provided. A hiker drowned attempting the crossing in 1985. Signs along the AT both north and southbound warn hikers not to attempt the crossing on foot.

My heel had bothered me some through this section but not to the degree it had through the Bigelows. The flat, less rugged Trail had helped considerably. Joan was waiting for me at the Trail crossing of the Kennebec; and, as I was crossing the river, it started to rain. The timing was great. I was ready for an R & R day, and this would be a good time to call my physician. I was not sure, though, that I wanted to know what he might tell me. If it were a fracture, he would most certainly take me off the Trail. It would not be so bad if I only had a few miles to Katahdin, but from Caratunk to Katahdin is about 148 miles including the last 100 miles through the Maine Wilderness.

We called my physician from Newport and gave him a detailed description of my problem. He seemed to feel that I had Achilles Tendinitis, a condition caused by overstressing the Achilles Tendon, and prescribed medication and treatment. Part of the treatment was to stay off my feet as much as possible, but Katahdin could not be reached that way.

The next morning I was back on the Trail headed for Monson feeling better about having talked to my doctor and was relieved he did not ground me. I felt I could deal with the tendinitis by taking the medication he prescribed and taking it easy for a couple of days. I realized, however, that the doctor's diagnosis was based on a telephone conversation and not by a physical examination, so there was a possibility that it still could be more serious.

The Trail from Caratunk to Monson is a 36-mile stretch preceding the "100-Mile Wilderness" and the last section I would be hiking through alone. It traverses a long wilderness area in central Maine between the village of Caratunk on the Kennebec River to ME 15, about four miles north of Monson. The AT crosses two mountains: Pleasant Pond (2,477 feet) and Moxie Bald (2,630 feet). Other features included: Pleasant Pond, Moxie Pond, Bald Mtn. Pond and Lake Hebron—yes, Lake Hebron is smaller than Moxie Pond—here we go again. The Trail then follows along the West Branch of the Piscataquis River with its picturesque pools and slate canyon before reaching Monson.

Joan and I moved our base camp from Farmington to New-port, our last before Katahdin. However, while Rod and I were hiking the "100-Mile Wilderness," our son Dave and daughter Melinda would arrive in Bangor and Dave would move it to the Millinocket area where they would join Rod and me to hike Katahdin.

It was about 60 miles from Newport to the trailhead at Caratunk, so we had to leave early for Joan to get me there by 7:30 AM. It was a cool morning in Maine—typical for this time of year. The feel of fall was definitely in the air, and the leaves were showing a lot of color. I had used the R & R day to rest and doctor my heel; and if I could reach Monson in three days, I would have two days to prepare for the "100-Mile Wilderness" before Rod arrived.

The morning hike went well with cool weather and a relatively easy walk to the Pleasant Pond Shelter where I stopped to rest and check the shelter journal for entries from "The Poet"—none there. The one-mile climb from the shelter to Pleasant Pond Mtn. summit was steep; and, when I reached its open rocky crest, a strong cold wind was howling around the huge boulders. In spite of the haze in the distance, the view was spectacular. To the west, the Bigelows stood out clearly. This range of mountains had been visible from the higher peaks along the AT for over a week. To the east were Moxie Pond and Moxie Bald Mtn.—areas I would be hiking through in the days ahead.

As I hiked further into central Maine, I became more and more moved with its pristine beauty and the vastness of the unsettled and underdeveloped areas. What a free-spirited feeling to stand on these stately peaks and look across this vast wilderness and not see a town, lights, roads, cleared land or any of the other marks made by man. There was, however, some evidence of timber clear-cutting by paper companies scattered around the countryside, but most were out of sight of the AT.

On the descent of Pleasant Pond Mtn., I met a southbound hiker who indicated there was no water at the Bald Mtn. Brook Shelter where I was planning to spend the night. He said I would have to obtain water at Moxie Pond and carry it 2 1/2 miles to the shelter. I had done this many times along the AT, especially if a dry camp were necessary along the ridges; but I never had to carry it this far. Upon arrival at Moxie Pond, I pumped one gallon into my water bag and filled my canteen. That was ten pounds of water, and my painful heel really did not need the extra weight. The five quarts would be enough for the evening meal, a sponge bath, breakfast and a little to start out the next day over Moxie Bald Mtn. where it was reported there was no water.

Upon reaching the blue blaze trail leading over to the shelter, I could see the stream was dry. Before I reached it, I made a close examination of the stream bed and, by walking off the trail, could see pools of water in some of the depressions along the stream. One really had to look close to see them and the hiker must have missed them, as they were out of sight from the Trail. Here I had carried an extra ten pounds for over 2 1/2 miles when it was not necessary. The shelter was newly constructed and in a peaceful setting by a small stream—too bad the stream was dry, but no doubt there would be an adequate water source here under normal conditions.

The Bald Mtn. Brook Shelter replaced the original Joe's Hole Brook lean-to which had been in a less desirable location. It was apparent that the MATC had put great effort into upgrading the shelters and, in many cases, had relocated and built new ones like this. They had also put in many long stretches of puncheons and bridged over wet areas which, without them, would have caused muddy, slow hiking. Impressive also were the hundreds of feet of stone steps they had constructed up over rocky escarpments near the summits of some of the higher peaks. This had involved a tremendous amount of work and time. It amazed me how they managed to lift and position some of the huge boulders used in building the steps, because some weighed hundreds of pounds.

The temperature dropped to 35 degrees over night at the shelter, and without doubt there was frost in the open areas. A southbound hiker from Pennsylvania joined me at the shelter. We shared many of our hiking experiences over various sections of the Trail, and he advised me of the beauty of the AT along the Piscataquis River, an area I would be hiking through the next day.

I reviewed my hiking plan which would take me across Moxie Bald Mtn., skirt Moxie Bald Pond and continue down Bald Mtn. Stream to the confluence with the west branch of the Piscataquis. The AT then follows the Piscataquis to the Horseshoe Canyon area where the next shelter and campsite were located. This would make a full day, and I was hoping my heel could hold up and not cause me problems as it had on the descent from Pleasant Pond Mtn. the day before.

The two-mile climb from the Bald Mtn. Brook lean-to to the summit of Moxie Bald Mtn. provided a strenuous morning work-out. Fortunately, the weather was cool, or I would have heated up quickly on the climb. As I approached the summit, the temperature dropped significantly and the wind was increasing. As I crested, the wind was very strong and cold—but what a view!— a 360-degree panorama. I could see from the Bigelows to the west and to Katahdin to the north and east. The views just seemed to get better and better, and I was greatly inspired by the pristine beauty here. Moxie is another interesting mountain with its summit projecting into the sky. There were large open areas of exposed granite with stunted Krumholtz Spruce struggling for survival in the scant soil in cracks and crevices between the expanses of granite. There is a blue blaze by-pass trail leading around the summit for hikers to use in case of severe weather.

On my descent of Moxie, I could look down into the blue waters of Bald Mtn. Pond with its spruce-covered peninsulas and islands and could see Katahdin in the hazy distance rising above the layers of blue ridges across the Maine countryside. My eyes became misty with tears—what an impressive and moving sight! The distant mountain would mark the end of a journey which I began in 1981. The end was in sight but about 12 days away and the "100-Mile Wilderness" was waiting and offering another major challenge. And then there was the constant pain in my heel with every step—could I make it through another 12 days?

I was also concerned about my weight loss, which was more than usual. Every day I had been drawing in the pack belt around my waist, and my appetite continued to falter. I had not been eating well, and that was not normal for me. Usually I was nibbling constantly throughout each day's hike in the quest to satisfy what seemed to be everlasting hunger, but not this time. The weight loss had affected my stamina, and I was fatigued most of the time. My hiking pace had slowed down to a point where I was often struggling.

During the earlier part of this hike and on all the others I had made on the AT, "the longer the stronger" rule applied. Upon finishing each of the sections, I was physically stronger even though I always had weight loss. This was not the case this time, because I was becoming weaker.

The eighteen-mile section from Moxie to Monson is relatively flat country with little elevation change and this would be another welcome break physically. I was also looking forward to the hike along the Bald Mtn. Stream and the picturesque canyon of the west branch of the Piscataquis River which the AT follows for several miles. The next two days would be the last I would be hiking alone, as Rod would be joining me at Monson. With the exception of the Mahoosuc Range in western Maine and other short sections where other hikers joined me along the Appalachian chain, I had basically hiked alone since the Humpback Rock Visitor Center on the Blue Ridge in Virginia. I was anticipating Rod's company while hiking the final segment to Katahdin—the "100-Mile Wilderness"—we both needed time together.

After descending Moxie, I stopped for a lunch break and to check the journal at the Moxie Bald Shelter. This is an older 6-hiker shelter, built in 1958 by the MATC, with a "baseball bat" floor (made of poles 3 to 4 inches in diameter laid side by side). It is situated on the peaceful shore of Moxie Bald Pond. It would have been a pleasure to spend more time here and perhaps take a dip in the pond had it been warmer and if time had permitted.

When I reached the Piscataquis River, the Trail followed beside it with many short but steep ups and downs skirting cliffs and steep drop-offs next to the river. The river sported many large boulders along its rocky stream bed with many riffles and swirling pools and travelled through a deep picturesque canyon bordered by steep cliffs. The Trail passed through a beautiful stand of large white pines along the river near Horseshoe Canyon. It was in this area where a new shelter had been constructed in 1989 on a ridge above the river, and this was my destination for the day. Upon my arrival at the shelter, I decided to stay in it rather than my tent as I just did not feel like setting it up. Most of the Trail had been moderate with no major climbs. However, the three-mile section of Trail skirting the canyon wall along the river just about depleted my already low energy level.

Two northbound hikers ("Stick" and "Bloodroot") joined me later that evening and pitched their tent near the shelter. After resting a while, I started looking for the spring to obtain my night's supply of water and found it dry. This meant the river would have to be my water source. I ate less than half the beef stew I had prepared for dinner because my appetite was not up to par. By now, I was convinced that the constant pain had affected my eating habits. I retired to my sleeping bag early; and while lying there, I realized this would be my last night staying alone for the remainder of the hike, and it was comforting to know Rod would be my hiking companion.

The chill of the mid September morning hovered around me when I peered out of the shelter as dawn broke. "Stick" and "Bloodroot" informed me they were headed for Monson for breakfast. I told them I wished I could join them there, but my hiking speed would not permit me to arrive in time for breakfast. This should be a short day as I would be hiking out on ME 15 four miles north of Monson, about a 9-mile hike.

When I reached the East Branch of the Piscataquis River, I was confronted by a beaver dam, recently built where the AT crossed the river. Scenes like this had become very common along the Trail in New England where the environment is favorable for them. I was always amazed at how well their dams are built, using trees of all sizes, positioned properly, cemented together with mud and how well they hold water.

When I reached the shores of Lake Hebron, I knew the end of this section was near. Many hikers take a blue blaze trail near Lake Hebron into Monson heading for the renowned Shaw's Boarding House on Pleasant Street or the Pie Lady on Main Street.

Both provide rooms, showers, excellent meals and a homey environment so hikers can rest and regroup before beginning the "100-Mile Wilderness."

I did not take the blue blaze into Monson but continued on across Buck Hill toward ME 15. I was anxious to complete the section and start making preparations for the Wilderness including resting and doctoring my heel. This was Tuesday, September 12, and Rod would be arriving on Thursday night in Bangor so we could begin the Wilderness on Friday. I had completed the hike to this point as scheduled, allowing me two days to prepare for the final segment.

When Joan picked me up, we drove into Monson and stopped briefly at the Pie Lady's Boarding House for a chat with a thru-hiker ("Tune") whom I had met near the Kennebec River. We then drove to Shaw's Boarding House, met them and signed their register. The Shaws are well known by AT hikers and probably have met and provided food and shelter to more hikers than any other establishment along the Appalachian Trail.

The town of Monson was bustling with activity. This was the time of year when waves of thru-hikers were coming through getting ready for the final thrust—kicking back, writing letters, making calls, resupplying, and in some cases waiting for others to catch up. One could feel the excitement in the air.

We drove into Newport, where Joan and I spent Wednesday and Thursday organizing the food and supplies in my pack for the final section. I also spent as much time as possible off my feet resting and using treatment techniques suggested by my physician. Rod had loaded his pack before we left home so we could bring it with us. I knew it was much too heavy and needed to be gone through and rechecked.

We picked Rod up at the Bangor Airport as scheduled and spent most of Friday morning helping him reorganize his pack to decrease the weight. He had included my old two-man tent, which weighed 5 1/2 pounds. I told him we could both use my small North Face Tadpole tent. It would be cozy for the two of us but we could manage. After reevaluating the food supplies, clothing, and other items in our packs, we felt we had taken out all that we dared, because we had to plan for ten days.

Joan doing one of her usual chores by helping to
prepare food and supplies for the next Trail hike.

TOP: The rock scramble on Sugarloaf Mtn.
where the injury occurred.
BOTTOM: East Peak of Bigelow Mtn. (Avery
Peak), Flagstaff Lake in background

TOP: Fire tower on Avery Peak. Large boulder
on left holds honorary plaque.
BOTTOM: A fine stand of Spruce near Pleasant
Pond through which the AT passes

14

"TRAIL MAGIC" IN THE WILDERNESS

"Words can't describe what's out here."
—Our son, Rod

We loaded our packs into the pickup for the trip to the trail-head at Monson. Since only two could ride in the cab, I told Rod to ride with his mother, as he had not seen her for a while and I would ride in the back with the packs. It was a 65-mile trip from Newport to Monson, so I thought I might as well settle back and enjoy the ride. We hoped to be on the Trail by 3:00 PM to make the three-mile hike to Leeman Brook Shelter, our planned destination for the first leg of the Wilderness hike. We were almost at the beginning of the last segment of my Appalachian Trail adventure. I remembered reading and hearing about the "100-Mile Wilderness" before starting at Springer Mtn., and today we were going to start hiking through it.

The small enclosed space in the back of our Ford Ranger pickup, which had partly been taken up by our packs had kept me confined with little room to shift my sitting position. I had been riding for 1 1/2 hours in this tight enclosure, but I didn't mind. It had given me time to think and reflect, and this had given Joan and Rod time to visit. He and I would have plenty of time to catch up on talk while we were hiking.

The truck started to slow down, and I quickly sat up and peered through the side glass of the pickup cap—we were arriving in Monson. The street and stores were familiar to me from my trip through town after Joan picked me up at the trailhead north of town a couple of days before. Joan pulled the truck up to the curb and stopped across from the Monson General Store. I was out in a flash, stretching to relieve my muscles and joints, cramped from sitting so long in one position.

I scanned up and down the street of this small north central Maine town of about 500 people, thinking of the many towns and communities I had passed through or near on the AT. This would be the last one. It was mid-September, with major weather changes inevitable in this part of Maine soon, and Katahdin was still about 116 miles away. From the many hikers in Monson and more that would be arriving, you could sense excitement and a feeling of urgency. All were eager to get back on the Trail to begin this final segment, and we would see and hike with some of them during the days that followed..

Rod wanted to buy some souvenirs for friends and family to send back with Joan, and he wanted them to come from Monson since this would mark the beginning of his hike. We also paid another visit to Shaws, and Rod purchased a pair of Gators from their small hiking store. After finishing our stops in Monson, Joan drove us the four miles north on ME 15 to the trailhead, the beginning of the "100-Mile Wilderness."

We loaded our packs—Rod's a hefty 65 pounds and mine a staggering 55 pounds—the most I had ever carried at any point along the AT. We walked over to the signs marking the trailhead for a photo session. Written on the signs were these messages: "Big Wilson Stream 9.9 miles, Barren Mountain 18.2 miles, Abol Bridge 97.5 miles, Katahdin 112 miles." The lower sign read: "Caution. There are no places to obtain supplies or help until you reach Abol Bridge. You should not attempt this section unless you carry a minimum of 10 days of supplies—Do not underestimate the difficulty of this section. Good Hiking MATC."

We reviewed plans with Joan for our pickup at Katahdin Stream Campground. If we were not there in the planned nine days, Joan was to check at Abol Bridge (the next road access), in case we may be there. We exchanged good-byes and began the first leg of the "100-Mile Wilderness."

During the first half mile, I began to have two concerns. The pain in my heel had not gone away. During the two previous days, I had been off of it most of the time, and it had not bothered me much. It was only when I walked on it that I felt discomfort. Now I was carrying 55 pounds and feeling pain with every step, and the weight of my pack was adding extra stress to my heel. My second concern was my lack of stamina. Granted, I was carrying extra weight, but I had just come off several weeks of very strenuous hiking which should have put me in tip-top form. I had managed very well until Sugarloaf, and it seemed that my strength had been diminishing ever since. I had lost a considerable amount of weight, but that was expected and happened on every extended hike made previously.

Beginning this section with these concerns gave me an uneasy feeling. However, it was very comforting to have Rod with me. I was determined to make this the grand finale of my AT hike and to insure that it would be an outstanding outdoor adventure for Rod.

We hiked to the Leeman Brook Shelter, passing three striking back country ponds which mirrored the spectacle of autumn colors in their clear waters. As we walked along exchanging conversation, Rod told me of his excitement about making this hike and that it would be extra special doing it with me and sharing in my completion of the Trail. He also talked about the excitement of his first major airplane flight from Cleveland to Bangor; and, last but not least, some very special things that were happening in his personal life. I shared some of my hiking experiences from this trip to date and told him of the magical feeling of hiking through the north woods. I confided how pleased I was to have him share the Wilderness with me and for him and Melinda and Dave (all three of our children) to share the grand finale of climbing Mt. Katahdin with me.

The Leeman Brook Shelter is located on a rocky bench overlooking the cascading Leeman Brook, a very pleasant setting. Since the shelter was unoccupied, we decided to stay in it rather than in the tent. After a hot hearty evening meal (in my case, beef stew again), we retired to our cozy sleeping bags just after dark. Being mid-September, there was a chill in the air, hinting that frost would be our companion in the north woods.

We lay there and talked for more than two hours, continuing our discussion of the Trail and changes in Rod's personal life. He had met a young lady in the spring, and the relationship had become quite serious. He said this hike would give him a lot of time to think and that this was the girl with whom he wanted to spend the rest of his life. He wanted to know how I felt about it and how I thought his mother would feel. I told him I was happy for him and I knew his mother would be as well. This pleased him; he said it was very important for him to have our blessings. I told him that hiking the Trail could be compared to the journey through life itself. Both have highs and lows, steep climbs and easy climbs, bright skies and dark skies, times of joy and times of disappointment, great views and no views at all, love and sadness—and the list goes on. You might say that hiking the Trail is a parallel to life's journey. We had both had a full active day; before we knew it, we drifted off into a deep sleep.

We did not get as early a start on our second day as hoped for. The activities of the previous day and the chill of the morning had kept us in our sleeping bags longer than we had planned. We hiked to Little Wilson Falls, the first major geological feature through this area. Little Wilson Creek plunges 80 feet down into a deep slate canyon and, according to literature, the falls is one of the highest on the AT. We met several hikers there, including a thru-hiking couple from England ("The Royal Berks"). We would be seeing them several times along the way, each passing the other at various points and also spending a couple of nights with them in the shelters.

We descended the ledgy trail from the Falls to the crossing of Little Wilson Creek and were both feeling the heavy weight of our packs over the rugged steep terrain. My heel was causing me a lot of pain and continued to slow me down, even on the climbs. I had told Rod that the second through the fourth days would probably be the most difficult for him, because his pack would be at its heaviest and conditioning during this time would cause soreness and a lot of fatigue. On the climb out of Little Wilson, he started to fall behind with frequent rest stops; that was okay with me, because I was having problems and needed the breaks myself.

We met two southbounders who gave us a report on the Big Wilson Stream crossing we would be making later in the day. They told us they made the crossing at night and regretted having done so, because they almost got in trouble. They advised us to use care because the stream was rough and swift, not to mention cold. Todd Schafer ("The Outlaw"), who spent a night with us near Andover had told me of a serious injury he sustained while crossing Big Wilson.

When we reached the stream I visually surveyed upstream and downstream and located what I thought was the safest and easiest area to cross. There really was not much choice, as it all looked about the same. The Trail literature had mentioned the danger of crossing the stream, especially in times of high water and indicated there was a bridge downstream three miles providing an option. Taking it, however, would require a six-mile hike (three miles down and three miles back to the Trail).

I took my boots off, tied them to the top of my pack and put on sandals to protect my feet. I worked my way across the stream one careful step at a time, making sure that each step was securely planted on the stream bed and not on a slippery rock that could cause a fall. With the help of my trusty staff, I made the crossing safely with Rod following suit. We warmed our feet and legs, chilled by the ice-like water, and put on dry socks and our boots.

The stream crossing had consumed a lot of our energy, making the climb up to the ridge out of the Big Wilson Valley seem difficult. When we crested the ridge, we took a break and decided not to attempt to reach the next shelter (Long Pond Stream) since it was late afternoon and we still had about three miles to go. My heel was causing me a lot of pain, and my strength certainly was not up to par. Rod was also struggling through his second day under the weight of his heavy pack. I told him I would move on and locate a campsite and for him to take his time.

We descended a very rough Trail which scalped the side of the mountain and provided occasional views of the Barren Range across the Long Pond Stream Valley. Rod dropped some distance behind, and I waited for him when I reached an old road crossing in the valley. We continued on to a small tent site by Vaughn Stream where we set up the tent above a 20-foot waterfall. It had been a difficult day for both of us. After preparing our evening meal by flashlight and candlelight, we stretched out in our small tent.

When I say small, that is just what it was, with only a little space on the side for gear; and we are two husky fellows with a lot of gear. Our sleeping bags covered the entire tent floor; and, when we got into them, the tent space was completely filled with a little breathing space above. Our packs had to be hung from a tree and protected by our pack covers. We talked a while about our day's experiences and the remarkable country we had hiked through and reviewed our hiking plans. I pointed out that we were 1 1/2 miles short of making our goal for the day. If we wanted to get back on our schedule, we would have to try to make it up the next day. That might not be easy because we were facing our first mountain range having rugged terrain and major elevation changes—the Barren Chairback Range. Rod made lengthy entries in his journal which he had started the night before.

We were on the Trail early the following morning, and the weather did not look favorable. So far, we had encountered outstanding weather, somewhat unusual for this time of year in north central Maine. I had talked to people who had hiked most of the Wilderness this time of year in cold wet conditions. We began the three-mile climb up Barren Mtn.; and by the time we reached the area known as The Slide, we hit fog and a cold wind. My ATC guide had mentioned a great view of the Long Pond region and Boarstone Mtn. from the top of The Slide, but the foggy weather had completely obscured the valley.

Rod was not feeling well and had fallen behind on the climb. He had not fully recovered from our previous difficult day. My problems were still plaguing me. The medication my physician had prescribed did not seem to be doing a thing—even the pain medication was not working. I waited for Rod to catch up; and when he did, we rested a while before continuing. When we reached the summit, it started to rain. The fog became more dense, making the ghostly structure of the fire tower on the summit barely visible. The next shelter was the Cloud Pond Shelter, about a mile off the summit. We decided to stay there, resulting in another short day. The weather conditions continued to deteriorate with no letup in sight, causing hiking to be slow and very slippery over the rugged terrain.

Neither Rod nor I were doing well, and the short day would give us both recovery time. We were joined later in the afternoon by three other northbounders who were also stopping early because of the nasty weather. Our original plan was to hike to the Chairback Gap Shelter. So we were now seven miles short of schedule, which could affect the date we would be hiking out at Katahdin Stream. The cold, wet foggy conditions continued throughout the evening and night.

The next morning we woke into a sea of fog and dripping trees. Cloud Pond is a high mountain tarn and appropriately named. We never had a good view of it due to the fog. The Trail was very wet and slippery when we left the shelter. According to my guidebook, the seven miles of Trail to the next shelter were very rugged with many ups and downs, and we needed extra time to traverse it.

After leaving the Barren Mtn. area and ascending the next peak, which was Fourth Mtn., the fog started to clear away; and the valleys and distant ridges began to open up. As indicated in the guidebook, the Trail was extremely rugged. We had to hike slowly and use extra caution through some of the areas. My heel was giving me a fit—I just could not make any time. Rod, however, was starting to kick in and was moving along with only minor difficulty on the climbs.

By the time we ascended Third Mtn., the fog had completely cleared, giving us a good view of Mt. Katahdin. We stopped at a stream between Third and Columbus Mtns. for water and exchanged greetings with a northbound thru-hiker ("Blind Faith") whom I had met in the Bigelows about two weeks before. After crossing Columbus Mtn., we descended into the Chairback Shelter and decided to spend the night there.

My heel was now giving me so much trouble that I could barely walk. By now, I was convinced that I had a fracture and was concerned about how much additional damage might occur because of the daily pounding it was getting. I had no choice—we were in the Maine Wilderness, and it was unlikely that we could hike out at Katahdin Stream Campground at the base of Katahdin by September 24. At this point, we had used up our extra day, and we would have to push it to make it even by the 25th. This certainly was not turning out the way I had planned. I wanted us to be able to take our time through the Wilderness and fully enjoy this magnificent back country. We were still determined to make the best of it and reach Katahdin Stream by the 25th, and we had one week to accomplish this.

We were joined later in the afternoon by "The Royal Berks." In an effort to keep me off my feet, Rod did all the evening chores, including going down a steep embankment to get water and building a nice cozy fire in the fireplace in front of the shelter. (The "Red Alert" had been lifted a few days before.) We had a restful evening enjoying the company of "The Royal Berks," the campfire, and the pleasant weather that had moved in.

After a very restful night, we hiked up to the summit of Chairback Mtn., where the views of the Maine Wilderness were outstanding. To the north was Katahdin, and I felt a surge of excitement as I eyed my goal and realized that in a few days my long walk would be over. The descent of Chairback Mtn. was on a series of rough rock steps. The MATC had ingeniously arranged massive boulders and rocks to form a staircase effect, making it more manageable. We crossed the logging road in the Pleasant River Valley, used by trucks to get logs to mills in central Maine, and were surprised to see cars and several non-hikers in the area. Vehicle access can be gained to this area via these logging roads and paper company check gates near the Katahdin Iron Works (the site of an iron-producing community during the mid-1800's). The old Iron Works site has been turned into a museum and is located at Brownsville Junction near ME11.

There are two noteworthy features near the AT crossing of the west branch of the Pleasant River. The first is The Hermitage, a magnificent stand of virgin white pine, some of which tower as high as 130 feet. The AT passes directly through this stand, which is owned by the Maine Chapter of the Nature Conservancy. The second highlight is Gulf Hagas, a 2.5-mile gorge carved by the west branch of the Pleasant River, featuring many cascades and waterfalls. Gulf Hagas can be accessed by a 5.2-mile loop trail leading off the AT. We would have liked very much to have made this side trip, if time and my physical condition would have permitted. From my readings and talks with hikers who have made this trip, I understand it to be one of the most dramatic features in the Maine Wilderness. Someday, I hope to come back to the area and hike it.

We hiked into the Carl Newhall Shelter, our goal for the day, and once again joined "The Royal Berks." Rod supplied a cozy fire, by which we all shared good fellowship and a restorative hot meal. The Trail literature mentioned reported moose sightings near the shelter. We did not see any, but I heard one calling several times during the evening and night.

At this point in our hike, we were one day behind the planned schedule and would likely be unable to make it up. If I had been in the condition I usually am at this point in a hike, this could have been accomplished. As for Rod, he was really moving along fine— even on the climbs. My main concern now was not to lose any more days. If we didn't, we would have a shot at Katahdin on September 26. If we lost another day, Dave would not be able to hike the mountain with us. Another concern crossed my mind— what about the weather on September 26. This was late September in north central Maine, and the mountain is one mile high, making it subject to very unpredictable weather this time of year, often ice and snow. I had heard that the rangers in Baxter State Park will not permit hikers to make the climb during these conditions.

The next day's hike, our fourth full day, would take us over the last mountain range we would be crossing—the White Cap Range. This range consisted of four peaks: Gulf Hagas Mtn. (2,683 feet), West Peak (3,181 feet), Hay Mtn. (3,244 feet) and White Cap (3,644 feet).

My pack thermometer registered 33 degrees Fahrenheit when we left the shelter on the ascent of Gulf Hagas Mtn. We applauded the cool weather on these climbs, and we had several ahead of us that day. Near the summit of Gulf Hagas, we met two southbounders ("Cliff Hanger" and "Ridge Rat") who reported that the view from White Cap was extraordinary and that Katahdin was clearly visible and waiting. The climbs over West Peak and Hay Mtn. went well although my climbing speed was slow. We were not disappointed when we reached the summit of White Cap, and the hikers' reports were accurate. Looking to the southwest on the horizon were the Bigelows which I had crossed about twelve days before. To the northeast across the picturesque Maine landscape, was the Big One—Katahdin—patiently waiting for my arrival.

We sat on the rocks on the exposed summit and rested with our shoes off, cooling our feet and enjoying the vast expanse of the Maine Wilderness below and beyond us. I told Rod there were few places left in this country where you could sit on a mountain top and not see some sign of man's presence. His reply was a statement that he often made while on this hike, "Words can't describe what's out here."

After some recovery time, I bound my foot and heel with one of my extra socks and secured it with duct tape in an effort to provide a cushion for my injury. I was willing to try anything, and this improvised brace worked fine as long as I was sitting, but I knew I could never reach Katahdin that way.

We descended White Cap to the Logan Brook Shelter, where we stopped for water and a break. While we were there, "The Royal Berks" came along and told us they would be spending the night there. They were not carrying a tent, so they had to go from shelter to shelter. The next one was about 11 1/2 miles on, a greater distance than they could cover during the remainder of the day. Rod and I continued on to the East Branch of the Pleasant River and pitched our tent by the AT. We had hoped to hike to the Mountain Pond Campsite which was 1 1/2 miles further, but I was in such pain I just could go no further.

I was also getting weaker, as I was still not eating properly. My normal constant munching generally helped keep my caloric intake commensurate with the high calorie consumption while hiking—often running as high as 5,000 a day—and I was not doing this. Again, Rod did all the chores—retrieved water, hung our wet clothes on a short line to dry (no fire though)—as I could barely stand.

We had passed southbound hikers for the past two days who spoke of a hiker's feast that was going on at Antlers Campsite, about 15.5 miles ahead. They encouraged us not to miss this, for there was a lot of good food, drink, fellowship and a place to kick back before completing the hike. When we asked specific questions about the feast, we were told we would find out when we got there. It was a balmy delightful evening, so we spread our tarp on the ground in front of the tent to prepare and eat our supper. Rod had been making lengthy entries into his journal, and he shared some of the contents with me. It sounded as though a marriage proposal was in the making in the near future. Before retiring for the night we reviewed our Trail guide and profile map and decided to make a serious attempt to reach Antlers the next day. We had cleared the western half of the Maine Wilderness, which was the mountainous part. Except for two low mountains ahead, the rest was flat lake country. We were determined to make Antlers, even if it meant some hiking by flashlight.

The next morning, we were on the Trail very early—in fact, just after daybreak. We delayed breakfast until we reached a campsite by Mountain Pond, the spot we intended to reach the night before. "Blind Faith" had tented there and was packing up to move on. We had our breakfast and were shortly on our way.

Near Crawford Pond, we met three southbounders who were dropped off just moments before by a bush pilot who had landed on the Pond. They were going to hike the western end of the Wilderness which we had just completed. After learning about my injury, they gave me an Ace bandage to bind it up to relieve some of the pain. The arrangement that I had used with the sock and duct tape had helped for a while but did not work out well because of its bulk. I put the Ace bandage on and left it on until we reached the Cooper Brook Shelter. Like the sock arrangement, this worked fine for a while, but the bulk in my boot was still a problem.

The Cooper Brook Shelter was situated in an unspoiled setting on a cascading stream and had a nice area in front for swimming, This would have been a great place to spend the night, but Rod and I still had about eight miles to Antlers, and we were firm in our objective. By making Antlers, we could accomplish two things. First, we would pick up a few of the miles we had lost during the earlier days. Second, there was some kind of wonderful feast awaiting us there, and we wanted to be a part of it.

The section of the AT from Pleasant River Campsite through our day's hike was the easiest we had had in the Wilderness so far, and that favored our reaching Antlers. We passed through more stands of very large white pines, and the hike through them was marvelous with a smooth trail and the very aromatic pine scent. The hardwoods were showing more and more color in their leaves each day and would be reaching full color a few days hence.

When we were within a mile of Antlers, we saw this sign posted on a tree—"Welcome all foot travelers to the Annual food-a-thon sponsored by Antlers Camp." Rod and I picked up our pace because we wanted to get there before dark. We passed the second sign,—"No catch no joke." Oh, yes, we were almost there. When we arrived at Antlers, we were greeted very graciously by "Cat" and Alex (hosts of Antlers Camp), who invited us to set our tent up under their large tarp if we so wished, or any site nearby. "Cat" also invited us, after we had set up our tent and taken care of our chores, to meet with the group for a feast around the campfire. We joined "Blind Faith," E. T.," "Trooper," "Raven," "Holiday," and "Dragline" (all hikers we had met earlier on the Trail). We were served chicken, fresh clams caught from Lower Jo Mary Lake, spaghetti, cooked veggies, snacks such as cheese, crackers, raisins, peanuts—even wine to drink. What a feast and what a great evening!

"Cat" made some loon calls, which were answered all around Jo Mary Lake. The loon tops my list of most-favored birds of the American forest. Each call I heard gave me a deep thrill, and I thought of Edward Howe Forbush's statement made in *A Natural History of American Birds*: "Of all the wild creatures in the northern forest, none seems best to typify the stark wilderness of primeval nature as the loon."

After a full evening of good food and wonderful fellowship, Rod and I retired to our cozy little tent, contented and thankful that we were able to be a part of all of this. As usual, we talked and reflected on our day. Rod made entries in his journal, and then it was time for sleep.

A note about Antlers Camp—this was the site of one of the early sporting camps which were scattered throughout the wilderness of Maine. These camps provided a wilderness retreat for those with means who wanted to hunt and fish in these great north woods. According to the literature, their popularity diminished by the 1950's, and the facilities fell to ruin and were being reclaimed by the forest. The buildings at Antlers were all gone, but the pine grove by Lower Jo Mary Lake is a favored campsite along the AT in the Maine Wilderness and a spot on our hike through Maine's north woods that Rod and I will never forget.

The next morning, after packing up our tent and gear, we were served a fabulous hiker's breakfast consisting of tasty and highly nutritional foods such as hot oatmeal, an eggs-and-bacon mixture, coffee, juice, homemade toast, plus all the munchies that were leftover. We noticed that the wine bottle was very low, for many of the hikers were quite thirsty the night before. Before leaving, we expressed our sincere thanks and appreciation to "Cat" and Alex for their most generous hospitality, and they invited us to stay another night. We wished we could have. This had been another one of those "Trail Magic" moments that tend to happen from time to time along the AT.

As we were leaving Antlers, I turned to Rod and told him that now I knew what Dan "Wingfoot" Bruce meant in a statement about Antlers he had written in his book, *The Thru Hiker's Handbook*. He wrote, "At least once a year, 'Manna from Heaven' (The Cat's got my tongue, so only a fortunate few will learn what this means)." I told him we were two of those fortunate few.

By reaching Antlers that day, we had picked up a few miles that were lost earlier, but we still had to maintain a good pace to reach Katahdin Stream on the 25th. This was September 22, and we had 45 miles to go to reach Katahdin Stream and another 5.2 miles to Baxter Peak on Mt. Katahdin. We hiked to the Potaywadjo Shelter which had a 14-foot diameter spring of the same name nearby. According to literature, this is the largest spring anywhere along the AT. I was very impressed with the volume and quality of water it was producing. While we were getting water from the spring, several hikers who we had spent the night with at Antlers passed us heading for Wadleigh Stream Shelter, which was also our destination for the day.

We continued on to where the AT touched the shoreline of Pemadumcook Lake (meaning "extended sandbar place")—how's that for another Indian name? My Trail guide lists this as one of the largest lakes the AT touches along its entire length, and as we stood on its shoreline, we were indeed amazed at its size. The weather had been cloudy since we left Antlers, and it looked like we would be getting some rain. While we were standing there, a fog moved in, obscuring part of the lake and its northern shoreline.

We began the hike up Nahmakanta Stream (meaning "plenty of fish"), which connects a lake of the same name to Pemadumcook Lake. It began to rain, and the fog settled in along the stream. I was hopeful we might see salmon spawning in the stream as our guide literature had mentioned, but the weather became so unpleasant that we kept moving. The AT meandered along the stream, ascending and descending drop-offs for about five miles to its head at the outflow of Nahmakanta Lake.

The weather did not improve as we skirted the western shore of the Lake for over two miles to the Wadleigh Stream Shelter. We had hiked in wet conditions for most of the day and were glad to find a place that was dry. There was one problem, though—the shelter was almost filled with hikers who had arrived before us and had staked their claims on the few square feet of floor space in the shelter. This meant we had to prepare our meal outside, having little protection from the rain under the shelter's overhang.

After our meal, the hikers ("Holiday," "Trooper," "E. T.," "Paluche," and Rob) made space for us in the shelter to bed down. We were grateful, because that night came the hardest downpour that I had seen since leaving Franconia. The ceiling of the shelter was supporting an array of packs, clothing, boots, cameras, etc., and gave the appearance of different sizes and shapes of stalactites hanging from the roof of a cave.

Rod and I chose to sleep with our head to the rear of the shelter where the roofline almost joined the floor making our heads just inches from the metal roof. The sound of the rain pounding on the roof sounded like a dozen drummers introducing a major sporting event. Two hikers had tented near the shelter, and we were hoping they would fair okay during this hard pounding rain. We were especially glad we had chosen not to tent, because the next day we would have been packing up a wet tent and gear; and I certainly did not need any extra weight to carry.

At daybreak, we peered out of the shelter and into a mist, the trees dripping from the night of heavy rain. There was excitement in the air, as the hikers were hurriedly preparing their breakfasts over their small gas stoves and packing up. Katahdin was near and everyone was anxious to get there. Most, like us, had families and/or friends meeting them at Katahdin Stream Campground to share in their great moment of completing the AT. Rod and I knew that, with their fast hiking pace, we would not see them again before reaching Katahdin Stream. We sent word with them to tell Joan if they saw her not to expect us at Katahdin Stream on the 24th as we had hoped; instead, we would arrive at Abol Bridge on that date.

We were late leaving the shelter and had a rather stiff climb up Mesuntabunt Mtn. ("Three Heads")—not a terribly high mountain, but one that nevertheless got the cardiovascular going by the time we reached the summit. The weather had cleared, and the views of Nesuntabunt Lake and Katahdin were outstanding. The distance to Katahdin had been reduced to 35 miles from the summit of this mountain. As we got closer, it was looming ever larger.

After descending to Pollywog Stream, we met a southbounder who shared a bit of information with us that would lead to another one of those "Trail Magic" happenings. He said that a bush pilot had flown in two men for a fishing trip on Rainbow Lake, located about six miles from our present location, and that they had treated him to food and drink. We really did not give much thought to it, as we had planned to tent at the south end of the lake near the dam, which would be about two miles from their camp.

We continued our hike to the Rainbow Stream Shelter where we decided to prepare our evening meal early, after which we would hike on to try to make up a few miles, making the next day's hike into Abol Bridge more manageable. The Rainbow Stream Shelter is rather special, because it was photographed by *National Geographic Magazine*. The picture was used in a feature story about the AT: "A Tunnel through Time" by Noel Grove and appeared in the February, 1987, issue of the magazine.

After an early dinner, we proceeded on toward the Rainbow Lake Dam area, where our Trail guide listed a tent site. Before reaching the dam, however, we hit a Trail relocation that crossed over the ridge away from the dam area, rejoining the AT about one mile further on. The relocation had completely bypassed the tent area near the dam. Near the junction of the relocation and the old AT, we passed two fishermen who told us we would have to hike back one mile to the tent sites near the dam, if that was where we wanted to go. They advised us it was only about one mile further on to the Rainbow Spring tent area, offering tent pads, an excellent spring and a great view of the lake.

That sounded good to us, so we moved on with Rod in the lead, soon out of sight. I had really been struggling for several days and enduring a lot of pain, and my strength and stamina were greatly diminished. My pack was still quite heavy—I had consumed less than half of my food supply in the eight days we had been hiking. In fact, we had given some of our excess food to a hiker back at the Cooper Brook Shelter in an effort to reduce some pack weight.

Before reaching the Rainbow Spring tent site, I could hear voices up ahead, and I thought it was Rod talking to some of the thru-hikers we had spent the night with at Wadleigh Stream Shelter. Upon my arrival, I found Rod visiting with the two gentlemen the southbounder had told us about. Their names were Randy and Bruce Mailloux, brothers from coastal Maine who fly by bush plane to Rainbow Lake each September to fish and enjoy the great natural beauty of the area. Now comes another bit of "Trail Magic." They told us to pitch our tent on a pad near theirs and invited us to join them by their campfire. We accepted and were given drinks while they grilled steaks over the open fire. The steaks were huge—two-inch-thick slabs of meat, which when grilled to perfection were butterflied making four steaks, two of which they gave to us. They had also prepared a pot of cooked vegetables.

We had eaten earlier at the Rainbow Stream Shelter, but that consisted mostly of Trail food, and I had not been eating right anyway. This meal was an absolute delight and truly the best meal we had had since the night before we left Newport to hike the

Maine Wilderness. Maybe this would give me back some of the energy I had lost by not eating well. After an enjoyable evening of good food and fellowship, Rod and I retired to our little tent and thought how thankful we were that we did not tent at the dam as we had originally planned and that we had met these two fine gentlemen.

The next morning the Mailloux brothers extended more of their hospitality by inviting us to a very hearty breakfast. We were served the full course—eggs, bacon, hot cereal, toast, coffee, juice, and all of this in the great Maine Wilderness. I thought of the gracious hospitality we had received from "Cat" and Alex at Antlers and its timing. It happened at a point in our hike when we needed and received an uplift. Now, here at Rainbow Spring, it happened again. Our bodies had received both a physical and spiritual recharge at a time when we sorely needed it.

We thanked Bruce and Randy for their charitable hospitality and a memorable evening of fellowship and began the final leg of the AT to Abol Bridge. The AT skirts the shoreline of Rainbow Lake for about another three miles. As we were hiking along, Rod and I understood why Bruce and Randy come here. Rainbow is a crystal clear lake, reflecting a shore lined with the multi-colors of fall foliage at its peak and a bright blue sky overhead. Its natural beauty is unexcelled.

It was in this area in 1954 that "Grandma" Emma Gatewood got lost on her first attempt to thru-hike the AT. After an unsuccessful attempt by searchers to locate her, she hiked out near here on her own. She regrouped her forces and in 1955 hiked the entire Trail beginning in Georgia and completing her hike in September at the young age of sixty-five. As if that were not enough, she hiked the AT two more times, the Long Trail, the Oregon Trail and a few others.

Within the first mile after leaving Rainbow Springs, my heel started to flare up, the usual pattern after hiking a while in the mornings. Rod insisted on carrying some of the items from my pack to relieve a bit of the weight. He was conditioned and had become a strong and remarkable hiking companion. I permitted him to take some of the weight for a while, but after a few miles I told him I could manage it.

We left the Rainbow Lake shoreline and ascended to Rainbow Ledges, a 1,500-foot hump between the Lake and the Penobscot River Valley. From these ledges, we had a marvelous view of the Maine landscape in full fall colors with the beautiful Rainbow Lake beneath us. To the north was Katahdin ("The Greatest Mountain") rising like a giant above a landscape of lakes and forests. Rod and I sat on a large rock staring at this magnificent mountain which was framed by an opening in the trees, and we were overwhelmed by its mass.

Before we left Rainbow Ledges, "The Royal Berks" came along, headed for the Hurd Brook Shelter—the last one in the Wilderness. We had not seen them for the last five days, as we were a few miles ahead of them. After a brief visit and photo session, we hiked off the Ledges with them to the shelter. It is about 3 1/2 miles from this last shelter to Abol Bridge. Since my pace was slow, I told Rod to move on and that I would be along. When I hiked out on the Golden Road at Abol Bridge, Rod was waiting for me by the highway. The Golden Road is a private paved highway controlled by a large paper company and is used primarily by large logging trucks to transport logs from the back country to mills in the Millinocket area.

Abol Bridge was the end of the "100-Mile Wilderness," and we had completed it on September 24 in about 9 1/2 days. Katahdin Stream Campground was 9.3 miles further, and there was no way we could make that distance on this day. We were wondering if the hikers whose help we had enlisted at Wadleigh Stream had delivered our message to Joan, indicating that we would not be hiking into Katahdin Stream Campground on the 24th of September but would instead be at Abol Bridge. We were also wondering if Melinda and Dave had arrived okay in Bangor. Dave was to drive our motorhome from Newport to the Medway/Millinocket area this morning. We trusted that things were unfolding as planned but were anxious to see everyone and wondered if they would drive to Abol Bridge later in the day.

Rod and I hiked up to the Bridge which was about one-quarter mile from the AT trailhead and provided a truly spectacular view of Katahdin from its walkway. The Bridge crosses the Penobscot River and has what is said to be the third best view of Katahdin from the AT. We crossed to the north end of the Bridge and stopped at the store by the highway, where we had cheeseburgers, drinks and inquired about their campground. Joan did not show up; and we figured she had not received our message, so we set up our tent in the Abol Bridge Campground.

We had not had a good hot shower since leaving Newport a week and a half earlier; and, needless to say, one was in order. My pack thermometer read 29 degrees Fahrenheit when we got up the next morning. We left early as we were anxious to hike the 9.3-mile final link to Katahdin Stream Campground.

The AT follows the banks of the Penobscot River upstream for about three miles. Near the middle of this section, beavers had built a dam across a brook, flooding the area where the AT crosses. We had to bushwack around the area, and this proved to be a major obstacle. The Trail then leaves the Penobscot and follows the Nesowadnehunk ("swift stream between mountains") upstream and enters the Baxter State Park's south boundary. Mt. Katahdin lies within this 201,018-acre tract, the largest area east of the Mississippi River devoted solely to wilderness use. This magnificent tract of wilderness land was donated to the state of Maine by its former Governor, Percival P. Baxter, with many stipulations.

We continued on up the stream, passing cascades and Big and Little Niagara Falls—two very beautiful and impressive waterfalls. As we hiked on toward Daicy Pond, we thought what a perfect day this would have been to make the climb up Katahdin. The sky was absolutely clear, and the air was cool and calm. If we could have maintained our original schedule, this was the day we would have made the climb. The next day would be the only shot at the mountain when our three children could hike it with me, so we hoped the fair weather would continue. We reached Daicy Pond by mid-day, registered at the Ranger Station and stretched out on the grass by the office to enjoy a remarkable view of Katahdin across the glassy water.

The Ranger came down and looked at my heel which had swollen and was causing me a great deal of pain. She was convinced I had a fracture and that I should be off of it. She also advised us that the weather forecast for the next day did not look favorable for our climb. Rain was expected to move in during the night and continue through the next day—not the forecast we wanted to hear at all. Besides this, I was concerned about whether I was physically up to making the climb. After about half an hour's rest, we began the two-mile hike to Katahdin Stream Campground. We skirted Daicy Pond with continued views of Katahdin and passed near Tracy and Elbow Ponds to where the AT joins Perimeter Road. It was only one-half mile to the Campground, and Rod said he would move on and see me there.

I did not have a sense of urgency to hurry this last one-half mile, even though I was anxious to see my family. I was just plodding along thinking, "Is this really happening?" It had been so long coming, and I became lost in thought with reflections of my hike and what it meant to both myself and my family. I thought of the pleasure of having Rod hike the Wilderness with me and the extraordinary mental and physical growth he had shown. He had truly demonstrated the skills of a seasoned hiker, and it was a comfort to have him by my side. I also thought of the sacrifices made by Melinda and Dave to share the final miles of the Trail with me. Then there was Joan, who was with me on that foggy morning in Georgia when I first began the hike and had remained totally committed to my goal of completing the Trail. She had been with me physically and spiritually across the fourteen states and would be at Katahdin Stream Campground during the afternoon to greet me.

I had been so deep in thought that I did not hear the car approaching from behind until it was a few feet from me. I stepped to the side of the road and allowed it to pass. The brake lights came on, bringing it to a stop. I walked up to the driver's side as the window lowered. Two ladies were in the car, and one remarked, "You look like you have a limp. Could we give you a ride?" I thanked them but replied that I had hiked a long way on the AT and had become a purist. If I accepted a ride, I would just have to return to this point again to make my hike official. I also told them that our son Rod was ahead of me and that we were headed for Katahdin Stream Campground where our family would be meeting us during the afternoon. After some conversation, the lady on the passenger side handed me a laminated card, and then they drove on. Written on the card was the following:

The "Thru-Hikers" Did it—
(I walked along with them!)

I've walked with the hikers, on their final climb,
In fact, I've done this time after time.
And once they sign the register, at Katahdin Stream—
"Silent is their chatter," as they near their dream
From hiking the Appalachian Trail—six months they
    struggled,
Managing not to fail to make those miles, even though,
"Day after day," was a very tough go.
Backpacking the items, so necessary to life:
Some left their jobs, family and wife,
To realize and experience those inborn urges,
To complete from start to finish, the Trail that merges
With so many others, denoted by "blue blazes"—
But they searched for the white ones, they searched
    "like crazy",
From Georgia's Springer Mountain to Mt. Katahdin in
    Maine—
To climb the Greatest Mountain, of all, they came!
And I've "walked" along with them,
"Though not one step!"—Yet,
      ——"In Spirit," I pray,——
        This—Trail Angel—
          did help!

      —Dorothy Mauldin O. W. G.
      "Ankle Express"

I read the lines in this poem and reread them before reaching Katahdin Stream Campground and was deeply moved. As I hiked into the Campground, I noticed that the shelters were all full. There were a lot of people in the area moving about, many of whom I am sure were friends and family members of thru-hikers. Some hikers had completed their climb of the mountain already and were in celebration with their family and friends, and some were still coming in even as I dropped my pack and sat down in the grass with Rod. "Blind Faith," "Ketchup," "French Fry," "Raven" and others were congratulating each other and making introductions to family members.

Joan, Melinda and Dave did not arrive until about 2:45 PM, accompanied by our friends, Dallas and Frances Chadwell, who had made the trip from West Virginia especially to share in our celebration of my completion of the Trail. Dallas had said many times that he wanted to be there for a video tape interview, which he did following our reunion greetings. The two ladies who offered me a ride on Perimeter Road came by, extended their congratulations and met our family. The one who had given me the poem was Dorothy Mauldin, poet from Marietta, Georgia, and was staying in one of the cabins at Daicy Pond. Dorothy is known by many thru-hikers as "Ankle Express," and her name has appeared in AT Trail literature.

As we were leaving Katahdin Stream Campground, I looked up at the massive mountain and saw its upper heights being crowded with clouds—a weather system was definitely moving in. We drove to the entrance gate of Baxter State Park, inquired from the Ranger what time the Park gate would open the next morning, and were told that it opened at 6:00 AM. We drove to our base camp at Medway, about 40 miles from Katahdin Stream Campground. We knew we would need to get a very early start the next morning to make the drive to the Campground. The eight miles from the Park gate to the Campground was rough and unpaved and would require extra time. After reaching our base camp, we enjoyed a wonderful evening of renewal with family and friends, had a great dinner and settled in for the night.

TOP: Herb and Rod at the beginning of the "100-Mile
      Wilderness" near Monson

Photo by Joan Eye

BOTTOM: Rod crossing Big Wilson Stream in the
         "100-Mile Wilderness"

TOP: Steep rock scramble off Chairback Mountain
BOTTOM: The feast at Antlers in the "100-Mile
Wilderness"

TOP: Herb and Rod enjoying a view of Katahdin from
    Rainbow Ledges—Baxter Peak is 20 miles from
    this point.
BOTTOM: Katahdin as viewed from Abol Bridge

15

THE GREATEST MOUNTAIN

*"Maybe had the weather been different we would have
summitted—maybe the next time—but the point is to
have a next time."*
— *Rick Wilcox, AMC Outdoors Magazine*

*"While on the mountain, I could not help but think of
the song, 'Our God is an Awesome God' "*
— *Our Son Dave*

I slept but was somewhat restless and woke up several times during the night. Around 4:00 AM, I felt the motorhome rock due to the blowing wind and heard pattering on the roof—not good weather signs for the day; but it was September 26. I woke everyone up and we had a quick breakfast. Before leaving, Melinda, Dave and Rod presented me with a poster they had made with a special message on it, expressing their feelings about me and my hike. The message was...

THE TRAIL IS LIFE'S PARALLEL

You had a dream to see the world in a different way,
Through skies of blue and clouds of gray,
Through forests green and over rocks so rugged,
With blistered feet at times, you just
Had to stay with the drive to hike on.

That is something that you have taught us, Dad.
Thank you for your courage, strength and endurance
to succeed. That is why in our minds you are
             "THE WISE MAN"
CONGRATULATIONS, DAD! WE LOVE YOU!
        Rod   Melinda   Dave
    "The Waterman"   "Nim"

I was deeply moved————!

We drove in fog and rain, stopping in Millinocket to get rain gear for Dave. We then continued on to the Park gate where the Ranger gave us a weather report and advised us not to go above tree line because rain and heavy winds were forecast, conditions which at higher elevations could be dangerous. I was disappointed, but safety concerns were utmost. I was not about to take a risk that would endanger any of us. We did decide, however, that we would climb to tree line and then assess whether the elements would permit us to go a little higher. When we reached Katahdin Stream Campground at 7:00 AM, no one had signed the register. However, we did see "The Royal Berks" hike over to the Ranger Station.

We began the ascent at 7:00 in fog and rain, and I knew then we would be lucky even to reach tree line, but the experience of hiking the mountain together (even if it meant part way) was important to me and them as well. The Wilderness hike had really conditioned Rod—he was physically and mentally ready for the challenge of the mountain. In fact, he chose to carry his big Kelty with extra food and water for all of us. My physical condition was poor, and I was struggling after we had hiked the mile to the bridge over Katahdin Stream. Dave was hiking with me up ahead, and Rod had teamed with Melinda. She was having some difficulty breathing due to her asthmatic condition that was being aggravated by the weather.

We climbed higher and the wind turned stronger and colder, with the fog becoming more dense. Visibility was just enough to see ahead a few feet. As we ascended along the Trail, we had been watching the countdown miles which were painted on the rocks along the Trail—4—3. Everything along the Trail was wet and dripping from the rain and density of the heavy fog; and, as it became steeper and rougher, Rod provided assistance to Melinda over the large slippery boulders. He would ascend first and then reach back with his staff so she could hold on to it as he pulled her up. I was enjoying watching them.

Dave was doing fairly well and had many questions about the Trail and the mountain. We stopped for a snack break just past the 3-mile marker. The weather continued to deteriorate—it was getting colder—and the wind was whipping the heavy fog past us through the scrub spruce trees and around the exposed boulders. I was really feeling a chill, and the dense fog and cold wind were causing breathing problems for Melinda.

We ascended past an area known as "The Cave," then up some huge boulders on Hunt Spur, where metal rungs had been placed to aid in the climb over them. We had reached tree line, and the weather had become extreme. Again, I had those flashbacks of Moosilauke, Old Speck, Saddleback and others when the wind was so strong I could barely stand. If it were this bad here, I could only imagine what it would be like another 1,700 feet up on Baxter.

Dave and I waited until Rod and Melinda caught up, and I told them we were not going to attempt to climb any higher. To make the attempt in conditions such as these was not worth the risk. I told them to find a spot on the rocks as much out of the weather as they could, because I wanted to take a few minutes to talk to them before we began the descent.

From the boulders on Hunt Spur on Mount Katahdin, I gave them the following message: "I have carried with me every day that I have hiked the AT all the way from Humpback Rocks in Virginia" (the point where my brother Osbra had hiked to with me from Springer Mtn. and unfortunately was unable to continue because of a quite sudden illness and death) "a flower that he grew in his garden and that was placed on his casket on the day of his funeral; and I brought it today to complete this journey for him, too. I am going to cast it into the wind on Mt. Katahdin symbolizing a journey that he has made spiritually with us, too. Osbra, you made it with us today, too. I am very grateful our children could join me in completing this journey—and this really isn't the end of the Trail but the beginning of a new one. It has been a journey that has helped me grow spiritually, physically and to develop an even greater appreciation of life and this great country and world in which we live. It has helped me to develop more patience, self-discipline and to fine tune the senses."

"I was blessed to have Rod do the last 100 miles with me, and it gave us a chance to spend quality time that we had not had due to our busy schedules. Due to Dave and Melinda's family and career commitments and our busy schedules, we have not had a lot of quality time with them either. Here on the mountain this morning, we have gathered to share these special moments together including Mom" (Joan) "who has sent this message (by tape recorder). 'Yes, I really am here, too. The completion of this hike has been a longtime goal for Dad and I guess you might say for our whole family. Dad has proven that it is important to have goals—goals are the reasons for getting up each morning and reasons to keep looking ahead in your life. I hope that each one of you can say some day that you have reached at least one of your future goals in life. Even though I am not physically with you today, I am there in spirit and prayer just as I have been with Dad all through his hike. Your support and mine have, if it is possible, made it a little easier for him. As you all know, the support we all give each other is what makes our family special; and I thank you for being there for him today. Love, Mom'—Now, my message to the three of you: I hope that my hiking the AT will inspire each of you to—just like Mom said—choose a goal, make a commitment and go for it. Live your dream—don't be afraid to get out there and do what you have dreamed of doing. I have fulfilled a dream that I had as a youngster and carried through my life."

The harsh weather really started to penetrate my weakened body, and Melinda continued to have breathing problems. The boys, however, were doing fine. Dave had taken Rod's pack and told him he would carry it off the mountain. We began the descent through the fog and mist into the valley with the three of them joking, playing and moving along as though they had been on a stroll, reminding me of their childhood. I was struggling and hoping I could reach the valley. The three of them had done exceptionally well and reached Katahdin Stream long before I did.

After I joined them, we all sat on the bridge over Katahdin Stream, reflecting on our day on the mountain. We were disappointed that we did not reach the summit but realized that it was not to be on this day. We were, however, grateful and will always cherish the time that we spent together on The Greatest Mountain. Each vowed that some day they would return and complete the hike to the summit. Even though we did not reach the summit of that mountain, we reached the summit in our love for each other—the Trail and the mountain saw to that—Trail Magic.

Joan arrived at the Campground about half an hour after we did and was pleasantly surprised that we were there already. She had spent a good part of the day with Dorothy Mauldin and her friend Joan in the Daicy Pond area and was excited at having seen a big bull moose near there.

As we were leaving Katahdin Stream Campground, I looked back toward the giant encased in a blanket of fog and thought— there are two miles up there that I have not seen—I'll be back. We returned to our base camp in Medway and made preparation to leave the following morning. Joan was to take Dave to the airport in Bangor for his flight home. In the meantime, Rod, Melinda and I were going to take the motorhome back to the Newport base camp, close enough to the airport to conveniently get them on their flight the following day.

After our sons and daughter left, Joan and I took several days to return to our home in Ohio. We both needed lots of R & R—Joan was pretty much wiped out from several hundreds of miles of travel to back country trailheads, preparing dinners, lunches and generally looking after all of us, including hikers we had met on the Trail. My physical condition was not good—I had lost 25 pounds which might have been okay if it had all been fat, but I had lost muscle along with it. I had become weak, and I still could not stand on my feet without pain in my heel.

When we arrived home, I was in my physician's office the following morning. After examination, he immediately sent me to an orthopedic surgeon, who x-rayed and found I had a stress fracture. He was not at all pleased that I had been hiking on it, especially for so long and for such a distance, which I figured to be about 180 miles. He ordered me to stay off of it and to make regular visits to his office so he could monitor the healing. This injury caused me to favor that foot with a limp for months. Even today, when I put weight on it after being seated or when I get out of bed, I feel discomfort.

After a few days of rest, we began to reflect on the hike, and I told Joan that other thru-hikers had talked of the "letdown" feeling they had after completing the Trail. I told her I was feeling that, too, and did not have a feeling of closure. I had finished the hike, but not the Trail. I still could not get those two miles out of my mind—the two miles from Hunt Spur to Baxter Peak, the official northern terminus of the AT—miles we did not complete because of the weather. I had hiked every mile and followed every white blaze since Springer, even hiked some of the sections twice and dozens of miles of blue blazes; but still there are those two miles, and important miles they are. My last two—I had to complete them!

TOP: Katahdin Stream Campground with
Mt. Katahdin in background
Photo by Rodney Eye
BOTTOM: Rod helps Melinda up over
boulders on Hunt Spur

TOP: Dave on ascent of Katahdin in boulders on
  Hunt Spur
BOTTOM: The meeting on Mt. Katahdin (Hunt Spur)
  Left to right—Rod, Melinda, Herb and Dave

Photo taken on automatic exposure

16

THE END AND A NEW BEGINNING

"Man is born to die, his works are short lived. Buildings crumble, monuments decay, wealth vanishes, but Katahdin in all its glory forever shall remain the mountain of the people of Maine."
—Percival P. Baxter, Governor of Maine 1921-1925

Joan and I returned to Maine the following September. Yes, we drove 1,000 miles from our home in Ohio to Mt. Katahdin so I could hike those two miles to Baxter Peak, the highest point on Katahdin. There were other motives, however, for our making the trip, including a yearning to return to those great north woods. I wanted to rehike some of the areas along the AT that had left a lasting impression on me. I guess, in short, once you have experienced the grandeur of New England, you just have to return.

On our way to Katahdin, we stopped at the campground in Newport, Maine, which we had used as a base camp the previous year. We liked the area and had established a friendship with the managers. We had planned to continue on to Medway the following day to establish a base camp there for my hike of Katahdin and perhaps the Gulf Hagas area in the Maine Wilderness. These plans were changed abruptly when we received a telephone call from our children informing us that Joan's mother had passed away. We put the motorhome in storage, arranged for a flight home and were home nearly a week before returning to Newport. During this time, the weather conditions had not been favorable for hiking and certainly not for making the climb up Katahdin.

It was September 19 when we left Newport and moved our base camp to Medway, where we had stayed the year before. We had been watching the weather with keen interest and received a good forecast for the next day, so we made plans for me to make the climb. We were up early and on our way to reach the Baxter State Park gate by its 6:00 AM opening time. The rays of the rising sun highlighted the rugged beauty of this magnificent mountain as we approached the Park gate. I had a surge of excitement and wished our children could be here to make the climb with me. My heel was not hurting; I had gained back a lot of the weight and with it strength; the weather was perfect; and the Ranger at the gate gave us a great forecast; it was go—all right!

As we were driving the eight miles from the Park gate to Katahdin Stream Campground, we thought how coincidental—it had rained here in Maine the entire time we were gone for Joan's mother's funeral; and now it was clear. We had lost a dear family member, but it was as though she had arranged for me to have a beautiful day for my climb.

The Campground was bustling with activity as it was the year before when we pulled in and parked. Many hikers were in preparation to make their final climb, and well-wishers were there to see them off. I signed the register at 7:02 AM and noticed that six other hikers had already signed in and were en route. I thought while hiking along Katahdin Stream, how different this hike was than last year's. The Trail was dry with no fog anywhere and no injuries. I felt great and was confident about making the climb, in contrast to last year when my physical condition was poor. My only regret was that I was hiking alone and wished family could have been with me on the mountain to share this very special day.

As I passed the 4-mile marker, my mind flashed back to last year, when we eagerly watched for the markers as we ascended. I reached the 3-mile marker, remembering how I was struggling at this point before. I reached the lower area of "The Boulders" at tree line, recalling that this was the point to which Melinda, Dave and Rod hiked with me a year ago, before bad weather forced us to turn back. As I stood there, a quote I had seen in the literature regarding inclement weather in the mountains came to mind— "Maybe had the weather been different, we would have summitted. Maybe next time—but the point is to have a next time."

From a large rock jutting out into space above tree line, I could see up the boulder-strewn spine of Hunt Spur, accepting that there would have been no way I could have made that ascent last year even if the weather had been good. When we were in this location twelve months ago, we could not see up the Spur because of the fog and, thus, could not have evaluated the difficulty of the climb ahead. Now I took my time, enjoying the remarkable view as I ascended higher, taking many pictures with the two cameras I was carrying.

I passed the 2-mile marker. The Trail had reached a level area for a short distance, from where I could look up the remainder of the rocky spine of Hunt Spur to an area near the top called "The Gateway." I reached the top of Hunt Spur and was completely overwhelmed with the view from there. I could see the route of the Trail up the rugged Spur from tree line and the distant valleys dotted with flashes of silver from the sun's reflection on the multitude of lakes of all sizes and shapes. To the west across the Katahdin Stream Valley, was "The Owl" and Barren Mountain, mountains in the Katahdin group. To the east was "The Tableland," a large plateau extending for about one mile from "The Gateway" to Baxter Peak. The flora on The Tableland and on Baxter Peak are of arctic varieties and, according to literature, are similar to those found in Greenland and northern Labrador.

I reached Thoreau Spring and the one-mile marker. I had often dreamed of reaching this spring and drinking from it—now I did so. In fact, after a thirst-quenching drink, I filled my canteen. Thoreau Spring was flowing freely, and I was amazed at how much water it was producing at such a high altitude (4,700 feet). The literature did, however, mention that during periods of extended dry weather the spring may not be dependable. The spring is a notable point on Katahdin, because it is here that the Abol Trail crossed the AT, providing another access to Baxter Peak. Also, it was near here to the south where Henry David Thoreau ascended during a storm, thinking he had reached the summit of Katahdin. Reports are that he never saw this spring nor ever reached the summit of the mountain.

I was within a mile of my goal on Baxter Peak and could see the large rock cairn marking the 5,267-foot summit. I did not hurry as I ascended the last few hundred feet, marveling at the magnitude of this massive giant. I had met a number of thru-hikers during the morning, and several had congregated about a hundred feet from the official wooden marker and rock cairn on the summit. As I passed them, they said they were holding back until other members of their group caught up so that they could all finish together.

I reached and touched the wooden marker indicating the northern terminus of the Appalachian Trail at 11:16 AM. There was no one physically present that I knew to shake my hand, applaud or congratulate me as the other hikers on the summit were doing, but I knew that spiritually my family members were there, and that Osbra was looking down on me, nodding with a smile. It was over—and I had a deep-rooted feeling of satisfaction, pride and, yes, closure. I turned and gazed with astonishment at the majestic scene from this, "The Greatest Mountain" and thought, "My God! This is awesome! Truly an awesome mountain—what a place to end my long walk."

I walked over to the large rock cairn and carefully removed two stones from near its base. I placed a rose and a carnation, which I had brought from the family bouquet at Joan's mother's funeral, in the open space. The rose was for Osbra and the carnation for Joan's mother—in their memory. I replaced the stones in their original positions. Near the rock cairn was a bronze plaque with the following inscription:

Mount Katahdin

"This tablet is placed here by the Forest Commissioner of Maine under order of the Governor and Executive Council dated March 16, 1932, to record the gift and conveyance to the State on March 3, 1931 and October 7, 1931 by Percival Proctor Baxter, Governor 1921-1925, of nine square miles of land in township 3 Range 9 Mt. Katahdin, within which area are located this the highest peak of the mountain 5267 ft. named Baxter Peak by the state legislature laws of Maine 1931 south peak 5246 ft Pamola Peak 4902 ft. The North Peaks 4734 ft. and 4612 ft. the Knife Edge, the Chimney the Tableland, Chimney Pond 2914 ft. Dry Pond 2799 ft. North West Plateau 4401 ft. Harvey Ridge 4182 ft. Hamlin Peak 4751 ft. Rum Mountain 3361 ft. and the great north and south basins.

This gift was made upon the express condition that the said tract so donated and conveyed shall forever be used for public park and recreational purposes, shall forever be left in the natural wild state, shall forever be kept as a sanctuary for wild beasts and birds, that no roads or ways for motor vehicles shall hereafter ever be constructed therein or thereon, and was so accepted by the State Legislature laws of Maine 1931 and by order of the Governor and Executive Council October 7, 1931."

I had eaten lunch many times on mountain summits while hiking up the beautiful Appalachian Range, but lunch on this mountain top was an unrivaled experience. While eating, I looked across the Knife Edge connecting Baxter Peak to Pamola and into the valleys dotted with those silvery speckled lakes, the vast areas of forest land surrounding them, the Tableland below me and all the peaks surrounding Katahdin, with no signs of man's intrusion. I thought of how much foresight Governor Baxter had in preserving this jewel for the people of Maine and for anyone who cares to venture onto this wilderness island. Again, the Wonderful World poem flashed back.

After a picture-taking session with other hikers who had summitted, I started my descent at 11:45, crossing the Tableland and down Hunt Spur to Katahdin Stream Campground. I signed the register by the AT near the campground at 3:56 PM, marking the end of my day on Katahdin and the official end of my hike on the AT.

I always had "an eye on the horizon" while hiking along this great footpath and have expressed my feelings about the various sections of the Trail throughout this text and feel no need to repeat them here. My closing statement can be made simply by saying that this was a journey of a lifetime and has left me with memories that will last forever.

When I reached the campground, Joan was waiting with open arms. She could not be with me physically on Baxter Peak at 11:16 AM, but she was there when I walked off the Trail as she was all those other times and was there when I walked on it in the beginning. Were there tears?—How could there not be?

TOP: Hunt Spur on Katahdin
BOTTOM: The Gateway—view down Hunt
Spur and into the surrounding Wilderness

TOP: Thoreau Spring and the surrounding Tableland
     on Katahdin
BOTTOM: Herb at the Baxter Peak sign marking the
     highest point on Katahdin and the Northern Terminus
     of the Appalachian Trail

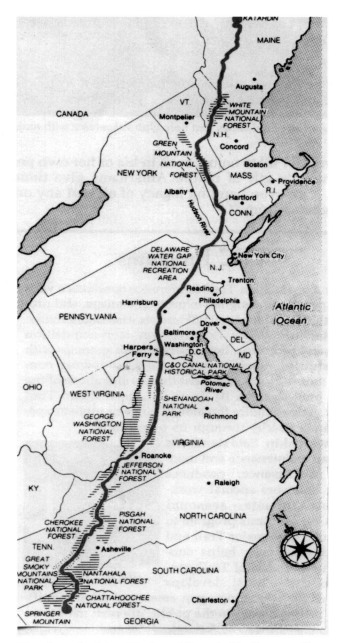

The Appalachian National Scenic Trail extending
from Springer Mtn., GA, to Mt. Katahdin, ME

REFERENCES CONSULTED:

AMC White Mountain Guide, 25th Edition (and Maps)
    1992 Appalachian Mountain Club, Boston, MA

The Appalachian Trail Data Book 1993, Compiled by Daniel D.
    Chazin, Appalachian Trail Conference, Harpers Ferry, WV.

Appalachian Trail Guides 1 through 10 (and Maps)
    Appalachian Trail Conference, Harpers Ferry, WV
    in conjunction with a Confederation of Trail Clubs.

Appalachian Wilderness The Great Smoky Mountains
    by Eliot Porter 1979 Dutton. New York

Backpacker Magazine's Guide to the Appalachian Trail,
    by Jim Chase 1989 Stackpole Books, Harrisburg, PA.

Ghost Towns of New England, by Fessenden S. Blanchard
    1960 Dodd, Mead. New York.

Hiking the Appalachian Trail, edited by James R. Hare
    1975 Rodale Press. Emmaus, PA.

In Defense of Nature, by John Hay
    1969 Little, Brown. Boston, MA.

National Geographic Magazine, Feb. 1987, "A Tunnel through
    Time The Appalachian Trail" by Noel Grove.

The 1989 Philosopher's Guide of the AT, by Darrell Maret
    1989 Appalachian Trail Conference, Harpers Ferry, WV

The Thru-Hiker's Handbook, by Dan "Wingfoot" Bruce
    1991 Appalachian Trail Conference, Harpers Ferry, WV